Michel Foucault

Hubert L. Dreyfus and Paul Rabinow

Michel Foucault:
Beyond Structuralism and Hermeneutics

*Second Edition
With an Afterword by
and an Interview with
Michel Foucault*

The University of Chicago Press

THE UNIVERSITY OF CHICAGO PRESS, CHICAGO 60637
© 1982, 1983 by The University of Chicago

All rights reserved. Published 1982
Second edition 1983
Printed in the United States of America

90 89 88 87 86 85 84 83   1 2 3 4 5

LIBRARY OF CONGRESS CATALOGING IN PUBLICATION DATA
Dreyfus, Hubert L.
  Michel Foucault, beyond structuralism and hermeneutics.

  Includes index.
  1. Foucault, Michel.   I. Rabinow, Paul.   II. Foucault, Michel.   III. Title.
B2430.F724D73   1983   194   83–9316
ISBN 0–226–16311–3
ISBN 0–226–16312–1 (pbk.)

To Geneviève and Daniel

Contents

Preface

This book was born out of a disagreement among friends. Paul Rabinow, attending a seminar given in 1979 by Hubert Dreyfus and John Searle which concerned, among other things, Michel Foucault, objected to the characterization of Foucault as a typical "structuralist." This challenge stirred a discussion that led to the proposal of a joint article. It became evident as the discussion continued through the summer that the "article" would be a short book. It is now a medium-length book and should have been longer.

The book was first to be called *Michel Foucault: From Structuralism to Hermeneutics*. We thought that Foucault had been something like a structuralist in *The Order of Things* and *The Archaeology of Knowledge* but had moved to an interpretive position in his later works on the prisons and on sexuality. A group of literary specialists and philosophers on whom we inflicted our ideas assured us with great conviction and no arguments that Foucault had never been a structuralist and hated interpretation.

The second title of our book was *Michel Foucault: Beyond Structuralism and Hermeneutics*. At this stage we argued that while strictly speaking Foucault had not been a structuralist, he thought that structuralism was the most advanced position in the human sciences. He, however, was not practicing the human sciences; he was analyzing discourse as an autonomous realm from the outside. This time we were on the right track. Foucault told us that the real subtitle of *The Order of Things* was *An Archaeology of Structuralism*. Our story now was that even though his language and approach were heavily influenced by the vogue of structuralism in France Foucault never posited a universal theory of discourse, but rather sought to describe the historical forms taken by discursive practices. We tried this version out on Foucault and he agreed that he was never a structuralist but that perhaps he was not as resistant to the seductive advances of structuralist vocabulary as he might have been.

Of course, this was more than just a question of vocabulary. Foucault does not deny that during the mid-sixties his work was deflected from an interest in the social practices that formed both institutions and discourse to an almost exclusive emphasis on linguistic practices. At its limit this approach led, by its own logic and against Foucault's better judgment, to an objective account of the rulelike way discourse organizes not only itself but social practices and institutions, and to a neglect of the way discursive practices are themselves affected by the social practices in which they and the investigator are imbedded. This is what we call the illusion of autonomous discourse. Our thesis is that this theory of discursive practices is untenable, and that in his later work Foucault has made the structuralist vocabulary that engendered this illusion of autonomous discourse the subject of critical analysis.

A second thesis was that just as Foucault was never a structuralist, although he was tempted by structuralism, so he was beyond hermeneutics although sensitive to its attractions. We were still on the track. It turns out that he was planning to write an "archaeology of hermeneutics," the other pole of the human sciences. Fragments of this project are evident in some of his writings on Nietzsche during this period. Foucault was never tempted by the search for deep meaning, but he clearly was influenced both by Nietzsche's interpretive reading of the history of Western thought as revealing nothing to give a deep interpretation of, and by the ideas that, nonetheless, madness, death, and sex underlie discourse and resist linguistic appropriation.

We argue that Foucault's work during the seventies has been a sustained and largely successful effort to develop a new method. This new method combines a type of archaeological analysis which preserves the distancing effect of structuralism, and an interpretive dimension which develops the hermeneutic insight that the investigator is always situated and must understand the meaning of his cultural practices from within them. Using this method Foucault is able to explain the logic of structuralism's claim to be an objective science and also the apparent validity of the hermeneutic counter-claim that the human sciences can only legitimately proceed by understanding the deepest meaning of the subject and his tradition. Using his new method, which we call interpretive analytics, Foucault is able to show how in our culture human beings have become the sort of objects and subjects structuralism and hermeneutics discover and analyze.

Clearly the issue of power is central to Foucault's diagnosis of our current situation. Yet, as we say in the text, it is not one of the areas he has most fully developed. In discussions with him, Foucault agreed that his concept of power remains elusive but important. He has generously agreed to take a step toward remedying this by offering for inclusion in this book a previously unpublished text on power, for which we are extremely grateful.

We would like to thank the many people, particularly those who attended our meetings in Berkeley, who provided generous attention and suggestions.

Hubert Dreyfus would especially like to thank David Hoy, Richard Rorty, Hans Sluga and, most of all, Jane Rubin for their help.

Paul Rabinow would especially like to thank Gwen Wright, Lew Friedland, Martin Jay and Michael Meranze for theirs.

The second edition has profited from the translating skills of Robert Harvey and the editorial suggestions of David Dobrin. Above all else, we would once again like to thank Michel Foucault for endless hours of stimulating conversation and patient and prompt revisions.

List of Abbreviations

In our study we will use the paperback editions and English translations of Foucault's works, corrected when we feel it is necessary to preserve the sense. While the translations are generally of an exceptionally high quality given the difficulty of the original text, we have found several places where the translations have reversed the sense the context obviously demands.

We will use the following abbreviations for the texts and interviews we cite.

AK   *The Archaeology of Knowledge*. Translated by A. M. Sheridan Smith. New York: Harper Colophon, 1972.

BC   *The Birth of the Clinic: An Archaeology of Medical Perception*. Translated by A. M. Sheridan Smith. New York: Vintage/Random House, 1975.

BW   M. Heidegger. *Basic Writings*. New York: Harper and Row, 1977.

CE   "Réponse au cercle d'epistemologie." *Cahiers pour l'analyse*, no. 9 (1968).

CF   "The Confession of the Flesh." Reprinted in Colin Gordon, ed., *Power/Knowledge: Selected Interviews and Other Writings by Michel Foucault, 1972–1977*. New York: Pantheon Books, 1980.

DL   "The Discourse on Language" in the American edition of *The Archaeology of Knowledge*.

DP   *Discipline and Punish: The Birth of the Prison*. Translated by Alan Sheridan. New York: Vintage/Random House, 1979.

EP   "The Eye of Power." Published as a preface ("L'Oeil de Pouvoir") to Jeremy Bentham, *Le Panoptique* (Paris: Belfond, 1977); reprinted in Gordon, ed., *Power/Knowledge.*

GM   Friedrich Nietzsche. *The Genealogy of Morals.* Translated by F. Golffing. Garden City, New York: Doubleday/Anchor Books, 1956.

HS   *The History of Sexuality. Volume I: An Introduction.* Translated by Robert Hurley. New York: Vintage/Random House, 1980.

ILF   "Interview with Lucette Finas." In M. Morris and P. Patton, eds., *Michel Foucault: Power, Truth, Strategy.* Sydney: Feral Publications, 1979.

IP   *L'Impossible Prison: Recherches sur le système pénitentiare au XIXᵉ siècle réunies par Michelle Perrot.* Paris: Editions du Seuil, 1980.

MC   *Madness and Civilization: A History of Insanity in the Age of Reason.* Translated by R. Howard. New York: Vintage/Random House, 1973.

NFM   "Nietzsche, Freud, Marx." In *Nietzsche.* Paris: Cahiers de Royaumont, 1967.

NGH   "Nietzsche, Genealogy, History" (1971). In D. F. Bouchard, ed., *Michel Foucault: Language, Counter-Memory, Practice: Selected Essays and Interviews.* New York: Cornell University Press, 1977.

OT   *The Order of Things: An Archaeology of the Human Sciences.* New York: Vintage/Random House, 1973.

SL   Lectures delivered at Stanford University, Palo Alto, California, October 1979.

Telos "Power and Sex: An interview." *Telos* 32 (1977).

TP   "Truth and Power." Translation of an interview with Alessandro Fontana and Pasquale Pasquino which appeared in *Microfisica del Potere,* reprinted in Gordon, ed., *Power/Knowledge.*

Introduction

This is a book about how to study human beings and what one learns from such study. Our thesis is that the most influential modern attempts to achieve this understanding—phenomenology, structuralism, and hermeneutics—have not lived up to their self-proclaimed expectations. Michel Foucault offers, in our opinion, elements of a coherent and powerful alternative means of understanding. His works, we feel, represent the most important contemporary effort both to develop a method for the study of human beings and to diagnose the current situation of our society. In this book we discuss Foucault's writings chronologically to show how he has sought to refine his tools of analysis and to sharpen his critical insight into modern society and its discontents. We also attempt to place Foucault's thought among other thinkers with whom his approach has common themes.

Foucault has shown at length that official biographies and current received opinions of top intellectuals do not carry any transparent truth. Beyond the dossiers and the refined self-consciousness of any age are the organized historical practices which make possible, give meaning to, and situate in a political field these monuments of official discourse.

The data contained in such official documents is nonetheless relevant and essential. Perhaps the most ironic and efficient (if not the best) way to begin a book on Michel Foucault is simply to reproduce the biographic dossier which is inserted at the back of the English translations of his works. A recent one reads as follows:

> Michel Foucault was born in Poitiers, France, in 1926. He has lectured in many universities throughout the world and served as Director of the Institut Français in Hamburg and the Institut de Philosophie at the Faculté des Lettres in the University of

Clermont-Ferrand. He writes frequently for French newspapers and reviews, and is holder of a chair [History and Systems of Thought] at France's most prestigious institution, The Collège de France.

In addition to his classic study, *Madness and Civilization*, M. Foucault is the author of *The Birth of the Clinic, The Order of Things, The Archaeology of Knowledge*, and, *I, Pierre Rivière*. His latest book, *Discipline and Punish: The Birth of the Prison*, was published by Pantheon in 1978.

This blurb was published at the back page of the English translation of *The History of Sexuality*. We might add that Foucault has also published a book-length introductory essay on the Heideggerian psychoanalyst Ludwig Binswanger, a book on the surrealist writer Raymond Roussel, and a short book on mental illness and psychology.

Shifting from dossier to official reception among the high intelligentsia, in a review in *The New York Review of Books* (26 January 1978) by Clifford Geertz, Professor of Social Sciences at the Institute for Advanced Study in Princeton, we read:

Michel Foucault erupted onto the intellectual scene at the beginning of the Sixties with his *Histoire de la Folie*, an unconventional but still reasonably recognizable history of the Western experience of madness. He has become, in the years since, a kind of impossible object: a nonhistorical historian, an anti-humanist human scientist, and a counter-structuralist structuralist. If we add to this his terse, impacted style, which manages to seem imperious and doubt-ridden at the same time, and a method which supports sweeping summary with eccentric detail, the resemblance of his work to an Escher drawing—stairs rising to platforms lower than themselves, doors leading outside that bring you back inside—is complete.

"Do not ask who I am and do not ask me to remain the same" he writes in the introduction to his one purely methodological work, *L'Archaeologie du Savoir*, itself mostly a collection of denials of positions he does not hold but considers himself likely to be accused of by the "mimes and tumblers" of intellectual life. "Leave it to our bureaucrats and our police to see that our papers are in order," he states. "At least spare us their morality when we write." Whoever he is, or whatever, he is what any French savant seems to need to be these days: elusive.

But (and in this he differs from a good deal that has been going on in Paris since structuralism arrived) the difficulty of his work arises not only from self-regard and the desire to found an intellectual cult only the instructed can join, but from a powerful and genuine originality of thought. As he intends nothing else than a Great Instauration for the human sciences, it is not surprising that he is more than occasionally obscure, or that when he does manage to be clear he is not less disconcerting.

The dossier presents the essential facts, the critical review situates them for us. We can now turn to Foucault's books.

We center our story on the problems Michel Foucault has grappled with in his works. Our book is not a biography, a psychohistory, an intellectual history, or a digest of Foucault's thought, although elements of the last two are, of course, present. It is a reading of his work, bearing in mind a certain set of problems, i.e., an interpretation. We have taken from Foucault that which is helpful in focusing on and dealing with those problems. Since we are using Foucault's work to aid us, we make no claim to comprehensiveness as to the breadth of issues which, at various times, have been the object of Foucault's studies. This seems to us fair since it is precisely how Foucault handles the master thinkers of the past.

Foucault thinks that the study of human beings took a decisive turn at the end of the eighteenth century when human beings came to be interpreted as knowing subjects, and, at the same time, objects of their own knowledge. This Kantian interpretation defines "man." Kant introduced the idea that man is that unique being who is totally involved in nature (his body), society (historical, economic, and political relations), and language (his mother tongue), and who at the same time finds a firm foundation for all of these involvements in his meaning-giving, organizing activity. We will follow Foucault's analysis of the various forms this problematic (which Foucault calls in *The Order of Things* the analytic of finitude) took over the next two centuries.

To situate Foucault, it is important to realize that the sciences of man have in the past two decades been split between two extreme methodological reactions to phenomenology, both of which inherit but seek to transcend the Kantian subject/object division. Both these approaches try to eliminate the Husserlian conception of a meaning-giving transcendental subject. The structuralist approach attempts to dispense with both meaning and the subject by finding objective laws which govern all human activity. The opposed position, which we gather under the general rubric hermeneutics, gives up the phenomenologists' attempt to understand man as a meaning-giving *subject,* but attempts to preserve meaning by locating it in the social practices and literary texts which man produces. To triangulate Foucault's movements it is important to pin down precisely all three positions: structuralism, phenomenology, and hermeneutics.

Structuralists attempt to treat human activity scientifically by finding basic elements (concepts, actions, classes of words) and the rules or laws by which they are combined. There are two kinds of structuralism: atomistic structuralism, in which the elements are completely specified apart from their role in some larger whole (for example, Propp's folk tale elements),[1] and holistic or diachronic structuralism, in which what counts as a *possible* element is defined apart from the system of elements but what counts as an *actual* element is a function of the whole system of differences of which the given element is a part. Foucault, as we shall see, explicitly distinguishes his method from atomistic structuralism, so we will be comparing and contrasting his archaeological method with the method of holistic structuralism to which it is more closely akin.

Lévi-Strauss succinctly states this method:

> The method we adopt . . . consists in the following operations:
> 1) define the phenomenon under study as a relation between two or more terms, real or supposed;
> 2) construct a *table of possible permutations* between these terms;
> 3) take this table as the general object of analysis which, at this level only, can yield necessary connections, the empirical phenomenon considered at the beginning being only one possible combination among others, the *complete system* of which must be reconstructed beforehand.[2]

Everything hinges on the criteria of individuation of the terms or elements. For holistic structuralists such as Lévi-Strauss, all possible terms must be defined (identified) apart from any specific system; the specific system of terms then determines which possible terms actually count as elements, that is, the system provides the individuation of the elements. For example, for Lévi-Strauss in *The Raw and the Cooked*,[3] raw, cooked, and rotten are identified as three *possible* elements; each *actual* system of elements then determines how in that system these three possible elements will be individuated. For example, they can be grouped into binary oppositions such as raw vs. cooked and rotten, or raw and rotten vs. cooked, or each of the three elements can count on its own.

Transcendental phenomenology, as defined and practiced by Edmund Husserl, is the diametric opposite of structuralism. It accepts the view that man is totally object and totally subject, and investigates the meaning-giving activity of the transcendental ego which gives meaning to all objects including its own body, its own empirical personality, and the culture and history which it "constitutes" as conditioning its empirical self.

1. Vladimir Ja. Propp, *Morphology of the Folktale* (The Hague: Mouton, 1958).
2. Claude Lévi-Strauss, *Totemism* (Boston: Beacon Press, 1963), p. 16. (Our italics.)
3. Claude Lévi-Strauss, *The Raw and the Cooked* (New York: Harper and Row, 1969).

Husserl's transcendental phenomenology gave rise to an existential counter-movement led by Heidegger in Germany and Maurice Merleau-Ponty in France. Foucault was steeped in the thought of both these existential phenomenologists. At the Sorbonne he heard Merleau-Ponty expound what he later calls the phenomenology of lived experience. In his lectures and in his influential book, *Phenomenology of Perception,* Merleau-Ponty attempted to show that the lived body rather than the transcendental ego organized experience, and that the body as an integrated set of skills was not subject to the sort of intellectualist analysis in terms of rules developed by Husserl. Foucault also studied Heidegger's classic rethinking of phenomenology, *Being and Time,* and sympathetically presented Heidegger's hermeneutic ontology in his first published work, a long introduction to an essay by the Heideggerian psychotherapist, Ludwig Binswanger.[4]

Heidegger's phenomenology stresses the idea that human subjects are formed by the historical cultural practices in which they develop. These practices form a background which can never be made completely explicit, and so cannot be understood in terms of the beliefs of a meaning-giving subject. The background practices do, however, contain a meaning. They embody a way of understanding and coping with things, people, and institutions. Heidegger calls this meaning in the practices an interpretation, and proposes to make manifest certain general features of this interpretation. In *Being and Time* he calls his method, which amounts to giving an interpretation of the interpretation embodied in everyday practices, hermeneutics. Heidegger's use of this term goes back to Schleiermacher who meant by hermeneutics the interpretation of the meaning of sacred texts, and to Dilthey who applied Schleiermacher's interpretive method to history. Heidegger, by generalizing Dilthey's work and developing it into a general method for understanding human beings, introduced the term and the approach into contemporary thought.

There are, in fact, two different kinds of hermeneutic inquiry in *Being and Time,* corresponding to Division I and Division II, and each of these has been developed by one of the two schools of contemporary philosophers who call their work hermeneutic.

In Division I Heidegger elaborates what he calls "an interpretation of Dasein in its everydayness."[5] There he lays out the way *Dasein* interprets itself in this everyday activity. This "primordial understanding" in our everyday practices and discourse, which is overlooked by the practitioners but which they would recognize if it were pointed out to them, is the subject of much recent hermeneutic investigation. Harold Garfinkel, a

---

4. Ludwig Binswanger, *Le Rêve et L'éxistence,* trans. Jacqueline Uerdeaux. Introduction and Notes by Michel Foucault (Paris: Desclée de Brouwer, 1955).

5. Martin Heidegger, *Being and Time* (New York: Harper and Row, 1962), p. 76.

sociologist,[6] and Charles Taylor, a political scientist,[7] explicitly identify themselves with this type of hermeneutic method. An off-shoot of this sort of hermeneutics of the everyday is the application of the same method to other cultures (for example, Clifford Geertz's brand of anthropology)[8] or to other epochs in our own culture (Thomas Kuhn's application of what he now explicitly calls the hermeneutic method to Aristotelian physics).[9]

In Division I of *Being and Time* Heidegger shows that the understanding in our everyday practices is partial and thus distorted. This limitation is corrected in Division II, which does not take the interpretation of Division I at face value but sees it as a motivated masking of the truth. As Heidegger puts it:

> Dasein's *kind of Being . . . demands* that any ontological Interpretation which sets itself the goal of exhibiting the phenomena in their primordiality, *should capture the Being of this entity, in spite of this entity's own tendency to cover things up*. Existential analysis, therefore, constantly has the character of *doing violence* whether to the claims of the everyday interpretation, or to its complacency and its tranquilized obviousness.[10]

Heidegger claims to find that the deep truth hidden by the everyday practices is the unsettling groundlessness of a way of being which is, so to speak, interpretation all the way down. This "discovery" is an instance of what Paul Ricoeur has called the hermeneutics of suspicion. One might have found that the underlying disguised truth was the class struggle as disclosed by Marx or the twists and turns of the libido as uncovered by Freud. In any such case, some authority which has already seen the truth must lead the self-deluded participant to see it too. (In *Being and Time* this authority is called the voice of conscience.) In each case too the individual must confirm the truth of this deep interpretation by acknowledging it. And since in each case the suffering is caused by the repressive defenses, facing the truth results in some sort of liberation, whether it be the increased flexibility that comes, as Heidegger claims, from the re-

6. Cf. Harold Garfinkel, *Studies in Ethnomethodology* (Englewood Cliffs, N.J.: Prentice-Hall, 1967).

7. Cf. Charles Taylor, "Interpretation and the Sciences of Man," in Paul Rabinow and William Sullivan, eds., *Interpretive Social Science* (Berkeley: University of California Press, 1979).

8. Cf. Clifford Geertz, *The Interpretation of Cultures* (New York: Harper and Row, 1973).

9. Thomas S. Kuhn, *The Essential Tension* (Chicago: University of Chicago Press, 1977), p. xiii.

10. Heidegger, *Being and Time*, p. 359.

alization that nothing is grounded and that there are no guidelines, or the power released by the realization that one's class is exploited, or the maturity gained by facing the deep secrets of one's sexuality.

Hans-Georg Gadamer, in *Truth and Method*,[11] gives deep hermeneutics a more positive direction as a method for reappropriating a profound understanding of Being preserved in traditional linguistic practices. According to Gadamer, reinterpreting this saving truth is our only hope in the face of nihilism.

Foucault is not interested in recovering man's unnoticed everyday self-interpretation. He would agree with Nietzsche and the hermeneutics of suspicion that such an interpretation is surely deluded about what is really going on. But Foucault does not believe that a hidden deep truth is the cause of the misinterpretation embodied in our everyday self-understanding. He captures all such positions as well as Gadamer's at an appropriate level of abstraction when he defines what he calls commentary "as the re-apprehension through the manifest meaning of discourse of another meaning at once secondary and primary, that is, more hidden but also more fundamental" (*OT* 373). Such an account of interpretation, he claims, "dooms us to an endless task...[because it] rests on the postulate that speech is an act of 'translation'... an exegesis, which listens... to the Word of God, ever secret, ever beyond itself" (*BC* xvi, xvii). Foucault dismisses this approach with the remark, "For centuries we have waited in vain for the decision of the Word" (*BC* xvii).

Obviously the terminology in this area is confused and confusing. In our discussion we will sort out the various kinds of interpretation or exegesis by using "hermeneutics" as a broad neutral term, "commentary" for the recovery of meanings and truths from our everyday practices or from those of another age or culture, and "the hermeneutics of suspicion" for the search for a deep truth which has been purposefully hidden.

We shall see as we follow Foucault's changing strategies for studying human beings that he has constantly sought to move beyond the alternatives we have just discussed—the only alternatives left to those still trying to understand human beings within the problematic left by the breakdown of the humanistic framework. He has sought to avoid the structuralist analysis which eliminates notions of meaning altogether and substitutes a formal model of human behavior as rule-governed transformations of meaningless elements; to avoid the phenomenological project of tracing all meaning back to the meaning-giving activity of an autonomous, transcendental subject; and finally to avoid the attempt of

11. Hans-Georg Gadamer, *Truth and Method* (New York: Seabury Press, 1975).

commentary to read off the implicit meaning of social practices as well as the hermeneutic unearthing of a different and deeper meaning of which social actors are only dimly aware.

Foucault's early works (*Madness and Civilization, Birth of the Clinic*) center on the analysis of historically situated systems of institutions and discursive practices. The discursive practices are distinguished from the speech acts of everyday life. Foucault is interested only in what we will call *serious* speech acts: what experts say when they are speaking as experts. And he furthermore restricts his analyses to the serious speech acts in those "dubious" disciplines which have come to be called the human sciences. In *The Archaeology of Knowledge* he seeks to purify his analysis of discourse by temporarily putting aside his institutional analysis. He argues that what can be roughly referred to as the sciences of man can be treated as autonomous systems of discourse, but he never gives up his earlier position that social institutions influence discursive practices. In the *Archaeology* he does, however, try to show that the human sciences could be analyzed as having an internal self-regulation and autonomy. Moreover, he proposes to treat the discourses of the human sciences archaeologically, that is, to avoid becoming involved in arguments about whether what they say is true, or even whether their statements make sense. Rather he proposes to treat all that is said in the human sciences as a "discourse-object." Foucault makes clear that his archaeological method, since it must remain neutral as to the truth and meaning of the discursive systems it studies, is not another theory about the relation of words and things. He does hold, however, that it is a theory about discourse—orthogonal to all disciplines with their accepted concepts, legitimized subjects, taken-for-granted objects, and preferred strategies, which yield justified truth claims. As he puts it, "I believed that I spoke from the same place as that discourse, and that in defining its space I was situating my remarks; but I must now acknowledge that I can no longer speak from the space from which I showed they spoke" (*CE* 21).

Foucault was never a structuralist strictly speaking, or a post-structuralist, and later he even backs away from his strong claims in the *Archaeology* that discourse is a rule-governed system similar to that presented by the various versions of structuralism, and that it is autonomous and self-referring, as post-structuralists were claiming at the time. However, it is important to confront the position in the *Archaeology* just because it shares certain fundamental assumptions with the structuralist approach. We will argue at length that the project of the *Archaeology* founders for two reasons. First, the causal power attributed to the rules governing discursive systems is unintelligible and makes the kind of influence the social institutions have—an influence which has always been at the center of Foucault's concerns—incomprehensible. Second, insofar as Foucault takes archaeology to be an end in itself he forecloses the possibility of bringing his critical analyses to bear on his social concerns.

In the face of this impasse, in which the method of the *Archaeology* alone did not allow Foucault to pursue the range of problems and concerns which informed his work, he spent some time rethinking and recasting his intellectual tools. After the *Archaeology* he turns sharply away from the attempt to develop a theory of discourse, and uses Nietzsche's genealogy as a starting point for developing a method that would allow him to thematize the relationship between truth, theory, and values and the social institutions and practices in which they emerge. This leads him to pay increased attention to power and the body in their relation to the human sciences. The archaeological method is not rejected, however. Foucault abandons only the attempt to work out a theory of rule-governed systems of discursive practices. As a technique, archaeology serves genealogy. As a method of isolating discourse objects, it serves to distance and defamiliarize the serious discourse of the human sciences. This, in turn, enables Foucault to raise the genealogical questions: How are these discourses used? What role do they play in society?

The *Archaeology* appeared in 1969. Foucault's next book, *Discipline and Punish,* appeared six years later. We intend to argue that in this book Foucault concentrates on the "carceral" practices which gave birth to the sciences of man and gave man and society a form which is amenable to objective (archaeological) analysis. Hence, many of the key terms such as "govern," "regulate," "transformation," "element," "rule," "series," "externality," and "system," upon which the *Archaeology* turns, are shown to be a grid of interpretation generated by specific historical practices.

Likewise, in *The History of Sexuality* (1977), Foucault challenges the hermeneutic belief in deep meaning by tracing the emergence of sexual confession and relating it to practices of social domination. He shows the significance of confessional practices such as psychotherapy or medical procedures as revealed by the enormous growth of interest in the psyche in all realms of life. Such practices, which were supposed to reveal deep meaning accessible only to an endless, allegorical interpretation, produce the proliferating discourse of "speaking subjects." We think Foucault is implying here that we cannot simply assume that there are deep meanings to investigate just because our culture tells us there are. This is just another way of saying that the notion of deep meaning is a cultural construction. Foucault thus gives us a concrete demonstration of the two strategic dimensions of the gradually developing totalizing practices which not only produce man as object and subject but, more importantly, preserve both in our objectified, meaning-obsessed society.

This combination allows Foucault to develop a general diagnosis of our current cultural situation. He isolates and identifies the pervasive organization of our society as "bio-technico-power." Bio-power is the increasing ordering in all realms under the guise of improving the welfare of the individual and the population. To the genealogist this order reveals itself to be a strategy, with no one directing it and everyone increasingly enmeshed in it, whose only end is the increase of power and order itself.

There are many other ways to read our history and Foucault is not the first to read it this way. He is clearly in a line of thinkers such as Nietzsche, Weber, late Heidegger, and Adorno. His contribution, however, is a heightened methodological sophistication and a unique emphasis on the body as the place in which the most minute and local social practices are linked up with the large scale organization of power.

Foucault combines the best of philosophical reflection with scrupulous attention to empirical detail. Nevertheless, he remains consciously, frustratingly elusive when it comes to capturing our current condition in general formulae, such as Heidegger's attempt to define the essence of technology as the positing, ordering, and putting at our disposal of all beings. But Foucault is being consistent to the consequences of his analysis, viz. that such generalities are either empty or that they can serve as the justification for promoting just what Foucault wants to resist. Once one sees the pervasiveness, dispersion, intricacy, contingency, and layering of our social practices, one also sees that any attempt to sum up what is going on is bound to be a potentially dangerous distortion.

Likewise, Foucault annoys many by insisting on a pragmatic intent in all significant historiography. Foucault says that he is writing the history of the present, and we call the method that enables him to do this interpretive analytics. This is to say that while the analysis of our present practices and their historical development is a disciplined, concrete demonstration which could serve as the basis of a research program, the diagnosis that the increasing organization of everything is the central issue of our time is not in any way empirically demonstrable, but rather emerges as an interpretation. This interpretation grows out of pragmatic concerns and has pragmatic intent, and for that very reason can be contested by other interpretations growing out of other concerns.

Now we can see the sense in which Foucault's work is and has always been beyond structuralism and hermeneutics. During the period of the *Archaeology* his reduction of the subject to a function of discourse and his attempt to treat serious discourse as an autonomous rule-governed system (although he never claimed to find universal ahistorical laws), led him to say his method was "not entirely foreign to what is called structural analysis" (*AK* 15). With his abandonment of archaeology as a theoretical project, however, Foucault not only distances himself from structuralism but situates the structuralist project historically within a context of the increased isolating, ordering, systematizing practices characteristic of what he calls disciplinary technology. He preserves the structural technique of focusing on both discourse and the speaker as constructed objects, however, as a necessary step to free himself from taking the discourses and practices of this society as simply expressing the way things are.

Before he took up structuralist techniques, in his earliest published work, the introduction to an essay by Binswanger, Foucault clearly identified himself with the tradition of hermeneutic ontology which originated in Heidegger's *Being and Time*. As his interest in the social effects rather than the implicit meaning of everyday practices developed, however, Foucault simply left the concerns of the hermeneutic position behind. His reading of Nietzsche was the vehicle through which he again turned to the necessity and dangers of the interpretive approach. Nietzsche's genealogy of the way power uses the illusion of meaning to further itself gave him good reason to be critical of hermeneutics both in its form of commentary on everyday life, and in its related form of deep exegesis of what everyday practices cover up. But this same genealogical analysis has led Foucault to the position he calls *dechiffrement*. This amounts to an understanding of social practices as having an intelligibility radically different from that available to the actors who, according to the hermeneutic account, find the practices superficially meaningful, deeply meaningful, or even deeply meaningless.

Foucault develops this interpretation—and this we claim is his most original contribution although he does not thematize it as such—by pointing to agreed-upon examples of how a domain of human activity should be organized. These exemplars, such as the Christian and psychoanalytic confessionals and Jeremy Bentham's Panopticon, show us how our culture attempts to normalize individuals through increasingly rationalized means, by turning them into meaningful subjects and docile objects. This helps explain how the study of human beings as subjects and objects has had such centrality in our culture, and why the current techniques used in this study—hermeneutics and structuralism—have proven so powerful. Thus Foucault manages both to criticize and to utilize—in a highly original way—the two dominant methods available for the study of human beings.

I *The Illusion of Autonomous Discourse*

1   Practices and Discourse in Foucault's Early Writings

The History of Madness

Madness and Civilization (1961) opens with a description of the exclusion and confinement of lepers in a vast network of leper houses scattered at the edges of European cities throughout the Middle Ages. Within these enclosures lepers were isolated from the inhabitants of the city and, at the same time, kept close enough to be observed. Their liminal position—at the edge but not beyond—was paralleled by the acute ambivalence with which they were regarded. Lepers were seen as dangerous and wicked; they had been punished by God but by the same token they were physical, bodily reminders of God's power and of the Christian duty of charity.

Dramatically and abruptly at the end of the Middle Ages the leper houses across Europe were emptied. But the physical site of social separation and moral connection was not to be left unoccupied. It was to be filled again and again by new occupants, bearing new signs and heralding new social forms. "With an altogether new meaning and in a very different culture, the forms would remain—essentially that major form of rigorous division which is social exclusion but spiritual reintegration" (*MC* 7). These twin themes of spatial exclusion and cultural integration which structure all of *Madness and Civilization* are captured in the first few pages.

Foucault follows his images of woe-begotten yet holy lepers with equally compelling descriptions of the Ship of Fools, *Narrenschiff*. During the Renaissance the mad were loaded onto ships and sent off to sail down Europe's rivers in search of their sanity. Bound on his ship, the madman was "a prisoner in the midst of what is the freest, the openest of routes..." (*MC* 11). The madman in the Renaissance began to make his appearance as a cultural figure of major concern, replacing death as a focus of deep and pervasive concern about order and meaning. At first, he appeared as part of a larger number of different types who were lumped together: the fool, the simpleton, the drunkard, the debauchee, the criminal, the lover.

The theme of disorder was cast in terms of excess and irregularity, not in terms of medical or bodily dysfunction. Foucault's elaboration on the emerging contrast of reason and madness occupies a very large section of *Madness and Civilization*. It is this new cultural content—reason and madness in the Classical Age, sanity and insanity in our age—which changes radically from period to period, and which seems to be a series of approximations to an unseizable ontological condition of pure otherness, that lies at the center of Foucault's analysis. Foucault seems to have thought that there was "something" like pure madness which all these different cultural forms were groping after and covering up—a view he later abandons.

Foucault's analysis of these cultural discontinuities is always juxtaposed to a description of a rather more continuous story of confinement and exclusion. The meaning changes with some frequency, but a long-term continuity of form of what can only be called power is (and was) the counterpoint to these dramatic shifts in cultural classifications. It is this tension, played out with significant shifts in emphasis, which runs throughout all of Foucault's works. The simple juxtaposition of continuity and discontinuity, power and discourse as parallel pairs is most clearly stated in *Madness and Civilization*. But the connections and the specific mechanisms which order discourse and power remain highly undefined. This need for specification is the center of Foucault's attention in his later books, first on the side of discourse, then on the side of power.

The seventeenth century marked the change already mentioned—from the Renaissance to the Classical Age. The leper houses across Europe were suddenly emptied of their lepers and turned into houses of confinement for the poor. Foucault wants to understand both the social forces at work throughout Europe which produced such a dramatic organization of the poor *and* the cultural classification system of the age which lumped so many people together into a single category. Why was it, Foucault asks, that within the space of several months in 1656 one out of every hundred people in Paris was confined?

Foucault isolates the establishment by the king of the Hôpital Général as a major historical event. At first glance, this regrouping of a series of buildings and welfare functions under a single rubric would seem to be little more than an administrative reform. These various Parisian buildings—one had housed an arsenal, another was a rest home for military veterans—were now given over to the charge of caring for the poor, the mad, the homeless. The king's edict provided that all the poor, " 'of both sexes, of all ages, and from all localities, of whatever breeding and birth, in whatever state they may be, able-bodied or invalid, sick or convalescent, curable or incurable' " (*MC* 39) had the right to be fed, clothed, housed, and generally looked after. A new series of high level administrators were appointed by the king, who had jurisdiction not only over the poor confined in the actual buildings but throughout the city of Paris. The edict declared the power of these administrators to be almost absolute: " 'They have all power of authority, of direction, of administration, of commerce, of police, of jurisdiction, of correction and punishment over all the poor of Paris, both within and without the Hôpital Général' " (*MC* 40).

Although doctors were assigned to make the rounds of the various houses of confinement, Foucault strongly emphasizes that they were not primarily medical institutions. It was the poor, the recalcitrant, the vagabonds as well as the madmen who were thrown together. Foucault is at pains to point out that the sudden emergence of "the great internment" should not be understood as the muddled prescientific appearance of what would later become our mental hospitals and medical clinics. Here and elsewhere Foucault is most definitely not telling the story of scientific progress. Rather, the story for Foucault is the other way round. It is in the first major moves toward social internment, toward the isolation and observation of whole categories of people, that the first glimmerings of our modern medical, psychiatric, and human sciences are to be seen. These human sciences will later develop their methods, refine their concepts, and sharpen their professional defenses, but they will continue to operate within institutions of confinement. Foucault interprets them as playing an ever more crucial role in the specification and articulation of the classification and control of human beings, not as giving us ever purer truth.

In *Madness and Civilization* Foucault explicitly identifies the establishment of the Hôpital Général as the direct policy of royal authority. He sees it as "an instance . . . of the monarchical and bourgeois order being organized in France during this period" (*MC* 40). The actors are identified, the actions given rather straightforward motivational accounting and the effects of their actions duly noted. In his later works, Foucault will rarely be this explicit about causal explanations of who acts and why; later, social, structural, and political dynamics will be problematized and recast. But, in *Madness and Civilization* it is only the discontinuous content of the cultural changes which remain free-floating and unexplained. The institutional and power side of things is given an explicit account. Foucault explains, for example, that by 1676 the king had extended this system of confinement and care throughout France. By the time of the French Revolution there was a great profusion and variety of these wel-

5

fare institutions both in France and elsewhere on the continent. But at the beginning, Foucault explains, "there must have formed, silently and doubtless over the course of many years, a social sensibility common to European culture, that suddenly began to manifest itself in the second half of the seventeenth century; it was this sensibility that suddenly isolated the category destined to populate the places of confinement" (*MC* 45). A new form of discourse and a new form of social institution emerged. So, Foucault tells us, "there must have existed a unity which justified its urgency" (*MC* 45). And indeed there was. The great confinement "organizes into a complex unity a new sensibility to poverty and to the duties of assistance, new forms of reaction to the economic problems of unemployment and idleness, a new ethic of work, and also the dream of a city where moral obligation was joined to the civil law, within the authoritarian forms of constraint" (*MC* 46).

Foucault lists the imperatives which made possible and necessary the appearance of the houses of confinement. First was the necessity of labor as both a moral and a social imperative. In the charter of the Hôpital the dangers of idleness and mendicancy for the city were stressed. As new forms of economic organization appeared, the hold of the guilds was weakened and social upheaval and dislocation followed. But whereas in previous periods of great unemployment the city protected itself against bands of vagabonds by putting guards at its gates, it now set up houses of internment within its walls. "The unemployed person was no longer driven away or punished; he was taken in charge, at the expense of the nation but at the cost of his individual liberty. Between him and society, an implicit system of obligation was established: he had the right to be fed, but he must accept the physical and moral constraint of confinement" (*MC* 48).

Foucault explains in a relatively straightforward way this linking of the welfare of the individual (and populations) to the administrative control of the state as the result of economic and social pressures. His analysis of the forms it took and particularly of the cultural idiom in which it played itself out is highly original, but the causal dimension of Foucault's analysis is not. He says, "Throughout Europe, confinement had the same meaning, at least if we consider its origin. It constituted one of the answers the seventeenth century gave to an economic crisis that affected the entire Western world: reduction of wages, unemployment, scarcity of coin . . ." (*MC* 49). In Foucault's later works the periodization, the relative importance of these socioeconomic imperatives, the complex relations to the "sensibility of the age" and to scientific discourse, and the specific mechanisms of its operations will be problematized and rarely set into such straightforward causal terms. But the thematic unity, at least, of Foucault's interests is clear enough.

Our modern relations with the insane emerged abruptly after the French Revolution. "Every psychiatrist, every historian yielded, at the beginning of the nineteenth century, to the same impulse of indignation; everywhere we find the same outrage, the same virtuous censure" (*MC* 221). This outrage turned on the newly perceived fact that the insane and the criminal were thrown together in the same houses of confinement. Clearly, or clearly to those holding this newly emergent sensibility, this was a shocking violation of categories. The modern separation of the insane from the criminal, the indigent, the debauched and their incorporation into the realm of the medical first appears in scores of shocked and outraged cries of humanitarian pain. Foucault quickly asserts that this was not some simple advance of humane treatment of others advancing under the guidance of science. No, "it was the depths of confinement itself that generated the phenomenon; it is from confinement that we must seek an account of this new awareness of madness" (*MC* 224). Although this sounds mysterious Foucault presents a straightforward account on two levels.

First, there was, as it were, an efficient cause. It was the protests of the imprisoned "criminal" nobility and intelligentsia who called attention to the mixing of the criminal and the insane. They demanded, for themselves, a separation of what they saw as an incompatible and suddenly incongruously promiscuous intermingling of different categories of persons. They called not for a freeing of the insane or even better treatment for them. They demanded only that ordinary criminals not be mixed with the insane lest they too leave the houses of confinement without their reason. "The presence of the mad appears as an injustice; but *for others*" (*MC* 228).

Second, a deep restructuring of both social sensibility and economic relations was taking place. Poverty, which had been seen as a vice and a danger to the social body, was now seen as a hidden but essential advantage for the nation. Those poor who were willing to work for low wages and to consume little constituted one of the essential ingredients of a nation's wealth. The notion of population as a crucial economic and social resource to be taken into account, to be organized, to be made productive comes to the fore.

Foucault treats the theme of population at greater length in several of his other books. In *The Order of Things* the analysis of labor and its changing discursive organization in the Classical Age and in our current Age of Man constitutes roughly one-third of the book, along with parallel analyses of life and language. In *Discipline and Punish* Foucault moves beyond his analysis of the discursive structure of labor and population and situates this analysis in the shifting development of what he now calls "bio-power." Bio-power (see chapter 6), our modern form of power, is

7

characterized by increasing organization of population and welfare for the sake of increased force and productivity. In this analysis the discursive and the institutional are once again brought back into a complex relationship. But in their later form less emphasis is given to the state and to capitalist growth, which Foucault takes for granted as an essential part of the story, and more attention is given to pinpointing exactly how this form of power is made to work on the local level.

It follows that if population was a potential component of the nation's wealth, then "confinement was a gross error, and an economic mistake" (*MC* 232). General confinement had to be abolished. It was replaced by a more scientific and humane specific confinement which separated certain categories of criminals (discussed by Foucault in *Discipline and Punish*) and the insane. The mad, it was now felt, must be liberated from their chains and cages and returned to health. What Foucault refers to as the mythic history of our progressive humanization of treatment of the insane hides "beneath the myths themselves...an operation, or rather a series of operations, which silently organized the world of the asylum, the methods of cure, and at the same time the concrete experience of madness" (*MC* 243). Foucault concentrates on the Quaker reformers in England associated with the name Tuke and the medical rationalists in France led by Pinel. His descriptions of the techniques developed and the general strategy for the treatment of madness used by these two schools are paralleled by those used for the treatment of criminal behavior by the same groups.

The strategy of the Quakers was to make each inmate or patient take responsibility for his crime or his illness. "Tuke created an asylum where he substituted for the free terror of madness the stifling anguish of responsibility; fear no longer reigned on the other side of the prison gates, it now raged under the seals of conscience" (*MC* 247). The emphasis was on getting the patient to accept his own guilt and responsibility. This involved a complex series of institutional arrangements. There was a structured hierarchy of relations in the asylum, in which the patients were at the bottom.

Since the patient was seen to be responsible for his illness, therapeutic intervention in the form of punishments became a standard mode of treatment. The goal of these interventions was to bring the patient to an awareness of his status as a subject, responsible for his own actions. Hence the subject, observed and punished by his warders, was led by a carefully structured series of procedures to do the same thing to himself. Once this internalization was accomplished, so the theory goes, the patient would be cured. "This movement by which, objectifying himself for the Other, the madman thus returned to his liberty, was to be found as much in Work as in Observation" (*MC* 247).

Pinel, in France, took a parallel but somewhat different approach to the insane. The asylum for him became "an instrument of moral uniformity and of social denunciation. The problem [was] to impose, in a universal form, a morality..." (*MC* 259). The mad must be made to see that they have transgressed the universal ethical standards of humanity. They must be brought back to an affirmation of social standards by a series of techniques of retraining, consciousness alteration, and discipline of both the body and the psyche.

Many of these techniques, including systematic extortion of confession, play a central role in Foucault's genealogy of the modern subject which he outlines in broad strokes in *The History of Sexuality*. Indeed, all these themes will recur in Foucault's later works—the constitution of human beings as subjects, the treatment of human beings as objects, the relationship of punishment and surveillance—and we take them up in more detail in chapters 7, 8, and 9. In *Madness and Civilization* Foucault isolates these themes as general social and cultural developments localized in specific institutions. In his later work, Foucault will shift the emphasis away from the level of institutions per se, and seek to isolate and identify a level of analysis below the threshold of the institution. He will seek to show that the very concepts of society, culture as world view and the individual (and not only madness, reason, science) are themselves produced as part of a more encompassing shift in relationships of power and discourse which had long been in preparation.

In *Madness and Civilization* the autonomy of Pinel's techniques is subordinated to the importance Foucault gives to the figure of the "medical personage." He is leading up to Freud and his emphasis on the patient-doctor relationship and he thus naturally reads previous developments in this light; later he will see Freud as part of a longer trend. However, this discussion of the medical personage introduces another major theme of Foucault's later works, the central importance that practitioners and systems of knowledge about human beings play in the development of structures of confinement and domination in our civilization. It is through the person of the doctor that madness becomes insanity and is thereby integrated as an object of investigation into the medical realm. "With the new status of the medical personage, the deepest meaning of confinement is abolished: mental disease, with the meanings we now give it, is made possible" (*MC* 270).

Both the Quakers and the French rationalists agreed on the importance of medical intervention. For both, the physician became the essential figure of the asylum. First, he had the power to regulate who entered the asylum and who left it. Second, he transformed the interior space of the asylum into a medical one. In *Madness and Civilization,* Foucault emphasizes the moral trustworthiness of the figure of the doctor rather than his scientific status. He says, "The doctor's intervention is not made by virtue of a medical skill or power that he possesses in himself and that would be justified by a body of objective knowledge. It is not as a scientist that *homo medicus* has authority in the asylum, but as a wise man . . . as a juridical and moral guarantee . . ." (*MC* 270).

Foucault in his later works will shift the emphasis back to the importance of the doctor's knowledge as itself the basis of his moral stature. He develops a highly sophisticated analysis of the human sciences—"dubious" sciences that never attain the level of Kuhnian normal science—and their political, social, and cultural functions. Foucault will argue that the fact that the human sciences (and those linked to psychiatry in particular) have contributed little objective knowledge about human beings and yet have attained such importance and power in our civilization is precisely what has to be focused and explained. Why and how this scientific shakiness becomes an essential component of modern power is an essential theme in Foucault's later works. In *Madness and Civilization*, though, Foucault underplays and in a sense reduces the importance and function of knowledge by saying, "If the medical personage could isolate madness, it was not because he knew it, but because he mastered it, and what for positivism would be an image of objectivity was only the other side of this domination" (*MC* 272). What is a mask in *Madness and Civilization* will later be seen as part of a complex strategic construct, an essential component of modern domination.

In *Madness and Civilization* Foucault traces the growth of scientific positivism as an overlay for the real explanation of the power to cure that lay behind objectivity—an explanation which only became clear a century later with the work of Freud. In the nineteenth century, practitioners had no place in their system for an explanation of their own successes. "If we wanted to analyse the profound structures of objectivity in the knowledge and practice of nineteenth century psychiatry from Pinel to Freud, we should have to show in fact that such objectivity was from the start a reification of a magical nature . . . . What we call psychiatric practice is a certain moral tactic contemporary with the end of the eighteenth century, preserved in the rites of asylum life, and overlaid by the myths of positivism" (*MC* 276).

The one thing that positivists could not account for was the effectiveness of their own operations. Foucault points to Freud as the next great locus of change in the saga of reason and madness. Freud, in Foucault's account, achieved his importance from isolating and highlighting, as a scientific object, the doctor-patient relationship as the essential component in the treatment of mental illness. "Freud demystified all the other asylum structures . . . but he exploited the structure that enveloped the medical personage; he amplified its thaumaturgical virtues . . ." (*MC* 277). The locus of operation of the power and effectiveness of the therapist was both given its true importance by Freud and, at the same time, covered over by a further myth of scientism. The authority of the psychoanalyst did not come from his science, as Freud well knew.

But even the ability of the psychoanalyst to understand the mental illness of the patient is obscured, according to Foucault. "Psychoanalysis can unravel some of the forms of madness; it remains a stranger to the sovereign enterprise of unreason" (*MC* 278). Foucault closes *Madness and Civilization* with some highly condensed references to some fundamental form of Otherness which lies beyond the grasp of reason and science and which in some unexplained way seems to give them their possibility. He points to the "lightning flash" of poets like Artaud, Hölderlin, and Nerval, who have somehow escaped the "gigantic moral imprisonment" and glimpsed this fundamental experience of unreason which beckons us beyond the bounds of society. Foucault wonders whether this Otherness is the opening for a "total contestation" of Western culture.

This reference to an absolute Otherness which founds and eludes history is made somewhat less obscure when we see Foucault's later analysis of what he refers to as "the retreat and return of the origin" in *The Order of Things* (328–35). Foucault analyzes this search for a fundamental experience outside of history which founds history as one of the essential forms of modern thought. With the early works of Heidegger clearly in mind, he shows that this philosophic move is characteristic of the most developed forms of modern thought and yet is bound to fail. Indeed, Foucault himself now seeks other ways than the recourse to an ontological boundary which defines us but is necessarily inaccessible to us, to formulate the problem of the limits of man's knowledge of his own being and hence the limits and functions of the human sciences.

In *Madness and Civilization* Foucault associated himself with those rare and special thinkers who had a glimpse of the "sovereign enterprise of unreason." Later he sought to ground his analyses in the body, giving publicly accessible concrete content to whatever remained of his temptation to find the ontological basis of our historical practices. In *The History of Sexuality*, for example, Foucault interprets the search for a secret, inaccessible sexuality behind appearances not as an attempt that correctly pursues the deep truth of the human condition, but rather as a mythic construction of modern thought that plays an important role in our contemporary form of knowledge and power. Foucault has thus given up the attempt—still pursued by those who hold that the hermeneutics of suspicion is the legitimate method of the human sciences—to articulate a deep meaning behind appearances. Rather, as we shall see at length, he now seeks to interpret those appearances as an organized set of historical practices which have produced the subject matter of the human sciences. It is only a slight distortion of the text to substitute "madness" for "the Word of God" and apply Foucault's own criticism of hermeneutics, which he calls exegesis, to his suggestion that madness is a deep secret experience, masked by rationality and discourse, of what it is to be human. Thus Foucault's account of madness as profound otherness comes dangerously close to being "an exegesis which listens, through the prohibitions, the symbols, the concrete images, through the whole apparatus of Revelation, to [madness], ever secret, ever beyond itself" (*BC* xvii).

This sentence from Foucault's next book, *The Birth of the Clinic,* shows how quickly he saw that his flirtation with hermeneutic depth was part of the humanistic tradition he was seeking to overcome and, as such, a dead end. Indeed, the bulk of the analysis in *Madness and Civilization* concerns publicly available practices and their effects, not secret ontological sources, and the book would have been strengthened by eliminating this recourse to ontology. But before Foucault again took up the most promising themes of *Madness and Civilization* he went through an overreaction to hermeneutics, from which he only emerges in his work of the 1970s.

The Archaeology of Medicine

Foucault's methodological overreaction to the search for deep truth behind experience resonates with the wave of structuralism that swept France in the sixties. In his next book, *The Birth of the Clinic* (1963), which appeared two years after the book on madness, Foucault set out to show that "the figures of knowledge and those of language ... obey the same profound law" (*BC* 198)—a structure which underlines the theories, discourse, practices, and sensibility of an age, insofar as they contribute to a "scientific" understanding of what it is to be human.

As one has come to expect from Foucault, this structure changes discontinuously at certain crucial junctures, and, even more exclusively than in *Madness and Civilization,* Foucault concentrates on the "ineradicable chronological threshold" (*BC* 195) between the Classical Age and the modern Age of Man. It will come as no surprise to those familiar with French reflections upon Western society that this "sudden, radical restructuring" (*BC* 62) coincides with the French Revolution.

Foucault accepts the medical profession's standard explanation of the timing and importance of this break, but he gives it a total reinterpretation. The official view is that, with Bichat, medicine finally broke away from fantasy and superstition and arrived at objective truth about the body and its diseases. From the modern perspective of careful perception and neutral description, the older medical accounts seem not only false but literally incomprehensible. What sense can one make of a report, such as the following, with which Foucault begins his book?

> Towards the middle of the eighteenth century, Pomme treated and cured a hysteric by making her take "baths, ten or twelve hours a day, for ten whole months." At the end of this treatment for the dessication of the nervous system and the heat that sustained it, Pomme saw "membranous tissues like pieces of damp parchment . . . peel away with some slight discomfort, and these were passed daily with the urine; the right ureter also peeled away and came out whole in the same way." The same thing occurred with the intestines, which at another stage "peeled off their internal tunics, which we saw emerge from the rectum. The oesophagus, the arterial trachea, and the tongue also peeled in due course; and the patient had rejected different pieces either by vomiting or by expectoration." (*BC* ix)

We do not know whether this report is empirically true or false; nor do we even know what would count as confirmation of such a report.

Foucault's strategy is to take our shocked realization that we don't know what this description, which was at one time taken seriously as an objective account, could even mean, and turn it into a devastating critique of our smug supposition that now, at last, medical science has converged on the objective truth. The point of the archaeological method, which is so important to Foucault at this stage of his work that it appears in the titles of three books, is that the archaeologist performs on all discourse and knowledge, especially our own, the same sort of distanciation of truth and meaning which we naturally bring to the medical accounts and other theories of the Classical Age. But there is also a positive side to the archaeological account. Once we treat the language and practices of a discipline from another age as mere meaningless objects, we can gain access to a level of description which shows that what remains incomprehensible is not without its own systematic order. Doctors like Pomme, giving their strange descriptions, were unknowingly governed by precise structural "codes of knowledge" (*BC* 90).[1] And once we see that the organization of medical knowledge in the Classical Age had a comprehensive formal structure, we can see that what we regard as the meaningful truth claims of modern medicine can likewise be treated as governed by similar arbitrary structures.

1. How general and structuralist Foucault's understanding of "code" is at this stage can best be seen in a remark he makes in the preface to *The Order of Things* three years later: "The fundamental codes of a culture—those governing its language, its schemas of perception, its exchanges, its techniques, its values, the hierarchy of its practices—establish for every man, from the very first, the empirical orders with which he will be dealing and within which he will be at home" (*OT* xx).

It is as if for the first time for thousands of years, doctors, free at last of theories and chimeras, agreed to approach the object of their experience with the purity of an unprejudiced gaze. But the analysis must be turned around: it is the forms of visibility that have changed; the new medical spirit to which Bichat is no doubt the first to bear witness in an absolutely coherent way cannot be ascribed to an act of psychological and epistemological purification; it is nothing more than a syntactical reorganization of disease. (*BC* 195)

It is important to see how far from any sort of hermeneutics Foucault has gone at this point. In the preface to *The Birth of the Clinic* he explicitly criticizes what he calls commentary, which includes both the search for the deep ontological ground hidden by discourse as well as any attempt to resuscitate the lost intelligibility of a discipline that was taken seriously in another age. Kuhn, for example, points out that at first sight Aristotelian physics seems puzzling and implausible, but rather than using this as a wedge to make us reconsider our assurance that our own physics at last makes sense, Kuhn sets out to make Aristotle plausible. After all, Kuhn notes, what Aristotle had to say about biology and politics was "both penetrating and deep." The proof of the success of his hermeneutic reawakening of Aristotle's way of looking at nature is that much "apparent absurdity vanished."[2] Nothing could be further from Foucault's method than such an attempt to revive lost meaning by filling out its horizon of intelligibility. If we follow this line of investigation, Foucault warns, "We are doomed historically to history, to the patient construction of discourses about discourses, and to the task of hearing what has already been said" (*BC* xvi).

Foucault wonders whether it is not possible to substitute "structural analysis" (*BC* xvii) for commentary. He promises to demonstrate in his "archaeology of medical perception" that another approach, which does not try to find a deeper meaning and a more essential truth in discourse by adding still more discourse, is possible. "It will be based neither on the present consciousness of clinicians, nor even on a repetition of what they once might have said" (*BC* xv). He wants to show that medical discourse, practice, and experience can be made intelligible in a different way, viz. by showing that they have a systematic structure.

We are concerned here not simply with medicine and the way in which, in a few years, the particular knowledge of the individual patient was structured. For clinical experience to become possible as a form of knowledge, a reorganization of the hospital field, a new definition of the status of the patient in

2. Kuhn, *Essential Tension*, pp. xi, xii, xiii.

14

society, and the establishment of a certain relationship between public assistance and medical experience, between help
and knowledge, became necessary; the patient has to be enveloped in a collective, homogeneous space....
    This structure, in which space, language, and death are
articulated—what is known, in fact, as the anatomo-clinical
method—constitutes the historical condition of a medicine that
is given and accepted as positive. (*BC* 196)

Using this method we see that when the classical structure of
medicine suddenly gave way to the modern structure of clinical perception what essentially changed was not semantic content but the syntactic
form. "The figures of pain are not conjured away by means of a body of
neutralized knowledge; they have been redistributed in the space in which
bodies and eyes meet. What has changed is the silent configuration in
which language finds support" (*BC* xi).
    In *The Birth of the Clinic*, Foucault moves away from his study of
social practices which attempt to make sense of and control the deep
subjective universal experience of madness, to examine those practices
which enable human beings to treat themselves as objects in the purest
sense. Now, instead of seeing discourse and practices as attempts to
systematize the deepest and most inaccessible reaches of human experience, Foucault, in line with his shift from a kind of hermeneutics to a sort
of structuralism, turns his attention to the analysis of the body as a corpse
laid out before the doctor's gaze, whose thing-like solidity leaves no place
at all for the search for hidden significance.

    It will no doubt remain a decisive fact about our culture that
    its first scientific discourse concerning the individual had to
    pass through this stage of death. Western man could constitute
    himself in his own eyes as an object of science, . . . only in the
    opening created by his own elimination: from the experience of
    Unreason was born psychology, . . . from the integration of
    death into medical thought is born a medicine that is given as a
    science of the individual. (*BC* 197)

The Birth of the Clinic, with its attempt to find the silent structure
which sustains practices, discourse, perceptual experience (the gaze), as
well as the knowing subject and its objects, represents Foucault's extreme
swing towards structuralism. But, although "unable to avoid . . . frequent
recourse to structural analysis" (*AK* 16), even at this point Foucault was
never quite a structuralist. He was not seeking *atemporal* structures, but
"*historical* . . . conditions of possibility" (*BC* xix, our italics). But in the
clinic book he does hold that archaeology could discover "deep structures" (*BC* 90) underlying medicine or presumably any other serious discipline which studied human beings.

15

2 The Archaeology of the Human Sciences

By the time he finished his history of madness and his archaeology of medical discourse and practice Foucault had a number of methodological options and possible domains of study available to him. He could have pursued the study of the meaning of discursive practices and their relative dependence on social institutions—the sort of history *Madness and Civilization* had opened up and to which he was later to return—or he could have developed the archaeological approach of *The Birth of the Clinic,* which sought to avoid meaning by emphasizing the structural conditions of the possibility of both practice and discourse. In either case, to do justice to the important methodological discoveries of both books, he would have had to purify his method by restricting the claims made in each. He could have followed his structuralist insights into the futility of seeking deep ontological meanings, extending the analysis of the historical practices underlying language and institutions of the madness book while eliminating its ontological claims. Or else, taking self-critically the analyses in *Madness and Civilization,* which show long-term strategies of control conditioning, and using the methods and results obtained in the "objective" sciences of man, he could have developed the archaeological description of *The Birth of the Clinic* while restricting its quasi-structuralist claims. Instead of seeking a code which would encompass and sustain the total domain of social, political, institutional, and discursive practices, he could have restricted his archaeological method to a more plausible (although ultimately untenable) attempt to discover the structural rules governing discourse alone.

In fact, this last option is the one Foucault chose. Under the influence of the structuralist enthusiasm sweeping Paris, he sought to purify and retain just those formal aspects of his work which now seem most

16

dubious both to us and to him. That is, he played down his interest in social institutions, and concentrated almost exclusively on discourse, its autonomy and discontinuous transformations. It is this attempt to divorce discourse as far as possible from its social setting and to discover the rules of its self-regulation which we will analyze and then criticize in the rest of part I.

While restricting his method to the analysis of discourse, Foucault broadened his domain of investigation to cover the central sciences of man. This was a natural extension since Foucault had always been interested in how human beings understand themselves in our culture. Having first tried to understand how Western civilization attempted to consider and make sense of what was radically "other" about human beings, he now turned to the systems of self-understanding Western thought had generated through reflection on those aspects of human beings that were most accessible to it. These aspects could roughly be classified as the social, the embodied individual, and shared meanings. In Foucault's classification they become the study of the various disciplines that have dealt with labor, life, and language. These are the subject matter of his book, *The Order of Things* (1966).

Foucault felt, as did many other intellectuals in France at the time, that the understanding of human beings had reached a crucial juncture. It seemed that at last the study of human beings, having taken several promising steps which in the end failed to live up to their own promise, had finally found a program that could be carried out. The structuralist projects of Lévi-Strauss, Lacan, and Chomsky seemed to have opened up a domain of formal analysis which could be profitably pursued by anyone who could free himself from traditional preconceptions. *The Order of Things*, subtitled *An Archaeology of the Human Sciences* (and originally entitled *The Archaeology of Structuralism*) is precisely an attempt to further these structuralist disciplines by determining "the possibilities and rights, the conditions and limitations, of a justified formalization" (*OT* 382).

The archaeology of the human sciences applies and purifies the method developed for the archaeology of medical perception. It attempts to study the structure of the discourses of the various disciplines that have claimed to put forth theories of society, individuals, and language. As Foucault puts it, "Such an analysis does not belong to the history of ideas or of science: it is rather an inquiry whose aim is to rediscover on what basis knowledge and theory became possible; within what space of order knowledge was constituted; on the basis of what historical *a priori* . . . ideas could appear, sciences be established, experience be reflected in philosophies, rationalities be formed, only, perhaps, to dissolve and vanish soon afterwards" (*OT* xxi, xxii). To do this job Foucault introduced his celebrated but short-lived notion, *episteme*, which he later defined as follows:

> By *episteme*, we mean ... the total set of relations that unite, at a given period, the discursive practices that give rise to epistemological figures, sciences, and possibly formalized systems.... The episteme is not a form of knowledge *(connaissance)* or type of rationality which, crossing the boundaries of the most varied sciences, manifests the sovereign unity of a subject, a spirit, or a period; it is the totality of relations that can be discovered, for a given period, between the sciences when one analyses them at the level of discursive regularities. *(AK* 191)

To carry out this enterprise Foucault attempts to isolate and describe the epistemic systems which underlie three major epochs in Western thought. These epochs are conventionally labelled: the Renaissance, the Classical Age, and Modernity. Foucault's archaeological level of analysis allows him to characterize them in a new and revealing way. After a brief, insightful account of resemblance as the basic organizing principle of the Renaissance, Foucault devotes much of *The Order of Things* to a detailed analysis of the episteme of the Classical Age, which turns on the relation of representation and mathesis. Only from this distance is he prepared for a look at Modernity. The archaeological method of detachment allows him to characterize Modernity as the Age of Man, and to show that "man" is a special kind of total subject and total object of his own knowledge, which gives to the sciences of man an especially tortured and ultimately stultifying structure.

In the next three chapters we will summarize Foucault's fascinating account of the Classical Age only insofar as it provides a necessary contrast to his analysis of Modernity. We will then attempt to explicate his crucially important and highly condensed account of man, and the intellectually powerful but ultimately self-defeating strategies which man has tried to use to understand himself. Finally, we will examine in some detail Foucault's methodological reflections on his first books, and we will argue that, although his metatheory about Western theories of human beings frees Foucault from the difficulties he correctly diagnosed in the sciences of man, he nonetheless turns out to be caught in just the sort of convoluted impasses he taught us to recognize. Only then will we be in a position to appreciate the new and fruitful role Foucault assigns to archaeology in his subsequent works.

The Rise of Representation in the Classical Age

The Classical episteme *can be defined in its most general arrangement in terms of the articulated system of a* mathesis, *a* taxonomia *and a* genetic analysis. *The sciences always carry within themselves the project, however remote it may be, of an exhaustive ordering of the world; they are always directed, too, towards the discovery of simple elements and their progressive combination; and at their center they form a table on which knowledge is displayed in a system. As for the great controversies that occupied men's minds, these are accommodated quite naturally in the folds of this organization.* (OT 74, 75)

According to Foucault, the Classical Age set itself the project of constructing a universal method of analysis which would yield perfect certainty by perfectly ordering representations and signs to mirror the ordering of the world, the order of being—for being, in the Classical Age, had a universal order. The place in which this ordering could be displayed was the table. There the universal method of analysis could lay forth in a clear and progressive fashion the representations which would give us the picture of the true order of the world. It is on this table that the particular sciences took their place, but it is the possibility of that table which defines the most general structures of the episteme.

Foucault points to Descartes as an emblematic figure who sought certitude through the search for a method that would guarantee it. The key terms become comparison and order. Comparison becomes a method with universalizing intent, based on finding simple natures in the subject being analyzed and then building from these simples. If the simples have been correctly isolated and the method of building is sure then we can progress from the most simple to the most complex with perfect assurance. We establish a series in which the first term is a nature that we intuit independently of any other nature. In this way all questions of identity and difference can be reduced, through the use of method, to questions of order. "It is precisely in this that the method and its 'progress' consist: the reduction of all measurement (all determination by equality and inequality) to a serial arrangement which, beginning from the simplest, will show up all differences as degrees of complexity" (*OT* 54). The correct ordering of elements, from simple to complex, in a calibrated progression, becomes crucial. This is an operation of method, the method of analysis. If it is carried out correctly, perfect certainty is achieved.

The key tool which will allow the method of analysis to produce the certain ordering of things in a table is the sign. "An arbitrary system of signs must permit the analysis of things into their simplest elements; it must be capable of decomposing them into their very origins; but it must also demonstrate how combinations of those elements are possible, and permit the ideal genesis of the complexity of things..." *OT* 62).

In the Classical Age man was not *the* maker, *the* artificer—God—but

19

as the locus of clarification, he was *an* artificer. There was a world created by God, existing by itself. The role of man was to clarify the order of the world. He did this, as we have seen, by way of clear and certain ideas. The key was that the medium of representation was reliable and transparent. The role of the thinker was to give an artificial description of the order which was already there. He did not create the world, nor ultimately the representations. He constructed an artificial language, a conventional ordering of signs. But it was not man who filled them with meaning. This is what Foucault means when he says that there was no theory of signification in the Classical Age. Man clarified but did not create; he was not a transcendental source of signification. Hence if we were to ask what was the special activity of the subject—the "I think"—we would get the relatively trivial answer that it was the tendency to attain clarity about concepts.

Hence nature and human nature are linked together. Human nature has a special role in relation to nature that turns on the human activity of knowing. "In the general arrangement of the Classical *episteme,* nature, human nature, and their relations, are definite and predictable functional moments" (*OT* 310). They are linked together by the power of discourse. Representation and being come together in discourse, that is, language insofar as it represents. But it follows therefore that "Classical language as the *common discourse* of representation and things, as the place within which nature and human nature intersect, absolutely excludes anything that could be a 'science of man.' As long as that language was spoken in Western culture it was not possible for human existence to be called in question on its own account, since it contained the nexus of representation and being" (*OT* 311). Since it was taken for granted that language by its very nature made possible successful representation, the role of human beings in relating representations and things could not itself be problematized.

This can be put another way: the activity of human beings in constructing the table could not itself be represented; there was no place for it on the table. Since a real being was in fact constructing this table there certainly should have been a place for him. There was a place for the human knower as a rational animal, high in God's hierarchy, but *not* for the representer per se; for man as a special, different kind of being, man as ordering subject could find no place on the table he organized. Foucault is concerned exclusively with the systematization of the actual statements of an age, and he sees the Classical Age as having no place for man as positing subject and posited object. Man cannot enter the classical picture without the whole scheme undergoing a radical transformation.

For Foucault the age of representation can be summed up by an analysis of what can and cannot be put in a picture when one tries to represent the understanding of being during the Classical Age. Foucault opens *The Order of Things* with a dense description of *Las Meninas,* a painting by Velázquez (1656). Foucault reads the painting in terms of representation and subject, the emblem of his story in *The Order of Things.* His explication of the painting serves to thematize the structure of knowledge in the Classical Age as well as the period which follows, the Age of Man. Foucault's analysis of the picture shows how all the themes of the classical view of representation are represented. Foucault's commitment to his archaeological method, as we shall see, rules out a reference to instabilities not explicitly found in the discourse of the age, but he nevertheless provides hints (which he expands much later in the book) of how the instabilities of the age already presage the appearance of man.

Let us follow Foucault in reading *Las Meninas.*

> The painter is standing a little back from his canvas. He is glancing at his model; perhaps he is considering whether to add some finishing touch, though it is also possible that the first stroke has not yet been made. The arm holding the brush is bent to the left, towards the palette; it is motionless, for an instant, between canvas and paints. The skilled hand is suspended in mid-air, arrested in rapt attention on the painter's gaze; and the gaze, in return, waits upon the arrested gesture. Between the fine point of the brush and the steely gaze, the scene is about to yield up its volume. (*OT* 3)

We see the painter depicted in a frozen moment as he stands back from his work and looks out at his model. If he was actually in the process of painting he would disappear behind the large framed canvas on which he is working. But, as depicted, he isn't working; he is caught between strokes, allowing him to be visible to us, the spectators. "Now he can be seen, caught in a moment of stillness, at the neutral centre of this oscillation. . . . As though the painter could not at the same time be seen on the picture where he is represented and also see that upon which he is representing something. He rules at that threshold of these two incompatible visibilities" (*OT* 3, 4).

The painter in the painting is staring at a space in which we, as spectators, are located. We can't be sure what he is painting, as his canvas has its back to us. However, by the structure of the painting we are fixed in the painter's gaze, joined to the picture by the fact that it is we who seem to be observed by the painter. "In appearance, this locus is a simple one; a matter of pure reciprocity; we are looking at a picture in which the painter is in turn looking out at us." However, "the painter is

Las Meninas by Velásquez. Copyright © Prado Museum, Madrid

turning his eyes towards us only in so far as we happen to occupy the same position as his subject. We, the spectators, are an additional factor" (*OT* 4). Clearly we occupy the place which the painter's model must also occupy.

"As soon as they place the spectator in the field of their gaze, the painter's eyes seize hold of him, force him to enter the picture, assign him a place at once privileged and inescapable, levy their luminous and visible tribute from him, and project it upon the inaccessible surface of the canvas within the picture" (*OT* 5). Model and spectator coincide: "In this precise but neutral place, the observer and the observed take part in a ceaseless exchange" (*OT* 4, 5).

Since we cannot see what is on the canvas, we cannot tell with certainty who occupies the model's place. This prevents the oscillation of gazes from being fixed. "The painter is observing a place which, from moment to moment, never ceases to change its content, its form, its face, its identity" (*OT* 5). Velásquez painting, the model being observed, and the spectator's viewing all this as a painting—are all brought into a relationship, a relationship which is necessary and assured by the unstable and elusive organization of the painting.

The light is another important factor. It floods the room from a window on the left, illuminating the scene, the paintings on the wall, and presumably the painting which is being painted. "This extreme, partial, scarcely indicated window frees a whole flow of daylight which serves as the common locus of the representation . . . . [It is] a light which renders all representation visible" (*OT* 6). We see the illumination but not its source. The source is outside the painting. As such, "it provides a ground which is common to the painting and to what lies outside it" (*OT* 10). Clearly, this is the light of the Enlightenment, which sets up a space in which objects and representations correspond. For the Enlightenment thinkers, "light, anterior to every gaze, was the element of ideality—the unassignable place of origin where things were adequate to their essence and the form by which things reached it through the geometry of bodies; according to them, the act of seeing, having attained perfection, was absorbed back into the unbending, unending figure of light" (*BC* xiii).

On the far wall at the back of the room, we see a series of pictures, largely hidden in shadow. There is, however, one exception which stands out with a particular glow. It is not a painting, but a mirror. All of the paintings in *Las Meninas* are obscured to us, either by their place or by their lack of illumination. Only the mirror seems to reveal what it represents: "Of all the representations in the picture this is the only one visible; but no one is looking at it" (*OT* 7). The painter is staring away from it; the other figures in the painting are also staring ahead towards us, or at least away from the direction which would enable them to see the mirror.

23

By the conventions of Dutch painting at the time, the mirror ought to reveal, in a distorted perspective, the contents of the painting in which it is set. But this is not what it is doing; in fact, it reveals nothing of what is represented in the painting itself. "At the far end of the room, ignored by all, the unexpected mirror holds in its glow the figures that the painter is looking at . . . ; but also the figures that are looking at the painter . . ." (*OT* 8). Foucault says that the mirror provides "a metathesis of visibility" by bringing into the picture a representation of those figures who are being painted.

What we see in the mirror is an image of two figures, King Philip IV and his wife, Mariana. They are indeed the models whom the painter is depicting. They can and do occupy that place for the painter. But this is a trick; for, we too, as spectators, occupy that place. The mirror should also reveal us—but this, of course, it cannot do.

Next to the mirror, in the painting, there is a softly lighted doorway framing a figure in full-length silhouette. He is seen in profile and seems to have just arrived. He is shown observing the scene in the painting, looking out at both the figures who are represented in the painting and the models who are being painted. Clearly, he is a representation of the spectator. As Foucault elliptically puts it, "Perhaps he too, a short while ago, was there in the forefront of the scene, in the invisible region still being contemplated by all those eyes in the picture. Like the images perceived in the looking-glass, it is possible that he too is an emissary from that evident yet hidden space" (*OT* 11). The spectating function, which is not represented in the mirror, is placed next to it—the passing spectator also intent upon the place that holds the attention of the painter and all the other figures in the painting.

This place is important, above all because of the triple function it fulfills in the picture. "For in it there occurs an exact superimposition of the model's gaze as it is being painted, of the spectator's as he contemplates the painting, and of the painter's as he is composing his picture (not the picture concealed on the canvas, but the one in front of us which we are discı ssing). These three 'observing' functions come together in a point exterior to the picture." This point is an ideal one, otherwise it would be impossibly overcrowded, but it is also a real one because it is the actual place occupied by the viewer. In any case, "that reality is projected within the picture—projected and diffracted in three forms which correspond to the three functions of that ideal and real point. They are: on the left, the painter with his palette in his hand [and his eyes on the model] (a self-portrait of Velázquez); to the right, the visitor, one foot on the step, ready to enter the room; . . . and lastly, in the centre, the reflection of the king and the queen, richly dressed, motionless, in the attitude of patient models [in the act of watching those who are watching them]" (*OT* 15).

Obviously, as Foucault reads it, the subject matter of *Las Meninas* is representation. What *Las Meninas* represents is the world of representations laid out in an orderly fashion on a table, in this instance, in the painting itself. What is represented are the functions of representation. What is not represented is a unified and unifying subject who posits these representations and who makes them objects for himself. This subject will emerge, in Foucault's account, with the emergence of man, with Kant. The crucial change to note is that the sovereign of the Classical Age is a model. But to be a model is to be a center of attention and only incidentally (as accidental as the image caught in the mirror) to be the object of representation. Likewise, he is a spectator who represents the scene to himself but he is not identified with this spectator role. Thus, he is not essentially the passive object of the painting nor the observer of its world. Lastly, he is not the painter who has organized and, in the last analysis, posited the scene.

In *Las Meninas* the aspects of representation—the subject matter of the painting—have been dispersed into three separate figures. Their representations are spread out in the picture itself. These aspects are the producing of the representation (the painter), the object represented (the models and their gaze), and the viewing of the representation (the spectator). Each of these separate functions can and has been represented by Velázquez. This dispersion of representation is necessary so that all these functions can be laid out in an organized table. This is what Foucault means when he says "representation . . . can offer itself as representation in its pure form" (*OT* 16).

The price paid for this success is that the activity of representation, the unified temporal unfolding of the functions of representation, cannot be represented on the table. And it is this tension which produces the instability in the painting and in the episteme. The central paradox of the painting turns on *the impossibility of representing the act of representing.* If the essential undertaking of the Classical Age was to put ordered representations onto a table, the one thing this age could not achieve was to put its own activity on the table so constructed. Hence the three functions of representation, but not the activity itself, have been successfully captured in the painting. First, the painter, who posits the painting, Foucault tells us, cannot be represented in the act of painting. He is pausing. He will disappear behind the canvas once he begins painting again. Second, the models are dimly and peripherally caught in the mirror. But centrally we see the characters all staring at the models; they are not directly represented in the act of modeling. If the king were to be brought into the painting all the internal tensions would collapse; the foreground would fill the frame and the perspective would be broken; the interplay and oscillation of spectator and model would be frozen. This in fact is what would

25

happen if the sovereign as both object and subject were the essential subject matter of the painting. But he isn't; representation is the subject matter of the painting. The king is only a model. Third, what the spectator sees is that there is a painting being painted; he views the representation as representation. But when Velázquez places the surrogate spectator in the back of the painting he is no longer observing the painting, but becomes an object painted. Nor does the mirror capture us as spectators looking at the painting being painted; it shows the royal couple. Hence the spectating function is also not represented as an act.

Foucault says essentially this when he says, "In this picture, as in all the representations of which it is, as it were, the manifest essence, the profound invisibility of what one sees is inseparable from the invisibility of the person seeing—despite all mirrors, reflections, imitations, and portraits" (*OT* 16). What one sees are the functions of representation spread out on the painting. What are profoundly invisible are representing as an activity and the source of light which makes it possible. They are nowhere represented—because they cannot be. This is precisely what Velázquez has shown: the visibility of all the ways representation works and the profound invisibility of showing it being accomplished. By first showing the spectator in the doorway, the mirror on the back wall, and the painter painting he has laid out the three functions of the subject. But in the painting itself no one sees them; they are placed behind the people in the picture who are gazing out at the model. Likewise, the person seeing, the true spectator outside of the pictures, is also profoundly invisible; he cannot be represented in the painting.

Hence the particular instabilities of representation. The painting is perfectly successful; it shows all the functions required for representation and the impossibility of bringing them together into a unified representation of their activity. Everything is referred to a single point where, by the internal logic of the painting and of the age, the artist, model, and spectator should all be. Velázquez can't picture this. Something essential has not been represented. However, this is not a failure; if the task of the painter was to represent everything that could be represented Velázquez did his job well.

Man and His Doubles: The Analytic of Finitude

The connection of the positivities with finitude, the reduplication of the empirical and the transcendental, the perpetual relation of the cogito *to the unthought, the retreat and return of the origin, define for us man's mode of being. It is in the analysis of that mode of being, and no longer in the analysis of representation, that reflection since the nineteenth century has sought a philosophical foundation for the possibility of knowledge.* (OT 335)

Suddenly, according to Foucault's story, somewhere at the end of the eighteenth century there occurred one of the most dramatic of those epistemic shifts which Foucault's archaeology is designed to chart. A "profound upheaval," "an archaeological mutation" (*OT* 312) occurred which signaled the collapse of the Classical Age and made possible the emergence of man. Representation suddenly became opaque. As long as discourse provided a transparent medium of representation whose linguistic elements corresponded to primitive elements in the world, representation was not problematic. God had arranged a chain of being and arranged language in preestablished correspondence with it. Human beings happened to have the capacity to use linguistic signs, but human beings as rational speaking animals were simply one more kind of creature whose nature could be read off from its proper definition so that it could be arranged in its proper place on the table of beings. There is no need for any finite being to make representation possible; no place in the picture for a being who posits it. "In Classical thought, the personage for whom the representation exists, and who represents himself within it, ... he who ties together all the interlacing threads of the 'representation in the form of a picture or table'—he is never to be found in that table himself" (*OT* 308). Man as that being who gets the whole picture as well as gets into the picture is unthinkable in the Classical episteme. "In the general arrangement of the Classical *episteme,* nature, human nature, and their relations, are definite and predictable functional moments. And man, as a primary reality with his own density, as the difficult object and sovereign subject of all possible knowledge, has no place in it" (*OT* 310).

Only when classical discourse no longer appears as a perfectable medium whose natural elements represent the natural elements in the world, only then does the representing relation itself become a problem. Foucault offers us no reasons for this major change. He merely charts the changes which occurred, refusing the traditional gambit of history or the social sciences. He does not explain. The reason for this obstinacy may be less a penchant for obscurantism than the simple fact that any explanation would only make sense within a specific frame of reference and hence within a specific episteme. Any explanation put forth to explain the change from one period to the next would add nothing to our understanding of the fundamentally abrupt and unexpected nature of these changes.

In the major change with which we are here concerned, man, as we know him today, makes his appearance and becomes the measure of all things. Once the order of the world was no longer God-given and representable in a table, then the continuous relation which had placed man with the other beings of the world was broken. Man, who was once himself a being among others, now is a subject among objects. But Man is not only a subject among objects, he soon realizes that what he is seeking to understand is not only the objects of the world but himself. Man becomes the subject and the object of his own understanding.

Man now appears limited by his involvement in a language which is no longer a transparent medium but a dense web with its own inscrutable history. Without a field of light which gives direct access to the structure of objects and the world, the knower, insofar as he is enmeshed in language, is no longer a pure spectator. "At the end of the eighteenth century, . . . seeing consists in leaving to experience its greatest corporal opacity; the solidity, the obscurity, the density of things closed in upon themselves, have powers of truth that they owe not to light" (*BC* xiii). Man is totally involved with, and his understanding is obscured by, the very objects he seeks to know: "All these contents that his knowledge reveals to him as exterior to himself, and older than his own birth, anticipate him, overhang him with all their solidity, and traverse him as though he were merely an object of nature.... Man's finitude is heralded—and imperiously so—in the positivity of knowledge..." (*OT* 313).

But the response of Kant and the age that followed was not to lament this limitation; rather they tried to turn it to advantage, making it the basis of all factual, that is, positive, knowledge. "The limitation is expressed not as a determination imposed upon man from outside (because he has a nature or a history), but as a fundamental finitude which rests on nothing but its own existence as fact, and opens upon the positivity of all concrete limitation" (*OT* 315). Since language no longer does the job of representing and thus making knowledge possible, the representing function itself becomes a problem. The job of making representation possible is taken over by man. "The analysis of man's mode of being as it has developed since the nineteenth century does not reside within a theory of representation; its task, on the contrary, is to show how things in general can be given to representation, in what conditions, upon what ground..." (*OT* 337).

Instead of an *analysis* of representations one now finds an *analytic*. From Kant on, an analytic is an attempt to show on what grounds representation and analysis of representations are possible and to what extent they are legitimate. "The pre-critical analysis of what man is in his essence becomes the analytic of everything that can, in general, be presented to man's experience (*OT* 341).... Where there had formerly been a correlation between a *metaphysics* of representation and of the infinite and an *analysis* of living beings, of man's desires, and of the words of his language, we find being constituted an analytic of finitude and human existence" (*OT* 317).

This attempt to treat factual limitations as finitude and then make finitude the condition of the possibility of all facts is an entirely new notion. "The modern themes of an individual who lives, speaks, and works in accordance with the laws of an economics, a philology, and a biology, but who also, by a sort of internal torsion and overlapping, has acquired the right, through the interplay of those very laws, to know them and to subject them to total clarification—all these themes so familiar to us today and linked to the existence of the 'human sciences' are excluded by Classical thought" (*OT* 310).

Thus man emerges not merely as both subject and object of knowledge, but even more paradoxically, as organizer of the spectacle in which he appears. The unthought of *Las Meninas* had reserved a place for him. As Foucault puts it in placing man in the empty space front and center in Velázquez's painting:

> Man appears in his ambiguous position as an object of
> knowledge and as a subject that knows: enslaved sovereign,
> observed spectator, he appears in the place belonging to the
> king, which was assigned to him in advance by *Las Meninas,*
> but from which his real presence has for so long been
> excluded. As if, in that vacant space towards which
> Velázquez's whole painting was directed, but which it was
> nevertheless reflecting only in the chance presence of a mirror,
> and as though by stealth, all the figures whose alternation,
> reciprocal exclusion, interweaving, and fluttering one imagined
> (the model, the painter, the king, the spectator) suddenly
> stopped their imperceptible dance, immobilized into one
> substantial figure, and demanded that the entire space of the
> representation should at last be related to one corporeal gaze.
> (*OT* 312)

As Foucault implies in putting man in the place of the king, man no longer merely claims to be capable of knowing the laws of the world which seem to limit him and his knowledge. These limitations are no longer viewed as imposed *upon* man, due to his intermediate place in the great table of beings, but as somehow decreed or imposed *by* man. Thus in a startling inversion man claims total knowledge by virtue of his limitations.

> To man's experience a body has been given, a body which is
> his body—a fragment of ambiguous space, whose peculiar and
> irreducible spatiality is nevertheless articulated upon the space
> of things; to this same experience, desire is given as a
> primordial appetite on the basis of which all things assume

value, and relative value; to this same experience, a language
is given in the thread of which all the discourses of all times, all
successions and all simultaneities may be given. This is to say
that each of these positive forms in which man can learn that
he is finite is given to him only against the background of its
own finitude. Moreover, the latter is not the most completely
purified essence of positivity, but that upon the basis of which
it is possible for positivity to arise. (*OT* 314)

Modernity begins with the incredible and ultimately unworkable
idea of a being who is sovereign precisely by virtue of being enslaved, a
being whose very finitude allows him to take the place of God. This
startling idea, which breaks forth full blown in Kant, that "the limits of
knowledge provide a positive foundation for the possibility of knowing"
(*OT* 317), Foucault calls the analytic of finitude. It is "an analytic . . . in
which man's being will be able to provide a foundation in their own
positivity for all those forms that indicate to him that he is not infinite"
(*OT* 315). Foucault recognizes this desperate move as definitive both of
man and of the modern age. "Our culture crossed the threshold beyond
which we recognize our modernity when finitude was conceived in an
interminable cross-reference with itself" (*OT* 318).

Having argued that man is an invention of modern thought, Foucault
proceeds to outline the rules for man's tortured transformations. There
turn out to be three ways in which man's factual limitations (the
positivities) are both distinguished from and equated with those conditions which make knowledge possible (the fundamental).

From one end of experience to the other, finitude answers
itself; it is the identity and the difference of the positivities, and
of their foundation, within the figure of the *Same* . . . .
It is within this vast but narrow space, opened up by the
repetition of the positive within the fundamental, that the
whole of this analytic of finitude—so closely linked to the
future of modern thought—will be deployed; it is there that we
shall see in succession the transcendental repeat the empirical,
the cogito repeat the unthought, the return of the origin repeat
its retreat . . . . (*OT* 315, 316)

We now turn to a discussion of each of the ways that the finite
limitations which Foucault calls the empirical, the unthought, and the
missing origin, respectively, are taken to be different from and yet
identical with (that is, to repeat) some ground or source of their own
possibility. First, however, we must include a few general remarks
concerning Foucault's method.

Since Foucault holds that what counts as truth is determined by the conceptual system or, more accurately, the discursive practices of a particular discipline, it makes no sense for him to say that a particular theory in the sciences of man is true or that it is mistaken. He cannot argue that since anthropological discourse is full of contradictions it is untrue, as if, were it only coherent, its theories would be true or at least have a chance of being confirmed. All that Foucault can say in criticizing the fundamental assumptions of discourse about man is that they lead to "warped" and "twisted" forms of reflection (*OT* 343), and the "proof" of his analysis would have to be that humanistic discourse is in fact "disintegrating"—that excitement and energy have gradually given way either to boredom and discouragement or factions and fads.

Foucault makes a strong case for this alleged decline. He seeks to show that with man's attempt to fully affirm his finitude and at the same time to completely deny it, discourse sets up a space in which the analytic of finitude, doomed from the start, twists through a series of futile strategies. Each new attempt will have to claim an identity and a difference between finitude as limitation and finitude as source of all facts, between the positive and the fundamental. Seen under this double aspect man appears: (1) as a fact among other facts to be studied empirically, and yet as the transcendental condition of the possibility of all knowledge; (2) as surrounded by what he cannot get clear about (the unthought), and yet as a potentially lucid cogito, source of all intelligibility; and (3) as the product of a long history whose beginning he can never reach and yet, paradoxically, as the source of that very history.

> In showing that man is determined, [the analytic of finitude] is concerned with showing that the foundation of those determinations is man's very being in its radical limitations; it must also show that the contents of experience are already their own conditions, that thought, from the very beginning, haunts the unthought that eludes them, and that it is always striving to recover; it shows how that origin of which man is never the contemporary is at the same time withdrawn and given as an imminence: in short, it is always concerned with showing how the Other, the Distant, is also the Near and the Same. (*OT* 339)

If all the possible permutations of this humanistic system of thought were fully played out we would expect to see three doubles (which Foucault calls transcendental/empirical, cogito/unthought, and retreat/return of origin) appear, characteristic both of man's mode of being and of the anthropological discourse which attempts to provide a theory of this dual mode of being. We would also expect to find each of these doubles in both a modern (nineteenth century) and a contemporary (twentieth century) form. There are, then, two ways of working out each double depending on which side absorbs the other; there are three doubles, and they each appear in two periods. That makes twelve possible ploys in all.

We will look only at the most distinctive moves, both in order to gauge the power of Foucault's specific critique of the human sciences and to prepare to test Foucault's general method. Ultimately we will want to decide whether the systematic study he calls archaeology is free from these doubles and thus provides a genuine alternative to the sciences of man. We will argue that Foucault's method at the time he wrote *The Order of Things* is close to structuralist theory, and, although beyond talk of man, still partakes of some of the very difficulties Foucault criticizes. This will lead us to an understanding of how and why the archaeological method is changed and improved upon, though not abandoned, in Foucault's subsequent work.

THE EMPIRICAL AND THE TRANSCENDENTAL

The threshold of our modernity is situated not by the attempt to apply objective methods to the study of man, but rather by the constitution of an empirico-transcendental doublet which was called man. (OT 319)

The possibility of turning the knower's messy involvement in the factual world of language, life, and labor into the pure ground of knowledge, of turning the post hoc into the a priori, finds its earliest instantiation in the radical Kantian distinction between the empirical and the transcendental. Kant attempts to rescue the pure *form* of knowing from history and factuality by relegating all contingency and obscurity to the side of the *content* of knowledge. But this simple distinction does not solve the problem of positivity, since it soon becomes apparent that not only the content but also the form of empirical knowledge can be seen as subject to empirical influences.

The nature of the form of knowledge was studied by thinkers who sought to assimilate the transcendental to the empirical. They developed the line suggested by Kant's transcendental aesthetic. Granted the form of our sensibilities supplies the conditions of the possibility of knowledge; why not give an empirical basis to all empirical science by investigating the specific structure of our senses? There have been endless variations on this naturalist-reductionist dream. Each would ground all knowledge in an empirical theory of perception. Other thinkers, concerned with the same problem, followed the lead of Kant's transcendental dialectic. They sought to assimilate the transcendental to the historical by laying out the history of man's thought so as to produce "a *history* of human knowledge . . . and prescribe its forms" (*OT* 319).

These positions assume that there is some truth in itself, accessible either through perception or through history, and that some discipline is in possession of a neutral discourse capable of revealing this truth. According to Foucault, "it is the status of this true discourse which remains ambiguous" (*OT* 320). Either one bases the truth of the categories used on the truth of a nature or history independent of discourse, in which case one has an uncritical positivism: "The truth of the object determines the truth of the discourse which describes its formation" (*OT* 320). Or else, discourse guarantees its validity by producing an eschatological truth, as in the case of Marx. Foucault sees these as not so much alternatives as a "fluctuation inherent in all analysis, which brings out the value of the empirical at the transcendental level. . . . Comte and Marx both bear out the fact that eschatology (as the objective truth proceeding from man's discourse) and positivism (as the truth of discourse defined on the basis of the truth of the object) are archaeologically indissociable: a discourse attempting to be both empirical and critical cannot but be both positivist and eschatological; man appears within it as a truth both reduced and promised. Pre-critical naïveté holds undivided rule" (*OT* 320).

The unstable tensions between a theory of man based on human nature and a dialectical theory in which man's essence is historical lead to a search for a new analytic of the subject. One sought a discipline which both has empirical content and yet is transcendental, a *concrete a priori*, which could give an account of man as a self-producing source of perception, culture, and history. This approach attains its most complete form in the twentieth century in what Foucault calls "the analytic of actual experience," or, following Merleau-Ponty, an "existential phenomenology." Foucault shows a deep appreciation of the attraction of the work of his former teacher. Such a phenomenology, he tells us, "does indeed provide a means of communication between the space of the body and the time of culture, between the determinations of nature and the weight of history" (*OT* 321). He adds, "It is easy enough to understand how the analysis of actual experience has established itself, in modern reflection, as a radical contestation of positivism and eschatology; how it has tried to restore the forgotten dimension of the transcendental; how it has attempted to exorcise the naïve discourse of a truth reduced wholly to the empirical, and the prophetic discourse which with similar naïveté promises at last the eventual attainment of a truly human experience" (*OT* 321, translation modified).

Foucault does not argue that such an existential phenomenology of the body is naïve or self-contradictory. He simply points out that this project is ambiguous: "The analysis of actual experience is a discourse of mixed nature: it is directed to a specific yet ambiguous stratum, concrete enough for it to be possible to apply to it a meticulous and descriptive language, yet sufficiently removed from the positivity of things for it to be possible, from that starting-point, to escape from that naïveté, to contest it and seek foundations for it" (*OT* 321). He adds that, therefore, it is unstable and can never be completed: "What is given in experience and what renders experience possible correspond to one another in an endless oscillation" (*OT* 336).

For Merleau-Ponty it was precisely the ambiguity and the incompletability of this project which made it interesting. However, for Foucault this incompletability shows that the project was hopeless from the start. In trying to make the body and its limitations the conditions of existence of all knowledge, the analysis of actual experience "is doing no more...than fulfilling with greater care the hasty demands laid down when the attempt was made to make the empirical, in man, stand for the transcendental" (*OT* 321).

There is no way to overcome the instability of the transcendental/ empirical double. Its congenital problems will only be (dis)solved when anthropological discourse is discarded. "The true contestation of positivism and eschatology does not lie, therefore, in a return to actual experience (which rather, in fact, provides them with confirmation by giving them roots); but if such a contestation could be made, it would be from the starting-point of a question which may well seem aberrant, so opposed is it to what has rendered the whole of our thought historically possible. This question would be: Does man really exist?" (*OT* 322).

This question would, indeed, set us on the way to a more adequate theory, provided man is the source of these difficulties, rather than the search for theory itself. Our eventual question will be: Can Foucault's new archaeological discourse avoid the transcendental/empirical double which haunts the discourse of anthropology? But, first, we must acquaint ourselves with the other doubles.

THE COGITO AND THE UNTHOUGHT

Man has not been able to describe himself as a configuration
in the episteme *without thought at the same discovering,*
both in itself and outside itself, at its borders yet also in its
very warp and woof, an element of darkness, an apparently
inert density in which it is embedded, an unthought which
it contains entirely, yet in which it is also caught. (OT 326)

Man's being and his reflection upon that being are burdened with parallel problems as man insists on taking his involvement in the world as the condition of its own possibility. Moreover, the relation between man's being and his reflection is itself a source of progressive puzzles, and worse, the seat of an inevitable moral paralysis.

Once man sees himself as involved in the world, and for that very reason its sovereign, he enters into a strange relation with his own involvements. His use of a language that he does not master, his inherence in a living organism he does not fully penetrate with thought, and the desires that he cannot control must be taken to be the basis of his ability to think and act. If man is to be intelligible to himself, this unthought must be ultimately accessible to thought and dominated in action, yet insofar as this unthought in its obscurity is precisely the condition of the possibility of thought and action it can never be fully absorbed into the cogito. Thus, "the modern *cogito* . . . is not so much the discovery of an evident truth as a ceaseless task constantly to be undertaken afresh . . ." (*OT* 324).

Again Kant establishes the ground rules of the game by claiming clarity as to the *form* of our thought and action, and announcing the imperative to obtain as much clarity as possible concerning the *content:* "Transcendental reflection in its modern form . . . find[s] its fundamental necessity . . . in the existence—mute, yet ready to speak, . . . of that *not known* from which man is perpetually summoned towards self-knowledge" (*OT* 323). But Kant already saw that total clarity concerning the content was in principle impossible. Modern thought takes up the problem after Kant, after even his residual classical confidence in the clarity of pure form has been dissipated: "The whole of modern thought is imbued with the necessity of thinking the unthought—of reflecting the contents of the *In-itself* in the form of the *For-itself,* of ending man's alienation by reconciling him with his own essence, of making explicit the horizon that provides experience with its background . . ." (*OT* 327).

Foucault passes quickly over the Hegelian and Schopenhauerian skirmishes with this unthought and focuses on the full blown contemporary Husserlian version of the struggle: "In Husserl's analyses the unthought was the implicit, the inactual, the sedimented, the non-effected—in every case, the inexhaustible double that presents itself to reflection as the blurred projection of what man is in his truth, but that also plays the role of a preliminary ground upon which man must collect himself and recall himself in order to attain his truth" (*OT* 327). Foucault accepts the current French version of Husserl as having evolved towards a form of the analytic of actual experience,[1] so he does not dwell on

1. Foucault's account of Husserl is similar to that found in Merleau-Ponty's Sorbonne lectures, "Phenomenology and the Sciences of Man." He accepts the claim that, as Merleau-Ponty put it in *Phenomenology of Perception,* Husserl had a final existentialist

Husserl's more and more implausible methodological contortions. Since, however, these contortions tend to confirm the contradictions of the modern cogito, they are worth looking at in detail.

Husserl's disciplined phenomenological descriptions led him to see that all explicit experience of objects takes for granted a background of practices and relations to other objects, all of which he called the object's "outer horizon." Husserl also saw that if human experience was to be made fully intelligible this background could not be left implicit but must be made the object of analysis. Thus, in *The Crisis of the European Sciences*,[2] his last work, he takes on the problem of making the background explicit and claims to have shown that all that is taken for granted in the constitution of objectivity can itself be treated as an object. Specifically, he claims that by means of a transcendental reduction which places the phenomenologist outside the horizon of his own thought, he can analyze the background that originally appears to be unthought and unthinkable as "truly" a sedimented set of beliefs which the phenomenologist has only to "reawaken" in order to be able to treat them as a belief system. Thus the Husserlian phenomenologist is in a doubly ambiguous position. He claims to show that the very practices whose nonrepresentability provides the background of all thought can nonetheless be treated as consisting of facts and beliefs, and he achieves this implausible tour de force by claiming to be able to stand fully inside and fully outside of his own cultural and perceptual field. This is the famous ego-split described by Husserl in *Cartesian Meditations* which gives rise to the phenomenologist as pure spectator of his own involvement.[3]

---

stage in which he gave up the attempt to convert all unthought skills and practices into explicit beliefs. (See *Phenomenology of Perception*, translated by Colin Smith, London: Routledge & Kegan Paul, 1962, p. 274.) Although this interpretation is still influential in France, further research has shown that this emphasis on Husserl's work as a project which "continually resolves itself, before our eyes into a description—empirical despite itself—of actual experience and into an ontology of the unthought that automatically short-circuits the primacy of the 'I think'" (*OT* 326) is an invention of Merleau-Ponty's, who was dedicated to reading his own ideas back into the posthumous, and then as yet unpublished, works of his master. Husserl, in fact, holds to the end the view of his own work that Foucault succinctly characterizes and then implies he rejects, viz. that he "revived the deepest vocation of the Western *ratio*, bending it back upon itself in a reflection which is a radicalization of pure philosophy and a basis for the possibility of its own history" (*OT* 325). Husserl always held that he could restore the intelligibility of the world by means of an analysis of the cogito's representations. Foucault's mischaracterization of Husserl's account of the cogito is, in fact, an accurate characterization of the thought of Merleau-Ponty.

2. E. Husserl, *The Crisis of the European Sciences and Transcendental Phenomenology* (Evanston: Northwestern University Press, 1970), see especially section 40.

3. E. Husserl, *Cartesian Meditations* (The Hague: Martinus Nijhoff, 1960), section 15.

Morality, too, in the Age of Man consists in getting clearer and clearer about those dim forces, whether in society (as in Marx and Habermas) or in the unconscious (as in Freud and Merleau-Ponty), which motivate action. "It is reflection, the act of consciousness, the elucidation of what is silent, language restored to what is mute, the illumination of the element of darkness that cuts man off from himself, the reanimation of the inert—it is all this and this alone that constituted the content and the form of the ethical" (*OT* 328). Thought itself thus becomes a kind of political action promising liberation, and thought is, indeed, active, although not in the way these defenders of the cogito suppose. As Sade and Nietzsche have seen, thought is a "perilous act" (*OT* 328). On the assumption that the only sources of motivation are either dark forces in the unconscious or clear objects of conscious reflection, one arrives at the need for reflective clarity about the sources of our actions. But the resulting objectified values become mere objects which we can choose or reject at will, and thus they lose their power to move us. As Sartre recognized, whoever achieves total clarity about himself and society would, indeed, be a sovereign chooser, but a sovereign that no longer had any reason to choose. According to the logic of this view we are either objects driven by unclear compulsions or lucid subjects who cannot act at all. Thus, "for modern thought, no morality is possible" (*OT* 328).

In sum, discourse about man faces the following dilemma: the background of taken-for-granted commitments and practices, precisely because it is unthought, makes thought and action possible, but it also puts their source and meaning out of our control. The attempt to reappropriate the background, however, is doomed to disillusionment; first there is the inevitable dissatisfaction with the Sisyphus-like task of clarifying the background as an infinite set of beliefs each of which itself makes sense only against a further background. This is a task which is popular right now as part of the attempt to treat man as an "information processing system," but it is a task which, as Foucault points out, can at best claim "the monotony of a journey which, though it probably has no end, is nevertheless perhaps not without hope" (*OT* 314). And second there is the despair of nihilism, for, if the background could be totally clarified, objectified, and represented, the resulting overcoming of enslavement and superstition, far from being a triumph, would spell the end of meaningful action.

THE RETREAT AND RETURN OF THE ORIGIN

We now find the effort to conceive of an ever-elusive origin, *to advance towards that place where man's being is always maintained, in relation to man himself, in a remoteness and a distance that constitute him.* (OT 336)

37

The final double that the analytic of finitude produces both in man's mode of being and in the sciences of man is two "linked, but opposite" (*AK* 25) stories about history and origins. The double arises, as in the first two cases, when language loses its transparency, and so loses touch with its beginnings. Rather than being the simple duplication of representation, as in the onomatopoeic theory, the origin of language becomes a genuinely historical question. The beginnings of language are shrouded in mystery and retreat further and further into the past in the face of empirical investigation.

This is one example of a general phenomenon. "It is always against a background of the already begun that man is able to reflect on what may serve for him as origin" (*OT* 330). Man discovers, in Heidegger's words, that he is "always already" in the world, in language, in society, and in nature. As Foucault puts it, "Man is cut off from the origin that would make him contemporaneous with his own existence: amid all the things that are born in time and no doubt die in time, he, cut off from all origin, is already there" (*OT* 332).

But language also gives a hint of how the retreat of the origin can be overcome. Man can never get behind his language to frame an objective account of how it began or how it works. Yet he uses language, so he must in some sense already understand it. He takes up and employs his mother tongue "without knowing it, and yet it must be known, in a certain way, since it is by this means that men enter into communication and find themselves in the already constructed network of comprehension" (*OT* 331).

Generalizing from this idea that language cannot be known objectively precisely because it is always already a kind of know-how, the analytic of finitude attempts to reappropriate the whole of history by showing that man always already has a history precisely insofar as his social practices enable him to organize all events, including events in his own culture, historically. And more generally still, it turns out that man's very ability to understand himself and objects, by making projects on the basis of what is given, has a three-fold structure which corresponds to the past, present, and future. Thus man's know-how opens up a temporal field in which time and history become possible.[4] "It is in him that things (those same things that hang over him) find their beginning: rather than a cut, made at some given moment in duration, he is the

---

4. At this point, without saying so, Foucault has plunged into the most difficult depths of early Heidegger. He presupposes a familiarity with Heidegger's position in *Being and Time* which he presents accurately and criticizes tellingly. (Heidegger himself rejected this early view of temporality in his later work. See, for example, *On Time and Being*, pp. 23 and 66.) There is no way to make Heidegger's position clear and Foucault's critique plausible short of writing a book on Division II of *Being and Time*, so let the reader beware.

opening from which time in general can be reconstituted, duration can flow, and things, at the appropriate moment, can make their appearance" (*OT* 332). In *Being and Time*, which is the culminating example of this strategy, Heidegger argues in detail that the origin or source of temporality can only be understood by understanding the structure of authentic *Dasein*. (*Dasein* is roughly equivalent to human being.)

In "What is Metaphysics," a lecture delivered two years after the publication of *Being and Time*, Heidegger develops the idea that *Dasein*, because it is the opening in which history as a series of events can occur and in which objects can be encountered, is set off from all beings as pure "transcendence." That is, man is a field or clearing (*Lichtung*—a pun in German which means both a clearing in a field and lighting) which encompasses all particular entities and gives access to them. Thus man cannot be identical with any object that shows up in the clearing established by his practices. Foucault puts it aptly, although even more metaphorically than Heidegger: "Though, in the empirical order, things are always set back from him, so that they are unapprehendable at their zero point, nevertheless man finds himself fundamentally set back in relation to that setting back of things, and it is by this means that they are able to weigh down upon the immediacy of the original experience with their solid anteriority" (*OT* 332).

But like all attempts to relate the positive and the fundamental (here the temporal beginning and the temporalizing clearing as two kinds of sources or origin) so as to make factual limitation the ground of its own possibility (in this case to make the historical practices found history as the source of their own beginning), this solution is unstable. The origin, once regained as man's historicizing practices, retreats again since these practices turn out to be inaccessible to the practitioners. Although man is defined by the cultural practices which establish the temporal clearing in which objects can be encountered, and this temporality is "preontologically close" to man since it is his very being, he cannot reflect on what these practices are precisely because they are too near to him and thus too encompassing. Thus man's primordial temporality is "ontologically farthest" from his understanding. And since Heidegger equates the clearing with Being (correctly understood) he can say in "The Letter on Humanism," "Being is farther than all beings and is yet nearer to man than every being" (*BW* 210).

Moreover (as Foucault shows with great perceptiveness and ingenuity) in Heidegger's version of the analytic of finitude, the origin, that is, the practices which set up history, themselves retreat into the past. In the last work of his early period, "On the Essence of Truth" (1930), Heidegger tries to give cultural, historical content to the empty

39

temporal horizon which in *Being and Time* is described as a "pure ecstatical unity." After all, not every culture has a sense of history, so the question arises: Just when do our historizing practices begin? Heidegger's answer is that the historical clearing which makes history possible is itself first opened up by the questioning of the first philosophers. The pre-Socratics start our history by setting up conflicting interpretations of what being means. "The primordial disclosure of being as a whole, the question concerning beings as such, and the beginning of Western history are the same; they occur together in a 'time' which, itself unmeasurable, first opens up the open region for every measure" (*BW* 129). And not only is the origin, even when fixed by Heidegger in the sixth century B.C., somehow still "unmeasurable," but *it* also begins to retreat into the more distant past. Critics pointed out, and Heidegger later acknowledged (*BW* 390), that the Western understanding of being and truth as he defined them are already found in Homer. So Foucault is justified in asking: "If the recession of the origin is thus posited in its greatest clarity, is it not the origin itself that is set free and travels backwards until it reaches itself again, in the dynasty of its archaism?" (*OT* 334). The attempt to pinpoint those practices which begin our history, rather than enabling us to get clear about the sources of our culture, finds those practices retreating further and further into the distant past until they become what Heidegger calls "the essential mystery" (*BW* 132).

As one would expect, given the logic of the analytic of finitude, Heidegger is finally forced to the conclusion that man is condemned to the fruitless project of attempting to get clear about the origin, which in this case amounts to trying to name being and thus drag the clearing into the open. Indeed, early Heidegger comes to hold that this ontological error is definitive of man. "Man errs. Man does not merely stray into errancy. He is always astray in errancy" (*BW* 135). The inevitable forgetting of the inevitable hiddenness of being, correlative with the attempt to get clear about man's finitude, leads, according to Heidegger, to man essentialy wandering in distress. "Dasein is a turning in need" (*BW* 137).

According to Foucault, in the final working out of the problematic or origin, the source of man's meaning is unobtainable, and this truth itself can only be learned by seeking and failing to find any source. Here "we find the experience of Hölderlin, Nietzsche, and Heidegger, in which the return is posited only in the extreme recession of the origin..." (*OT* 334). These thinkers experience that "ceaseless rending open which frees the origin in exactly that degree to which it recedes..." (*OT* 334).

At this stage, since man has always already failed to find this source in the past, the only hope seems to lie in the future. Since the origin or basis of man's history cannot be some empirical event in the past which is its beginning, nor an empty temporal field, nor an "original" event such as the words of the pre-Socratics which set up the practices which in turn set up history, it turns out that the meaning of man's origins is *always* yet to be understood. Whatever the practices were which, in the archaic past, gave man his understanding of being and history will only be revealed in an equally mythical and distant future. In Foucault's gloss: "The origin, becoming what thought has yet to think . . . would be forever promised in an imminence always nearer yet never accomplished. In that case the origin is that which is returning, . . . the return of that which has already always begun, the proximity of a light that has been shining since the beginning of time" (*OT* 332).

As Heidegger put it in "The Letter on Humanism," "The essence of man is too little heeded and not thought in its origin, the essential provenance that is always the essential future for historical mankind" (*BW* 203, 204). According to Heidegger the thought which seeks to understand our future is a "gentle releasement" (*BW* 138). Foucault echoes Nietzsche as he rests his case: "Thus, for the third time, the origin is visible through time; but this time it is the recession into the future, the injunction that thought receives and imposes upon itself to advance with dovelike steps towards that which has never ceased to render it possible" (*OT* 332).

Thus the logic of the analytic of finitude is preserved. Man discovers that he is not the source of his own being—that he can never get back to the beginnings of his history—and at the same time he seeks to show, in an "extremely complex and extremely tangled" (*OT* 333) way, that this limitation is not something that truly limits him, but rather is the transcendental source of that very history whose beginning escapes empirical enquiry.

CONCLUSION TO THE DOUBLES

The three kinds of the double form an overlapping series. From the moment man emerged as finite all three doubles were presumably equally possible strategies for conceiving this finitude in such a way as to preserve it and surmount it. But the doubles seem to have exhausted themselves one at a time, for, according to Foucault, "it is within this vast but narrow space, opened up by the repetition of the positive within the fundamental . . . that we shall see *in succession* the transcendental repeat the empirical, the cogito repeat the unthought, the return of the origin repeat its retreat" (*OT* 315, 317, our italics).

At first, philosophers and human scientists became enmeshed in various attempts to ground knowledge by showing that the transcendental and the empirical can be both the same and yet essentially different. But they found that if one reduced man to his empirical side one could not account for the possibility of knowledge, and if one exclusively emphasized the transcendental one could not claim scientific objectivity nor

41

account for the obscurity and contingency of man's empirical nature. Thus, during the time this issue occupied serious thinkers there was an "interminable to and fro of a double system of reference" (*OT* 316)—a stage which Foucault associates with the positivism of Comte and the eschatological discourse of Hegel and Marx.

After a time, however, this intellectual see-saw became boring, and more recent thinkers have sought "a discourse that would be neither of the order of reduction nor of the order of promise: a discourse whose tension would keep separate the empirical and the transcendental, while being directed at both..." (*OT* 320). The whole problematic was thus stabilized by a different sort of doubling in which naturalism and transcendentalism coexisted in an ambiguous balance: Husserl doubles the natural attitude by the transcendental attitude without trying to reduce one to the other; Heidegger treats *Dasein* or human practices as both fact and condition of possibility (ontic/ontological in his terminology) without seeing this as an opposition that has to be resolved; Merleau-Ponty makes the body simply that ambiguous entity which is both a fact and yet makes all facts possible. But accepting the ambiguity seems to spell the end of this line of argumentation.

While the transcendental/empirical issue is on the way to its final ambiguous impasse, the new idea is gaining ground that one can obtain clarity about man by subjecting his intrinsically obscure factual condition to lucid philosophical reflection. Foucault summarizes this new approach: "It is now a question ... not of the possibility of understanding, but of the possibility of a primary misunderstanding; not of the unaccountable nature of philosophical theories as opposed to science, but of the resumption of a clear philosophical awareness of that whole realm of unaccounted-for experiences in which man does not recognize himself" (*OT* 323). This strategy, in which the issue is no longer science vs. philosophy, but obscurity vs. clarity, is employed by Hegel, Marx, and Freud but does not become a central philosophical theme until Husserl's phenomenology.

Finally, when this infinite task of clarification is seen as the hopeless task it has been all along, a third, even more difficult project of making sense of what is irreducibly obscure comes to the fore. The hermeneutic approach, which attempts to find meaning in history, develops and exhausts two equally futile possible strategies: total return or total withdrawal of the origin. On the one hand, Hegel, Marx, and Spengler thought of history as the movement towards some sort of completion, a fulfillment of man's true meaning, for better or for worse. They thus conceived of the return of the original truth as the end of history. Thought finally would completely appropriate its origin and attain perfection only to disappear as it undermined its own motivation. On the other hand, thinkers such as

Hölderlin, Nietzsche, and Heidegger held that a more profound understanding of human beings was once present in the mythical past, but that now man can only get in touch with this original understanding by becoming acutely aware of what he has lost—aware of the origin as pure absence. The origin is near only in proportion to the pain of its extreme recession, and, in the limit, it and man may be forgotten altogether. Both views end—whether in fulfillment or despair—with the annihilation of man and history. To understand his own meaning man must grasp his origin, and yet it necessarily escapes him.

To sum up: the three strategies available to the analytic of finitude for uniting the positive and the fundamental are reduction, clarification, and interpretation. Although aspects of all three strategies can be found at any stage of the sciences of man, each strategy becomes in turn the center of serious attention and is developed until its self-defeating character becomes obvious and serious thinkers lose interest in it.

This is Foucault's final formulation of the strategies which first became available to nineteenth and twentieth century thinkers in their search for "a philosophical foundation for the possibility of knowledge" (*OT* 335) "when the Western *episteme* broke up at the end of the eighteenth century" (*OT* 335). So this analysis can be regarded as a test of Foucault's archaeological method. Obviously, looking for the possible permutations allowed by the episteme gives us astonishing synoptic insight into the tortured turnings of two hundred years of complex and tangled thought. Still, before our final evaluation, we must ask if and how Foucault in his own attempt at methodological reflection manages to break with each of the three interrelated impasses he has revealed as inherent in modern humanism. A discourse free of the doubles would offer new hope for an understanding of human beings. Foucault himself has taught us, however, that a discourse that reproduces the doubles must still be based on a subtle acceptance of man, or on some even deeper misguided move, and should be abandoned still-born rather than pursued through a new series of shifts to ever subtler and more self-defeating reformulations. In the next chapter we analyze Foucault's explicit attempt to give a theoretical account of his archaeological method, and in the last chapter of part I we will argue that this quasi-structuralist theory runs into problems similar to those Foucault so clearly sees in the sciences of man.

3 Towards a Theory of Discursive Practice

A Phenomenology to End All Phenomenologies

In *The Order of Things* Foucault convincingly argues that the sciences of man, like their classical precursors, could not have a comprehensive theory of human beings, and are similarly doomed to "disintegration." He does not, however, at this stage think that these difficulties should lead us to call into question the very attempt to arrive at a theoretical understanding of human beings. Rather, like Kant who woke from his dogmatic slumber and deduced the categories which were to put physics on a sure footing, Foucault wishes to wake us from our "anthropological sleep" in order to open our eyes to a successful study of human beings. He has been engaged in "an enterprise by which one tries to throw off the last anthropological constraints; an enterprise that wishes, in return, to reveal how these constraints could come about" (*AK* 15). We have already seen Foucault practicing this new method in his analysis of the breakdown of the sciences of man; *The Archaeology of Knowledge* presents this new method in detail and sketches the theory of discourse on which it is based.

When, after a decade of scholarly activity during which he reassessed madness and medicine and undermined the foundations of the sciences of man, Foucault took time to reflect on the powerful new techniques he had developed, he found that in the course of his analyses he had discovered a vast uncharted territory—"a domain that has not so far been made the object of any analysis..." (*AK* 121). "Irreducible to interpretations and formalizations" (*AK* 207), this domain is inaccessible both to that descendant of the sciences of man that takes meaning seriously, that is, hermeneutics, and that which abandons meaning altogether, that is, structuralism. Foucault's methodological treatise, *The Archaeology of*

Knowledge, takes possession of this new domain and lays out the equipment necessary for its exploration.

Unlike most alien territories this one is so close to us that it is very difficult to find. Foucault arrived there through a series of groping steps which he retraces for pedagogical reasons as a circle from discursive formations to statements, and back to discursive formations. We will attempt to reorder the steps as a logical sequence.

Reflecting on his analysis of discourse Foucault finds that his "central theme" (*AK* 114) has been what he takes to be a previously unnoticed type of linguistic function—the statement (*énoncé*). The statement is neither an utterance nor a proposition, neither a psychological nor a logical entity, neither an event nor an ideal form.

Statements are not propositions, since the same sentence with the same meaning can be different statements, that is, have different truth conditions, depending on the set of statements within which it appears. The identity of the statement is

> relative and oscillates according to the use that is made of the statement and the way in which it is handled . . . . At a certain scale of macro-history, one may consider that an affirmation like "species evolve" forms the same statement in Darwin and in Simpson; at a finer level, and considering more limited fields of use ("neo-Darwinism" as opposed to the Darwinian system itself), we are presented with two different statements. The constancy of the statement, the preservation of its identity through the unique events of the enunciations, its duplications through the identity of the forms is constituted by the functioning of the *field of use* in which it is placed. (*AK* 104, translation modified)

On the other hand, statements are not utterances either. Several different utterances can be repetitions of one identical statement, as for example, when a stewardess explains an airline's safety procedures in several languages. Indeed, the statement is not even a grammatical entity restricted to sentences. Maps can be statements if they are used as representations of a geographical area, and even a picture of the layout of a typewriter keyboard can be a statement if it appears in a manual as a representation of the way the letters of a keyboard are standardly arranged.

Foucault argues further that statements are also not speech acts, but, as he admits, he was wrong in thinking that statements were different from the "speech acts" discovered and catalogued by the English philosopher, John Austin, and systematized in the speech act theory of John

Searle.[1] Indeed, a comparison of Foucault on statements and Searle on speech acts can be highly illuminating.

Searle notes that speech acts have a literal meaning regardless of other levels of possible interpretation. Foucault too holds that statements are performances which can be taken at face value regardless of both the possible ambiguity of the sentences used in their formulation (such ambiguous sentences are the subject of commentaries on texts) and the causal factors involved in their utterance (such causal factors are studied hermeneutically, for example in the psychoanalysis of everyday life).

> Polysemia—which justifies hermeneutics and the discovery of another meaning—concerns the sentence, and the semantic fields that it employs; the same group of words may give rise to several meanings and to several possible constructions; there may be, therefore, interwoven or alternating, different meanings operating on the same enunciative base. Similarly, the suppression of one verbal performance by another, their substitution or interference, are phenomena that belong to the level of the formulation . . . but the statement itself is not concerned with this duplication or this suppression. (*AK* 110)

Searle and Foucault thus agree that the existence of literal meaning exempts us from having to look for deep meaning. To situate the statement the archaeologist need only accept it at face value, and place it in its actual context of other surface statements. Searle, however, is interested in how the hearer *understands* a speech act. This requires more than situating it among other speech acts. To understand a speech act the hearer must hear it in a local context and against a shared background of

1. Foucault notes the striking similarity of statements to speech acts—"Can one not say that there is a statement wherever one can recognize and isolate an act of formulation—something like the speech act referred to by the English analysts?" (*AK* 82)—but he denies the identity of statements and speech acts, using the mistaken argument that several sorts of statements, such as descriptions or requests, can be components of a single complex statement and yet remain statements; whereas, according to Foucault's understanding of speech act theory, speech acts cannot have other types of speech acts as their components. "More than a statement is often required to effect a speech act: an oath, a prayer, a contract, a promise, or a demonstration usually require a certain number of distinct formulas or separate sentences: it would be difficult to challenge the right of each of these formulas and sentences to be regarded as a statement on the pretext that they are all imbued with one and the same speech act" (*AK* 83).

Searle, however, has challenged this alleged difference between speech acts and statements, pointing out in a letter to Foucault that in speech act theory too, one type of speech act, for example an assertion, can be part of another speech act, for example, a promise. His objection has been accepted by Foucault: "As to the analysis of speech acts, I am in complete agreement with your remarks. I was wrong in saying that statements were not speech acts, but in doing so I wanted to underline the fact that I saw them under a different angle than yours" (Foucault's letter to Searle, 15 May 1979).

practices which are not merely other statements.[2] Foucault presupposes, but is not interested in, this everyday straightforward sort of under-standing.

It now becomes clear why Foucault could so easily overlook the identity of statements and speech acts. His interests are, indeed, entirely different from Austin's and Searle's. He is not concerned with *everyday* speech acts. Thus he is not interested in speech act theory—the attempt to work out the rules which govern the production of each type of speech act. Nor is he interested in the way a local, pragmatic context and a background of nondiscursive practices determine the conditions of satis-faction of ordinary speech acts, such as the assertion, "The cat is on the mat," or the request, "Please shut the door." Rather, Foucault is inter-ested in just those types of speech acts which are divorced from the local

2. Spelling out the analogies and differences between archaeology and transforma-tional grammar casts much needed light on Foucault's conception of the "interdependence" of nondiscursive social practices and autonomous discursive formations. In Chomsky's account general rules govern which strings of words can, in a given language, be produced or accepted as well-formed sentences. However, formation rules or linguistic *competence,* discovered by seeking rulelike regularities in what people acutally say and accept as gram-matical, are not alone sufficient to explain what types of sentences actually get produced and counted as grammatical. To explain the fact that not all possible types of grammatical sentences ever get uttered and could not be understood if they were, Chomsky appeals to extralinguistic limitations on human mental processing such as memory capacity, fatigue, and attention span, which operate in the speaker to further limit *performance* to those grammatical sentence types he can actually utter and understand. On another level, ar-chaeology, which takes a domain of linguistic performance as its field of possibilities, shows why certain types of speech acts that are acceptable on linguistic grounds nonetheless are not produced in a given period, because they cannot be taken seriously. This further limita-tion on linguistic performance is explained by archaeological formulation rules which cap-ture what might be called *serious competence.* These competence rules governing discursive practice, like Chomsky's generative rules of syntax, are autonomous, meaningless, and restrictive; their only function is to exclude some possible statements as possibly not seri-ous, and thus open "a blank, indifferent space, lacking in both interiority and promise" (*AK* 39).

This restriction to serious competence requires in its turn an archaeological version of the notion of performance. Nondiscursive practices then must enter as performance vari-ables (analogous to Chomsky's psychological variables) to further restrict the output of discourse. These social factors would have only a limiting function. They would in no way influence the rules which in a given period determine what types of statements can be taken seriously. Their only function would be to further restrict the rarefication produced by these formation rules. Foucault acknowledges this similarity of archaeology to transformational grammar rather cryptically: "By seizing, out of the mass of things said, upon the statement defined as a function . . . of the verbal *performance,* [archaeology] distinguishes itself from a search [for] . . . linguistic *competence:* while such a description constitutes a generative model, in order to define the acceptability of statements, archaeology tries to establish rules of formation, in order to define the conditions of their realization; between these two modes of analysis, there are, therefore, a number of analogies, but there are also a number of differences (in particular, concerning the possible level of formalization)" (*AK* 207).

situation of assertion and from the shared everyday background so as to constitute a relatively autonomous realm. (Just how autonomous will be the subject of later discussion.) Such speech acts gain their autonomy by passing some sort of institutional test, such as the rules of dialectical argument, inquisitional interrogation, or empirical confirmation. "It is always possible one could speak the truth in a void; one would only be in the true, however, if one obeyed the rules of some discursive 'police' which would have to be reactivated every time one spoke" (*DL* 224).

By passing the appropriate tests statements can be understood by an informed hearer to be true in a way that need make no reference to the everyday context in which the statement was uttered. This exotic species of speech act flourished in especially pure form in Greece around 300 B.C., when Plato became explicitly interested in the rules that enabled speakers to be taken seriously, and, by extrapolating the relative context independence of such speech acts to total independence, invented pure theory. But, of course, any culture in which methods allow privileged speakers to speak with authority beyond the range of their merely personal situation and power could be the subject of an archaeological study. In any such speech act an authorized subject asserts (writes, paints, says) what—on the basis of an accepted method—is a serious truth claim.

This systematic, institutionalized justification of the claim of certain speech acts to be true of reality takes place in a context in which truth and falsity have serious social consequences. To avoid Foucault's misleading tendency to refer to this atypical subset of statements which interests him simply as *statements,* let us call these special speech acts *serious speech acts.* Any speech act can be serious if one sets up the necessary validation procedures, community of experts, and so on. For example, "It is going to rain" is normally an everyday speech act with only local significance, but it can also be a serious speech act if uttered by a spokesman for the National Weather Service as a consequence of a general meteorological theory. As we shall see in part II, Foucault claims that our culture has a tendency to convert more and more of our everyday speech acts into serious ones. This is, according to Foucault, the manifestation of a will to truth, which "daily grows in strength, in depth and implacability" (*DL* 219).

The method of justification and refutation confers on these serious speech acts their claim to be knowledge *(savoir),* and makes of them objects to be studied, repeated, and passed on to others. Among all the things that get said, sketched, and scrawled such serious assertions are relatively rare, and it is precisely because of this rarity and because they claim to make serious sense that they are cherished: "Statements are not, like the air we breathe, an infinite transparency; but things that are transmitted and preserved, that have value, and which one tries to appropriate; ... things that are duplicated not only by copy or translation, but by exegesis, commentary, and the internal proliferation of meaning" (*AK* 120).

Foucault is not interested in adding to the commentary that such serious speech acts evoke, nor is he interested in collecting and formalizing those sets of assertions whose truth claims have been verified. The former is the job of a certain kind of exegetics, and the latter the job of philosophers of science who seek to rationalize successful disciplines. Nor is Foucault interested in how serious speakers and hearers understand each other on specific occasions. No doubt he would agree with writers from Wittgenstein to Kuhn to Searle that the specific understanding of specific speech acts involves a taken-for-granted shared background of practices, since no one can ever fully say what he means so as to exclude in advance every possible misunderstanding. At the time he is writing *The Archaeology of Knowledge*, however, Foucault is exclusively interested in types of serious speech acts, the regularities exhibited by their relations with other speech acts of the same and other types—which he calls discursive formations—and in the gradual and sometimes sudden but always regular transformations such discursive formations undergo. In the service of this interest, Foucault develops in *The Archaeology of Knowledge* a method which allows him to avoid consideration of the "internal" conditions governing speech act understanding, and to focus purely on what was actually said or written and how it fits into the discursive formation—the relatively autonomous system of serious speech acts in which it was produced.

Studying discursive formations requires a double reduction. Not only must the investigator bracket the *truth* claims of the serious speech acts he is investigating—Husserl's phenomenological reduction—he must also bracket the *meaning* claims of the speech acts he studies; that is, he not only must remain neutral as to whether what a statement asserts as true is in fact true, he must remain neutral as to whether each specific truth claim even makes sense, and more generally, whether the notion of a context-free truth claim is coherent.

In *The Birth of the Clinic* we saw an example of the bracketing of a specific claim to serious meaning in Foucault's treatment of Pomme's description of the woman soaked for ten months whose various inner organs peeled off. In the *Archaeology*, however, what is bracketed is the whole notion of serious meaning. Not that the archaeologist fails to understand statements as meaningful speech acts—he is not bracketing all meaning like a structuralist or a behaviorist until all he has left is mere meaningless sounds. He is bracketing precisely the claim of serious speech acts to *serious* meaningfulness, to being what Kuhn called "penetrating and deep." It makes no difference to the archaeologist whether this meaningfulness is conceived of as the "gift" of a transcendental subject as in Husserl, or whether the meaning is provided by the place of the utterance in a totality of utterances which in turn make sense against a background of interconnected shared practices, as in Wittgenstein. Foucault is suspending the claim of serious speech acts to a context-free truth, by suspending their claim to intelligibility. Going Husserl one better, Foucault treats both reference *and* sense merely as phenomena. "In the examination of language, one must suspend not only the point of view of the 'signified' (we are used to this by now), but also that of the 'signifier'" (*AK* 111).

Phenomenologists like Husserl and Merleau-Ponty bracketed the legitimacy of context-free truth claims, but they never suspended belief in their *sense*. Rather their enterprise was devoted precisely to establishing the *conditions of their possibility*. Thus, although Husserl bracketed the natural attitude's assumption that statements refer to transcendent objects, his aim was to use this bracketing to study and ultimately to ground this claim to truth. Husserl claimed to be able to show the origin of meaning and truth in the perceptual gestalts of the everyday world, and then to trace the teleological development of situational truth claims into the full-fledged context-free truth claims of science. This aspect of Husserl's phenomenology was further developed by Merleau-Ponty in his *Phenomenology of Perception*. Foucault rejects both attempts as a form of the analysis of actual experience, still caught in the transcendental/empirical double.

Foucault thus claims to leave behind both transcendental and existential phenomenology. Like Husserl and Merleau-Ponty, he sets out to describe in minute detail how serious truth claims emerge, but his detachment is twice as radical as theirs. The phenomenologists wanted to ground the validity of serious speech acts in perception after first grounding perception and showing its primacy, whereas Foucault takes such an attempt to ground truth by giving a "history of the referent" as not having achieved total phenomenological detachment: "What we are concerned with here is not to neutralize discourse, to make it the sign of something else, and to pierce through its density in order to reach what remains silently anterior to it, but on the contrary to maintain it in its consistency, to make it emerge in its own complexity" (*AK* 47).

In other words, Foucault, unlike Husserl and Merleau-Ponty, does not consider the dependence of discourse on objects which are anterior to it something that needs to be grounded if serious speech acts are to be taken seriously; he simply does not take serious speech acts seriously at all. He not only remains neutral as to the truth of each and every serious truth claim (the transcendental reduction), but also neutral as to the necessity of a transcendental justification of the possibility of serious truth claims (transcendental phenomenology). His double reduction, by remaining neutral with respect to the very notion of truth, opens up the possibility of a *pure description* of discursive events. "One is led ... to the project of a *pure description of discursive events* as the horizon for the search for the unities that form within it" (*AK* 27).

Strictly speaking, the very notion of horizon belongs to the hermeneutic discourse the archaeologist abandons. Rather than explicating a *horizon* of intelligibility Foucault is simply describing an open logical *space* in which a certain discourse occurs. To open up this logical space Foucault replaces the exegesis of the meaningful monuments left by humanity, which had been the concern of traditional humanism, with the quasi-structuralist construction of sets of meaningless elements.

> In that area where, in the past, history deciphered the traces left by men, it now deploys a mass of elements that have to be . . . placed in relation to one another to form totalities. There was a time when archaeology, as a discipline devoted to silent monuments, . . . objects without context, . . . aspired to the condition of history, and attained meaning only through the restitution of a historical discourse; it might be said, to play on words a little, that in our time history aspires to the condition of archaeology, to the intrinsic description of the monument. (*AK* 7)

This decontextualizing which does away with the horizon of intelligibility and meaning dear to hermeneutics leaves only a logical space for the possible permutations of types of statements. Archaeology describes serious speech acts only insofar as they fall within this space. "The analysis of statements, then, is a historical analysis, but one that avoids all interpretation: it does not question things said as to what they are hiding, what they were 'really' saying, in spite of themselves, the unspoken element that they contain . . . ; but, on the contrary, it questions them as to their mode of existence, . . . what it means for them to have appeared when and where they did—they and no others" (*AK* 109).

The Husserlian phenomenologist is interested in reconstructing within his bracketing whatever meaning was there beforehand. He would therefore consider it a failure if he had not completely taken up the unthought horizon of meaningfulness into his explicit cogito. Foucault, on the other hand, is not interested in capturing in his analysis everything that the participant lives through within the horizon. It is no objection to his method that in his analyses the meaningful relations between statements drop out altogether. As Foucault notes, even Husserlian neutrality may be too weak a word for such radical detachment: "Perhaps we should speak of 'neutrality' rather than exteriority; but even this word implies rather too easily a suspension of belief, . . . a 'placing in parenthesis' of all position of existence, whereas it is a question of rediscovering that outside in which, . . . in their deployed space, enunciative events are distributed" (*AK* 121).

One might question whether, from such a detached viewpoint, one could even identify speech acts so as to describe discursive formations and study their claim to be deeply meaningful. Foucault, however, claims that he does not need to share the beliefs of those who take these serious speech acts seriously in order to locate them among all the things that are said and written. He can count on the seriousness of those involved in the actual discourse to select, and thus limit, what is taken seriously at any given period, and to defend it, criticize it, and comment upon it. Foucault can then simply study the carefully preserved rare serious statements and the plethora of commentary upon them.

The doubly detached ultimate phenomenologist can thus locate what is serious and meaningful to an age, without its being serious and meaningful to him. Foucault defines his position by explicitly repudiating the three anthropological doubles: "If, by substituting the analysis of rarity for the search for totalities, the description of relations of exteriority for the theme of the transcendental foundation, the analysis of accumulations for the quest of the origin, one is a positivist, then I am quite happy to be one" (*AK* 125).

Foucault delights in the freedom from the philosophical baggage characteristic of the sciences of man that is afforded by this extreme phenomenological positivism. And it is, indeed, refreshing to be able to understand and explain the phenomenon of the human sciences without becoming embroiled in the serious debates and contradictions such scientific explanations of human behavior inevitably generate. In *The Order of Things* Foucault demonstrated how exhilarating and illuminating such an enterprise can be. We must now examine in detail the method that enabled Foucault to attain his insights while keeping his distance. Only then can we ask what explanatory power Foucault claimed for this method, and whether that claim was justified.

Beyond Structuralism: From Conditions of Possibility to Conditions of Existence

An important feature of the serious speech act is that it cannot exist in isolation. Searle notes in his discussion of what he calls the network of speech acts that some speech acts, such as casting a vote for the Presidency, only becomes possible in a network of other speech acts. Foucault makes a similar point about statements. Speaking of what he calls the enunciative function, which is what makes statements serious, he notes, "[It is] characteristic of the enunciative function...[that] it cannot operate without the existence of an associated domain" (*AK* 96).[3] The crucial question is how to treat this relation between individual speech acts and the domain which determines their seriousness. Since he rejects both hermeneutics, which claims to understand *utterances* on the basis of

3. English translation leaves out the "not".

a common background of meaning, and formalization (to be distinguished from structuralist formalism), which attempts to reconstruct a deductive system of scientific *propositions*, Foucault proposes, as the only remaining alternative, that the domain in which speech acts can be taken seriously "is not a secret, the unity of a hidden meaning, nor a general and unique form; it is a rule-governed system" (*CE* 29).

If statements are unified into rule-governed systems then there must be elements for the rules to relate. This model of intelligibility is familiar from the mathesis of the Classical Age where all organization was understood as a complex combination of primitive representations. Foucault has, of course, abandoned the notion of representation both in its classical and Kantian forms, but the idea of a decomposition of a whole into its parts and their systematic relations remains. Foucault thus calls his new method "archaeological analysis" (*AK* 151)—"a method of analysis purged of all anthropologism" (*AK* 16).

The goal of producing an analysis of the interrelated network of serious speech acts as a system of elements ordered by rules of transformation, Foucault notes, resembles structuralism: "My aim is to uncover the principles and consequences of an autochthonous transformation that is taking place in the field of historical knowledge. It may well be that this transformation, the problems that it raises, the tools that it uses, the concepts that emerge from it, and the results that it obtains are not entirely foreign to what is called structural analysis" (*AK* 15). But Foucault notes on this same page that although his work is not opposed to structural analysis, "this kind of analysis is not specifically used" (*AK* 15), and he remarks two hundred pages later, that archaeology's "methods and concepts cannot possibly be confused with structuralism..." (*AK* 204). In the foreword to the English translation of *The Order of Things*, written a year after the *Archaeology*, he becomes even more emphatic, insisting that he has "used none of the methods, concepts, or key terms that characterize structural analysis" (*OT* xiv). What is this subtle but significant difference?

As we have noted, there are two kinds of structuralism: atomistic structuralism, in which the elements are completely specified apart from their role in a system, and holistic structuralism, in which what counts as a *possible* element is defined apart from the system, but what counts as an *actual* element is a function of the whole system of differences in which the given element is involved. Foucault first considers atomistic analysis, with its independently defined primitives: "At first sight, the statement appears as an ultimate, undecomposable element that can be isolated and introduced into a set of relations with other similar elements...the atom of discourse" (*AK* 80). But the archaeologist is led to distinguish the domain of serious speech acts from a domain such as grammar in which isolable elements (in this case classes of words) are assembled into higher order units according to abstract formal rules. "Whereas grammatical construction needs only elements and rules in order to operate . . . there is no statement in general, no free, neutral, independent statement; but a statement always belongs to a series or a whole . . . . It is always part of a network of statements . . ." (*AK* 99).

Serious speech acts obviously cannot be isolated from the rest of the "enunciative network." They are constituted as serious by the current rules of a specific truth game in which they have a role. Foucault calls the specific truth games, whose structures have yet to be defined in detail, enunciative fields. He can then clearly distinguish his position from all forms of atomistic structuralism which deals with isolable elements: "Generally speaking, one can say that a sequence of linguistic elements is a statement only if it is immersed in an enunciative field, in which it then appears as a unique element" (*AK* 99).

Archaeology, then, has nothing in common with atomistic structuralism; its elements are the *product* of a field of relations. Its relation to holistic structuralism, however, is much more complex. Foucault clearly has in mind this subtler and more influential brand of structuralism, in which what counts as a possible element is a function of the system, when he notes that the goal of structuralism is "to define recurrent elements, with their forms of opposition, and their criteria of individuation [which] . . . make it possible to lay down laws of construction, equivalences, and rules of transformation" (*AK* 201). But since Foucault's elements are statements or serious speech acts, if he were to follow this method he would have to define or identify the set of types of possible serious speech acts apart from any specific system and then leave it to each specific system of speech acts to determine which possible serious speech acts actually counted as serious. Although this project may seem to make sense for a structuralist concerned with what he stipulates are meaningless elements, it turns out not to make sense for the archaeologist who, although he brackets meaning, depends upon the fact that statements are assumed to be meaningful by the users.

The archaeologist finds that his elements (statements) are not only *individuated* by the whole system of statements, but that they can be *identified* as elements only in the specific system in which they make sense. Thus, although speech acts for Foucault as well as for Searle have some sort of fixed "information content" or "sentence meaning," whether or not two speech acts mean the same thing (that is, determine the same truth conditions) depends not merely upon the words that determine their information content but upon the context in which they appear. For Searle, who is interested in everyday speech acts, this context is the background of everyday practices; for Foucault, who is interested in serious speech acts, it is the system of other serious speech acts (the discursive formations) in which the particular speech act in question makes serious sense. Thus, Foucault, like the holistic structuralists, holds that the *individuation* of the statement depends on an associated field. For Foucault, "If the information content and the uses to which it could be put are the same, one can say that it is the same statement in each case" (*AK* 104). But Foucault's pragmatic holism is more radical than the structuralists' holism. Even the *identity* of a statement depends on the use that is made of it. As we have already seen, "not only can this identity of the statement not be situated once and for all in relation to that of the sentence, but it is itself relative and oscillates according to the use that is made of the statement and the way in which it is handled" (*AK* 104).

We are now in a position to state with precision how both structuralist and archaeological holisms differ from atomism, and yet also differ essentially from each other. Structuralist *atomism* identifies and individuates elements in isolation. It denies that the whole is different from the sum of its parts. Structuralist *holism* identifies elements in isolation and then asserts that the system determines which of the complete set of possible elements will be individuated as actual. In this case, one might say that the actual whole is less than the sum of its possible parts. *Archaeological holism* asserts that the whole determines what can count even as a possible element. The whole verbal context is more fundamental than its elements and thus is more than the sum of its parts. Indeed, there are no parts except within the field which identifies and individuates them.

Just as one cannot abstract the possible elements from the system of actual elements when describing serious speech acts, so one also cannot set up an abstract table of all possible permutations of statements but can only describe specific rules of transformation. While the structuralist claims to find cross-cultural, ahistorical, abstract laws defining the total space of possible permutations of meaningless elements, the archaeologist only claims to be able to find the local, changing rules which at a given period in a particular discursive formation define what counts as an identical meaningful statement. Strictly speaking, if a rule is a formal principle defining the necessary and sufficient conditions that a speech act must satisfy before it can count as serious, there are no rules at all. Rather, the rules governing the system of statements are nothing but the ways the statements are actually related: "A statement belongs to a discursive formation as a sentence belongs to a text, and a proposition to a deductive whole. But whereas the regularity of a sentence is defined by the laws of a language *(langue)*, and that of a proposition by the laws of logic, the regularity of statements is defined by the discursive formation itself. The fact of its belonging to a discursive formation and the laws that govern it are one and the same thing..." (*AK* 116).

There is no complete system; no way to determine in advance the conditions of possibility of which the present system is one possible instantiation. One can only describe specific systems and determine which kinds of serious statements actually occur. Indeed, archaeology is a purely descriptive enterprise. It seeks "to describe statements, to describe the enunciative function of which they are the bearers, to analyse the conditions in which this function operates, to cover the different domains that this function presupposes and the way in which those domains are articulated..." (*AK* 115).[4]

Foucault's way of summing up these important differences is to stress that whereas the structuralist studies possibilities, the archaeologist studies existence. "The statement is not therefore a structure (that is, a group of relations between variable elements, thus authorizing a possibly infinite number of concrete models); it is a function of existence that properly belongs to signs and on the basis of which one may then decide... whether or not they 'make sense,' according to what rule they follow one another or are juxtaposed, of what they are a sign, and what sort of act is carried out by their formulation (oral or written)" (*AK* 86, 87).

We can conclude that although there are reasons for calling the method of the archaeologist an *analysis*, since it deals with "elements" and "rules," this form of analysis has little in common with classical mathesis or its modern structuralist descendants and variations. Indeed, this method of decomposition into context-dependent categories of statements and their context-dependent transformations rather than atomic elements and abstractable rules of formation could better, following Kant, be called an *analytic*, since it seeks to discover the a priori conditions that make possible the analysis practiced in each specific discipline including structuralism.

But this comparison too must be qualified. Although Foucault seeks a description of the a priori "conditions of the emergence of statements," (*AK* 127) these are not formal transcendental conditions. "Nothing... would be more pleasant, or more inexact, than to conceive of this historical *a priori* as a formal *a priori* that is also endowed with a history: a great, unmoving, empty figure that irrupted one day on the surface of time, that exercised over men's thought a tyranny that none could escape, and which then suddenly disappeared in a totally unexpected... eclipse: a transcendental syncopation, a play of intermittent forms" (*AK* 128). Just as there are no basic elements (actual or possible) in which the analysis bottoms out (so that Foucault's method cannot be called structuralist),

---

4. Foucault sometimes makes the stronger claim that the archaeologist can determine which serious statements *can* actually occur, or which ones *must* actually occur, but we must postpone until later an examination of whether he has a right to claim such explanatory power for archaeology.

there are no top level (empty) transcendental rules for an epoch and, a for-tiori, no rules which would describe in an atemporal form the principles governing the changes between epochs.[5] In short, Foucault's method, having no grounding in lowest level isolable elements, is not an analysis, and having no highest principles of ordering, is not transcendental.

In spite of its rejection of conditions of possibility and its discovery of conditions of existence, archaeology still resembles structuralism in two important ways. One such resemblance—namely, the rejection of all recourse to the interiority of a conscious, individual, meaning-giving subject—is shared with so many other movements (psychoanalysis, ethnology, linguistics, Heideggerian existential phenomenology, Wittgen-steinian "behaviorism") that it is clearly a resemblance to the general movement beyond anthropology of which structuralism is merely one manifestation. The other similarity is more specific and striking: both Foucault and the structuralists are not interested in whether the phenomena they study have the serious sense supposed by participants. Thus they reject the view, shared by pragmatists such as Dewey, her-meneutic phenomenologists such as Heidegger, and ordinary language philosophers such as Wittgenstein, that in order to study linguistic prac-tices one must take into account the background of shared practices which make them intelligible.

In *Being and Time* Heidegger called this background the clearing. In his later writings he called it the open and referred to the fundamental difference between this practical background and a network of beliefs or statements as the ontological difference. Foucault is explicitly rejecting both Husserlian phenomenology and Heideggerian hermeneutics when he opposes to the exegetical account the exteriority of the archaeological attitude. The archaeologist isolates sets of statements "in order to analyse them in an exteriority that may be paradoxical since it refers to no cor-relative form of interiority. In order to consider them in their dis-continuity, without having to relate them . . . to a more fundamental opening or difference" (*AK* 121, translation modified). What Foucault claims to have discovered is a new domain of serious statements which, although experienced as dependent on nondiscursive practices by those within them, can be described and explained by the archaeologist as an autonomous realm.

The archaeologist insists that one cannot study individual possible

5. This devotion to the description of concrete structures understood as conditions of existence bears a striking similarity to what Heidegger, in *Being and Time,* calls an exis-tential analytic. But there is an important difference here too. For although both Heidegger and Foucault attempt to disengage and relate the "factical" principles which structure the space governing the emergence of objects and subjects, Heidegger's method is hermeneutic or internal, whereas Foucault's is archaeological or external.

or actual serious speech acts in isolation from each other, but he claims that one can study sets or systems of such statements in isolation from the practical background. Even context need not involve the background practices. What counts as the relevant context is itself determined by the system of serious statements in which a particular statement is being used. "It is against the background of a more general relation between the formulations, against the background of a whole verbal network, that the effect of context may be determined" (*AK* 98). Thus the archaeologist can study the *network* of discursive practices and treat it as an ensemble of interconnected elements while bracketing what Foucault will later call the "thick tissue" of nondiscursive relations which forms the background of intelligibility for those actually speaking.

Foucault insists on the purely linguistic character of his subject matter and accordingly on the autonomy of the field of stability and the field of use. Precisely because serious speech acts form a system, the archaeologist can simply study from the outside the enunciative function, that is, whatever it is that makes people at a certain period take certain speech acts seriously. Foucault, like a structuralist, is sure that this function is *a function only of other serious speech acts*. Seen from the inside, statements seem to make serious sense only against a background of scientific and nonscientific practices, but seen from the outside, this shared background of practices turns out to play no essential role in determining which speech acts will, at any given time, be taken to make serious sense. What gives speech acts seriousness and thus makes them statements is their place in the network of other serious speech acts and nothing more.

Foucault is surely right in arguing that statements such as "Species evolve" have meaning only in a discursive formation that specifies their truth conditions. But one cannot conclude from this context-dependence that serious speech acts owe their seriousness to this web of discursive practice alone. Such a structuralist conclusion confuses necessary and sufficient conditions. Foucault's own researches ultimately led him to reject this non sequitur. At the time of the *Archaeology,* however, what Foucault shares with the structuralists is the isolation and objectification of a chosen domain of theoretical investigation—a domain which is supposed to have its own autonomous lawfulness.

The Analysis of Discursive Formations

To test the possibility of a discipline situated in the middle domain between everyday nondiscursive practices and the formalizable disciplines such as mathematics and some of the natural sciences, Foucault chooses to test his new archaeological method on the set of statements that make up the so called sciences of man. If this domain could be carved out, analyzed, and explained as an autonomous realm using only pure description without appeal to meaning or formalization, then archaeology would be shown to be a contribution to a new discipline. One might hope that such a discipline, by disconnecting itself from common sense understanding, might be the first step towards a successful theory of an important aspect of human beings.

Foucault proposes to begin like a pure empiricist, simply selecting as his raw data an ensemble of what were taken to be serious speech acts during a given period. (Presumably the work of preselection has been done by the curators of the Bibliothèque Nationale. The fact that these collectors have already made a decision as to what is serious and have applied their own classification to the resulting corpus, based on their discursive and nondiscursive practices, is no problem for Foucault. The archaeologist does not take this original set of statements and the concomitant classification into disciplines that it presupposes at face value; rather the statements simply supply the raw data for an independent systematization.)

Once we doubly bracket serious speech acts so that we cannot appeal to their meaning and truth, and therefore cannot evoke the thought processes of the great thinkers nor the sciences' progress towards knowledge, we need a new way to systematize discourse. Indeed, according to Foucault, the traditional unities fail even on their own terms. He observes that there is no essential characteristic of any discipline defined in the traditional way that remains the same through change. Disciplines do not define their objects, types of description, legitimate practitioners, concepts, and methods in the same way from period to period, and even within a given period the objects of a science are constantly undergoing shifts, transformations, substitutions.

Foucault is not the first to have noted this problem. Wittgenstein would say that disciplines are not exempt from the general truth that we do not classify objects, whether they be chairs and games or botany and physics, by identifying an essence or list of essential features. Rather "we see a complicated network of similarities overlapping and criss-crossing: sometimes overall similarities, sometimes similarities of detail." Our concepts, Wittgenstein contends, are like a thread made up of fibers. "The strength of the thread does not reside in the fact that some one fibre runs through its whole length, but in the overlapping of many fibres." Instead of a definition, then, we capture this "family resemblance" by selecting a perspicuous example and organizing other cases as more or less like this example.[6]

6. Ludwig Wittgenstein, *Philosophical Investigations* (Oxford: Basil Blackwell Publishers, 1953), pp. 32, 49.

Historians of science such as Thomas Kuhn who have focused on discontinuities, have, like Foucault, had to face the problem of accounting for unity through change. Kuhn's solution, influenced by Wittgenstein, is to introduce the notion of a paradigm—a specific exemplar of successful work—and to attempt to account for the unity of a scientific community, with its objects, methods, and so on, in terms of its shared allegiance to such a paradigm rather than its allegiance to a specific set of beliefs.

Foucault is strangely silent on the subject of Kuhn's paradigm-based description, which would seem to address his own problem of accounting for the unity of a body of knowledge while avoiding both the hermeneutic recourse to a hidden common referent and the formalist attempt to find necessary and sufficient conditions for identity. Perhaps this is because at the time he, like many other readers of Kuhn, understood a paradigm to be a set of beliefs, a general conceptual framework, shared by the practitioners of a given discipline. Thus in an interview which postdates *The Archaeology of Knowledge,* Foucault seems to conflate systematicity, theoretical form, and paradigms.[7] By thus assimilating Kuhn's promising proposal to a familiar position, Foucault is led to accept as the only possible account a more traditional identity of disciplines as based on a shared set of rules for what the practitioners count as acceptable. "Disciplines constitute a system of control in the production of discourse, fixing its limits through the action of an identity taking the form of a permanent reactivation of the rules" (*DL* 224). Kuhn, on the other hand, is quite explicit that "the determination of shared paradigm is not...the determination of shared rules.... Rules...derive from paradigms, but paradigms can guide research even in the absence of rules."[8]

Of course, Foucault does not hold that the supposed self-imposed normative rules which define a discipline for its practitioners account for its constancy through shifting objects and methods, for these normative rules change too. But when he comes to propose a principle of unity through discontinuities which makes no appeal to the intentions of individual subjects, he again passes over the possibility that disciplinary unities might be the result of unreflectively shared practices, and assumes that the unities must be found on the level of rule-governed discourse.

On the assumption that serious speech acts are to reveal the principles of their own autonomous unity to a new descriptive study, Foucault must now introduce the conceptual machinery the archaeologist will use to catalogue this new domain. In equipping such an investigation for research into the very heart of the old sciences of man, precaution must be taken at every stage to assure that the analysis of serious speech acts

7. *L'Arc* 70, p. 18.
8. Thomas S. Kuhn, *The Structure of Scientific Revolutions,* 2d ed. (Chicago: University of Chicago Press, 1970).

avoids the old anthropological categories. Foucault seeks to assure the purity of his approach in two ways.

First, since the surest defense is an effective offense, he proposes as a provisional strategy to analyze the very discourse whose pervasive influence he is trying to avoid: the sciences of man. This discourse offers the advantages of "a field in which the [discursive] relations are likely to be numerous, dense, and relatively easy to describe," (*AK* 29) and yet a field in which the discipline has not reached the stage of formalization. So Foucault sets out to analyze "all the statements out of which [the anthropological] categories are constituted—all the statements that have chosen the subject of discourse . . . as their 'object' and have undertaken to deploy it as their field of knowledge" (*AK* 30).

Second, the new categories for describing sets of serious speech acts must be constantly contrasted with descendants of both sides of the transcendental/empirical double: the empirical categories used to explain utterances and the transcendental categories used to analyze propositions. With these precautions Foucault proceeds to introduce his four new descriptive categories for the analysis of discursive formations: objects, subjects, concepts, and strategies.

OBJECTS

The most obvious way to catalogue discursive formations would be to group together those serious speech acts which refer to a common object. This is what Foucault attempted in his book on madness, selecting for archaeological study those statements which had as their object a certain experience. But by the time of the *Archaeology* he realizes that, far from being differentiated by their objects, discursive formations *produce* the object about which they speak. Madness was not, as he had earlier assumed, an object or limit experience outside of discourse which each age had attempted to capture in its own terms. Foucault is no longer "trying to reconstitute . . . some primitive, fundamental, deaf, scarcely articulated experience, . . . which . . . was later organized (translated, deformed, travestied, perhaps even repressed) by discourses" (*AK* 47). Rather, Foucault now sees that a "mental illness was constituted by all that was said in all the statements that named it, divided it up, described it, explained it, traced its developments, indicated its various correlations, judged it, and possibly gave it speech by articulating, in its name, discourses that were to be taken as its own" (*AK* 32). It follows that for Foucault "there can be no question of interpreting discourse with a view to writing a history of the referent" (*AK* 47).

Perhaps, then, what unifies the field of study are the transcendental conditions defining the objectivity of the discourse, and thus governing the production of transcendent objects. But this Kantian move from the empirical to the transcendental also fails to capture the phenomenon. Neither a fixed, unified object nor the transcendental rules governing the meanings given by a transcendental subject can account for the systematically changing object, madness.

Foucault succinctly sums up these two options. The tendency to think of language in terms both of referents, and of words pointing to objects, must be resisted. He points out that "from the kind of analysis I have undertaken, *words* are deliberately absent as are *things* . . ." (*AK* 48). Archaeology is thus "a task that consists of not—of no longer—treating discourses as groups of signs (signifying elements referring to contents or representations) but as practices that systematically form the objects of which they speak" (*AK* 49). Since "one cannot speak of anything at any time" (*AK* 44), what is required is a way of talking about "the space on which various objects emerge and are continuously transformed" (*AK* 32).

How are we to talk about this space? At first Foucault's account seems to be a concrete and restricted version of the general views shared by Wittgenstein and Heidegger. All three thinkers hold that a whole constellation of practices enables those who share these practices to single out and talk about objects. Foucault even emphasizes the importance of nondiscursive social practices in his list of relations that make it possible to pick out objects and give them public reality. "These relations are established between institutions, economic and social processes, behavioral patterns, systems of norms, techniques, types of classification, modes of characterization" (*AK* 45). He stresses, as do the other thinkers interested in the practical background which makes objectivity possible, that this space in which objects can be encountered is not to be found by analyzing the concepts of the objects it forms: "These relations are not present in the object; it is not they that are deployed when the object is being analysed . . . . They do not define its internal constitution, but what enables it to appear, . . . to be placed in a field of exteriority" (*AK* 45).

It might seem that Foucault simply applies this general thesis concerning the importance of background practices to the enunciative functions which make possible serious speech acts and their objects. Foucault, however, next makes a structuralist move which sharply distinguishes his account of the background of practices from that of Wittgenstein and Heidegger. Although he is clearly aware that nondiscursive practices play a role in "forming" objects he insists that the crucial role is played by what he calls *discursive* relations. These relations are not the logical and rhetorical relations that hold between propositions, but presumably the relations that hold between speech acts used in specific contexts to perform certain actions. As Foucault puts it: "[Discursive relations] are, in a sense at the limit of discourse: they offer it objects of which it can speak, ... they determine the group of relations that discourse must establish in order to speak of this or that object, in order to deal with them, name them, analyze them, classify them, explain them, etc." (*AK* 46).

To establish the special role of discursive practice, Foucault points out, first, that the discursive relations which make serious reference possible are neither objective nor subjective. They are not what Foucault calls primary relations—relations independent of discourse and its objects "which may be described between institutions, techniques, social forms, etc." (*AK* 45). Nor are these relations "secondary relations"—those found in the way practicing subjects reflectively define their own behavior. "What, for example, the psychiatrists of the nineteenth century could say about the relations between the family and criminality does not reproduce ... the interplay of real dependencies; but neither does it reproduce the interplay of relations that make possible and sustain the objects of psychiatric discourse" (*AK* 45). Of course, "institutions, political events, economic practices and processes" (*AK* 162) affect what can be seriously said, and, of course, individual speakers who want to be taken seriously must talk about the sort of objects collectively agreed upon by the scientific community of which they are members, but what determines the shared canons of seriousness are not the real or primary relations nor the reflective secondary ones, but the way these primary and secondary relations are organized by discursive practice. "When one speaks of a system of formation, one does not only mean the juxtaposition, coexistence, or interaction of heterogeneous elements (institutions, techniques, social groups, perceptual organizations, relations between various discourses), but also the relation that is established between them—and in a well determined form—by discursive practice" (*AK* 72).

This thesis, that the discursive practices have a certain priority because they "establish" relations between the other types of relations, is one of the most important but least discussed claims in the *Archaeology*. Any theory which claims, on the one hand, that discursive practice is autonomous, and yet at the same time wants to show that "the autonomy of discourse and its specificity do not give it [discourse] the status of pure ideality and total historical independence" (*AK* 164, 165) must explain just how discursive relations interact with primary and secondary ones. As Foucault puts it: "Thus a space unfolds articulated with possible discourses: a system of *real* or *primary relations,* a space of *reflexive* or *secondary relations,* and a system of relations that might properly be called *discursive.* The problem is to reveal the specificity of these discursive relations, and their interplay with the other two kinds" (*AK* 45, 46). But Foucault has remarkably little to say on this point in the

Archaeology. He simply names the problem by telling us that "the field of statements is...a practical domain that is autonomous (although dependent), and which can be described at its own level (although it must be articulated on something other than its self)" (*AK* 121, 122).

This position is plausible insofar as one distinguishes between causal dependence and descriptive intelligibility. Then Foucault could be understood as holding that although what gets said is obviously causally dependent on many nondiscursive factors, one does not need to bring in these outside factors in order to systematize and thus make intelligible why certain types of serious speech acts are performed and others are not. This kind of intelligibility only requires that one find and lay out the rules of discursive practice. Thus Foucault can say, "In the end, we are sent back to a setting-up of relations that characterizes discursive practice itself; and what we discover is...a group of *rules* that are immanent in a practice, and define it in its specificity" (*AK* 46).

But, as we just saw, Foucault seems to want to make a stronger claim than that the rules of discursive practices have autonomous intelligibility. He claims that discursive relations have a certain effect on all other relations. Foucault's best example of the way discursive practices, while dependent upon nondiscursive factors, still influence these nondiscursive elements, is found in his discussion of the relation of medical discourse and other factors influencing medical practice. We have seen that in *The Birth of the Clinic* the question of the priority of discourse did not arise since Foucault assumed that all practices—institutional, technical, and political, as well as those that were specifically discursive—were, at any given time, all manifestations of the same underlying structure or code. Now, however, he has drawn back from this sweeping historical structuralism and restricted his analysis to the structure of discursive practices, and even more specifically, to the rules governing serious speech acts. The question must then arise: What is the relation of the rules governing medical discourse to the other forces which affect medical practice? Foucault's answer is that discourse "uses" the various social, technical, institutional, and economic factors which determine medical practice by taking them up and giving them "unity." Thus, although what gets said depends on something other than itself, discourse, so to speak, dictates the terms of this dependence. What that means can best be seen if we reproduce Foucault's example in detail.

Foucault begins by listing the nondiscursive relations (both primary and secondary) which seem to influence medical discourse.

> If, in clinical discourse, the doctor is in turn the sovereign,
> direct questioner, the observing eye, the touching finger, the
> organ that deciphers signs, the point at which previously for-
> mulated descriptions are integrated, the laboratory technician,

it is because a whole group of relations is involved. Relations between the hospital space as a place of assistance, of purified, systematic observation, and of partially proved, partially experimental therapeutics, ... relations between the doctor's therapeutic role, his pedagogic role, his role as an intermediary in the diffusion of medical knowledge, and his role as a responsible representative of public health in the social space. (*AK* 53)

He then proceeds to show that what is new in modern medical practices cannot be the result of transformations of these techniques, institutions, or concepts.

Clinical medicine must not be regarded as the result of a new technique of observation—that of autopsy, which was practiced long before the advent of the nineteenth century; ... nor as the effect of that new institution, the teaching hospital— such institutions had already been in existence for some decades in Austria and Italy; nor as the result of the introduction of the concept of tissue in Bichat's *Traite des membranes*. But as the establishment of a relation, in medical discourse, between a number of distinct elements, some of which concerned the status of doctors, others the institutional and technical site from which they spoke, others their position as subjects perceiving, observing, describing, teaching, etc. (*AK* 53)

He concludes (and this is Foucault's strong claim):

It can be said that this relation between different elements (some of which are new, while others were already in existence) is *effected by* clinical discourse: it is this, as a practice, that *establishes* between them all a system of relations ... and if there is a unity, if the modalities of enunciation that it uses, or to which it gives place, are not simply juxtaposed by a series of historical contingencies, it is because [clinical discourse] *makes constant use* of this group of relations. (*AK* 53, 54, our italics)

Whatever is meant by discourse "establishing" a "system of relations," it should be clear that in the *Archaeology* the assertion that discourse is autonomous covers more than the claim that discourse can be made intelligible on its own terms. It is rather the extreme and interesting (if ultimately implausible) claim that discourse unifies the whole system of practices, and that it is only in terms of this discursive unity that the various social, political, economic, technological, and pedagogical factors come together and function in a coherent way. This claim is striking because one might have thought that the institutional practices would have to be already coherent and unified in order for unified discursive practices to develop, or at least, that there would have to be some common cultural practices underlying both the institutional and discursive practices in order for both these sets of practices to mesh with each other. Just as, according to Kuhn, what focuses and unifies scientific practices as well as scientific discourse into one enterprise is a shared exemplar.

To make Foucault's structuralist view plausible in the face of these obvious objections, it helps to take a more familiar example. The functioning of the university is dependent upon a great many primary relations—these include economic, political, familial, institutional, architectural, and pedagogical practices—but these diverse elements can coalesce into the modern university only because of something which has been called "the idea of the university." But this concept, which administrators, professors, and students share to some extent, is itself a "secondary relation" conditioned by something else. This final unifying factor cannot be described in objective nor in mentalistic terms. It is rather a certain currently acceptable way of talking (describing, discussing, demanding, announcing) which is taken seriously in a domain called higher education. This specific type of discourse is no doubt related to what administrators, professors, and students think about university education, but these ways of *thinking* no more organize all the factors that make up the university system than do the various social and economic forces. What organizes the institutional relations and the thinking is finally the system of rules which govern what sort of *talk* about education (and which talkers) can, in a given period, be taken seriously. It is these rules "governing" what can be seriously said that, counter-intuitive as it may first seem, ultimately "effect" or "establish" university life as we know it.

Of course, even if the rules of discourse do establish a given system of relations this does not preclude questions about the way the discourse and its rules are dependent upon the social and economic practices they unify. A modern university could not be set up in a country with a feudal system merely by teaching an elite to talk like the California Board of Regents. The current institutions and practices must somehow sustain the discourse. Foucault acknowledges that "archaeology also reveals relations between discursive formations and non-discursive domains..." (*AK* 162). In Foucault's terms there must be something on which discourse can be "articulated." So one must then ask how these primary factors affect the discourse. Their effect cannot be simply a relation of meaning nor one of objective causality. "These rapprochements are not intended to uncover great cultural continuities, nor to isolate mechanisms of causality. Before a set of enunciative facts, archaeology does not ask what could have motivated them (the search for contexts of formulation); nor does it seek to rediscover what is expressed in them (the task of hermeneutics)" (*AK* 162). "Articulation" is a *sui generis* sort of relation with which archaeology must deal. "[Archaeology] tries to determine how the rules of formation that govern [a statement]—and which characterize the positivity to which it belongs—may be linked to non-discursive systems: it seeks to define specific forms of articulation" (*AK* 162).

Foucault assures us that "to reveal in all its purity the space in which discursive events are deployed is not to undertake to re-establish it in an isolation that nothing could overcome; it is not to close it upon itself; it is to leave oneself free to describe the interplay of relations within it and outside it" (*AK* 29). Foucault does not, however, give us any further account of articulation relations in the *Archaeology*. We are told that "if [archaeology] suspends . . . causal analysis, if it wishes to avoid the necessary connexion through the speaking subject, it is not in order to guarantee the sovereign, sole independence of discourse; it is in order to discover the domain of existence and functioning of a discursive practice" (*AK* 164). But we are left with only the promise that archaeology will tell us, for example, how "medical discourse as a practice concerned with a particular field of objects, finding itself in the hands of a certain number of statutorily designated individuals, and having certain functions to exercise in society, is articulated on practices that are external to it, and which are not themselves of a discursive order" (*AK* 164).

We will argue in part II that only when Foucault gives up his semi-structuralist claim that discourse has some sort of priority which enables it to "use" nondiscursive relations can he discover the legitimate domain of the functioning of discursive practices, and give an account of the unique way discourse is both dependent upon and yet feeds back and influences the nondiscursive practices it "serves."

ENUNCIATIVE MODALITIES

Just as Foucault thought, mistakenly, in *Madness and Civilization* that he could individuate a field of discourse by locating its fixed objects, so in preparing *The Birth of the Clinic* he at first thought that he could isolate fixed, homogeneous stages of medical science by discovering certain constant styles of statements, certain basic ways subjects spoke. And just as a careful analysis of a discursive formation did not reveal a well-defined, dense set of objects, but rather a series full of gaps, substitutions, and transformations, so the attempt to define one specific group of statements, as if this group constituted one "great continuous text," had to give way to the description of a field of heterogeneous types of statements.

To understand the variety of styles of statements, Foucault found that the archaeologist has to take into account other systematically changing discursive practices, such as who has the right to make statements, from what site these statements emanate, and what position the subject of discourse occupies. In the case of medicine, Foucault had to describe, among other things, how doctors are certified, hospitals are organized, and how the position of the doctor as observer, interrogator, data collector, researcher, and so forth, changes.

Moreover, in the study of statements, as in the study of their objects, Foucault found that his analysis took him to the limits of discursive practice. He had to "recognize that clinical discourse was just as much a group of hypotheses about life and death, of ethical choices, of therapeutic decisions, of institutional regulations, of teaching models, as a group of descriptions" (*AK* 33). But true to the theoretical preconceptions which dictate the method of the archaeology, Foucault manages to subordinate this discovery and save the relative autonomy of discourse by claiming that the ethical, pedagogical, and therapeutic practices, while indeed presupposed by the serious speech acts involved in medical description, are themselves made possible by more broadly conceived discursive relations. The range of nondiscursive pedagogic practices which, for example, would have to include the importance of apprenticeship in passing on everything from medical preconceptions concerning life and death to such specific skills as reading tuberculosis X-rays, is ignored. Foucault's focus becomes narrowed to the specific question, Who can be taken seriously? that is, Who has the right to speak with the presumption that what he/she says is true? And this in turn leads right back to the more general system of discursive relations that make possible the formation and transmission of serious speech acts by serious speakers. "Medical statements cannot come from anybody; their value, efficacy, even their therapeutic powers, and, generally speaking, their existence as medical statements cannot be dissociated from the statutorily defined person who has the right to make them, and to claim for them the power to overcome suffering and death" (*AK* 51).

In his determination to avoid the traditional attempt to trace medical lore back to the "founding act" of the reflectively aware "thinking, knowing, speaking subject," Foucault thus passes over the shared everyday medical practices passed on by teaching models and picked up by apprenticeship below the level of explicit reflective awareness. He substitutes for the nondiscursive "teaching models" he mentions in passing, explicit formulations of criteria of competence: "The status of doctor involves criteria of competence and knowledge; institutions, systems, pedagogic norms; legal conditions that give the right . . . to practice and to extend one's knowledge" (*AK* 50). By ignoring exemplars and other such medical background practices which help form serious speakers, Foucault can move from his justified claim that the "enunciative domain refers

neither to an individual subject, nor to some kind of collective consciousness, nor to a transcendental subjectivity'' to the stronger but unjustified
claim that ''the different forms of speaking subjectivity [are] effects
proper to the enunciative field'' (*AK* 122).

Hermeneutic thinkers such as Heidegger and Kuhn would agree
with Foucault that subjects are surely not the source of discourse. All
would agree that the source is ''an anonymous field'' (*AK* 122) of practices. But those doing hermeneutics would insist that this field is not
purely discursive. It does not consist merely of ''the totality of things
said, the relations, the regularities, and the transformations that may be
observed in them'' (*AK* 122). Changing nondiscursive skills sustain the
changing styles of statements, the modalities of enunciation, and the kinds
of subjects which are possible. This level of practice is not directly available to the reflective awareness of empirical subjects, however, nor can it
be ''reanimated'' as the implicit belief system of a transcendental consciousness, as Husserl claimed. Granting its importance, then, is not to
fall back into ''reanimating'' the history of the medical mentality.

For Foucault at this stage, however, the only alternative to his own
view seems to be traditional philosophies of the subject, and these are
rightly rejected: ''I showed earlier that it was neither by 'words' nor by
'things' that the regulation of the objects proper to a discursive formation
should be defined; similarly, it must now be recognized that it is neither by
recourse to a transcendental subject nor by recourse to a psychological
subjectivity that the regulation of its enunciations should be defined'' (*AK*
55). Only a modified structuralism that attributes autonomous efficacy to
the discursive field remains. Foucault is thus led to ground his account of
enunciative modalities in a ''law operating behind all these diverse statements'' (*AK* 50)—a law which avoids reference to objects or subjects, but
at the cost of setting aside all specific characteristics of current social
practices as well.

THE FORMATION OF CONCEPTS

If one seeks to show that the unity of a particular discursive formation is determined by its use of some fixed set of concepts, one, of course,
again finds the traditional account inadequate. As Foucault showed in *The
Order of Things*, concepts shift, incompatible concepts overlap, and all
are subject to conceptual revolutions. Again Foucault posits a completely
external description in opposition to the traditional interest in the internal
rules for constructing concepts available to the psychological subject.
Like Kuhn he seeks a level of analysis which takes account of concepts,
their continuities, small shifts, and radical reordering without recourse to
an immanent rationality, that is, without recourse to the notion that one
theory is replaced by another because the second is superior according to

some general rational principles. But unlike Kuhn, who argues that not rules but shifting adherence to paradigms accounts for the continuity and discontinuity of concepts, Foucault chooses to remain at the level of the systems of discursive practices which he claims are autonomous and rule-governed. "Such an analysis . . . concerns, at a kind of *preconceptual* level, the field in which concepts can coexist and the rules to which this field is subjected" (*AK* 60).

The status of Foucault's explanatory principles, however, is as shifting as the concepts they purport to regulate. This time, instead of being described as a *law* operating *behind* the discursive phenomena, they are described as *rules* operating *within* the discursive level itself: "Instead of outlining a horizon that rises from the depths of history and maintains itself through history, the 'preconceptual' thus described is, on the contrary, at the most 'superficial' level (at the level of discourse), the group of rules that in fact operate within it" (*AK* 62). This presumably means that whereas in accounting for modes of speaking Foucault proposed to base his analysis on laws which were not available to the practitioners whose style of statement they determined, in accounting for shifting concepts Foucault hopes to describe the very rules which are followed by individual speakers. He will describe these rules, of course, not as ways individuals assure themselves that they are making sense and will be taken seriously, but rather, from his neutral archaeological perspective, as simply the rules of the anonymous truth game. "In the analysis proposed here, the rules of formation operate not only in the mind or consciousness of individuals, but in discourse itself; they operate therefore, according to a sort of uniform anonymity, on all individuals who undertake to speak in this discursive field" (*AK* 63).

It is hard to resist the growing suspicion that Foucault is much clearer about the traditional humanistic methods he rejects than about the status of the principles of formation he is attempting to introduce. One important point about these principles of formation is clear, however. Whether they are the same rules the speakers follow viewed from the outside as relations between meaningless events, as Foucault seems to hold here, or whether, as in the case of enunciative modalities, these principles are a law behind the phenomena, totally different from the rules in the minds of the practitioners and discoverable only by archaeological observation, the principles with which Foucault is concerned are principles of a rarefaction.

The archaeologist does not take serious speech acts seriously. Thus for him the plethora of discourse generated by trying to assert truths about objects taken to be real and by attempting to interpret what serious subjects are trying to say about these objects is revealed as restricted to a narrow domain. Rarefaction does not mean merely that the total corpus of serious speech acts uttered can be accounted for by a few rules or laws. Nor does it mean that any of the mass of speech acts (research reports, data banks, biographies, and autobiographies) are somehow rejected by the archaeologist. It means rather that, viewed from outside, the group of speech acts which at any given time can be taken seriously occupy small discontinuous regions.

Regions of what? one may well ask. And one is tempted to say: Regions of the domain of all possible serious speech acts. But then one would run into the structuralist claim that one can identify beforehand all possible elements, and all possible rules governing their combination, so as to determine the total field of possible permutations. One cannot determine conditions of possibility, only conditions of existence. So the rarity of actual serious speech acts must be defined without recourse to the contrasting notion of the plenitude of possible serious speech acts.

The notion of rarefaction presumably points to the fact that in other times with other discursive formations speech acts which for us are bizarre and incomprehensible were taken seriously, whereas speech acts which we take seriously now would, if anyone chanced to utter them, have seemed the ravings of a madman or a visionary in other times. Foucault wants to argue that the islands of density in which serious speech acts proliferate are the result of principles which operate from within or from behind discourse to constrain what can count as objects, what sorts of things can seriously be said about them, who can say them, and what concepts can be used in the saying.

THE FORMATION OF STRATEGIES

One last traditional attempt to understand the unities and discontinuities of what were once called disciplines is to look for underlying themes. Foucault has no difficulty showing the problems of this approach. The same theme, such as evolution, can be articulated in two different fields of objects and concepts. In the eighteenth century, ideas about evolution were based on the notion of the continuum of species interrupted by natural catastrophe, while in the nineteenth century evolutionists were not concerned with laying out a continuous table of species but with the description of discontinuous groups. A single theme, but two types of discourse. Conversely, in economics the same set of concepts is taken up into two different strategies for explaining the formulation of value—one based on exchange, and the other on remuneration.

What then replaces themes in accounting for the unity of a certain segment of continuity and systematic change? Foucault proposes that a group of serious speech acts is individuated by the points of choice a discursive formation makes available, "the different possibilities that it opens of reanimating already existing themes, of arousing opposed strategies, of giving way to irreconcilable interests, of making it possible, with a particular set of concepts, to play different games" (*AK* 36, 37). This suggests that a given discursive formation opens up a certain room for maneuver, what Foucault calls "a field of possible options" (*AK* 66). Foucault holds that this changing space in which certain possibilities for action emerge, are exploited, and then are abandoned, should replace the teleological notions of the development of themes or theories.

The questions such a view must answer are: How are these strategic possibilities distributed in history? What opens up this space and how do we account for its transformations? Again Foucault is quick to find the flaws in the approach dictated by the Kantian double—both the transcendental approach which claims a necessary development of progressively better solutions to the same problem, and the empirical approach which makes the appearance and disappearance of possibilities the result of contingent ideas and influences. Foucault proposes as an alternative account of the changing candidates for serious research strategies a description of the systematic way the various strategies are related. He seeks the "rules for the formation of... theoretical choices.... A discursive formation will be individualized if one can define the system of formation of the different strategies that are deployed in it; in other words, if one can show how they all derive... from the same set of relations" (*AK* 65, 68).

Foucault has not devoted a book to describing a system of formation of strategies and its implicit rules. His dense but illuminating systematization of the analytic of finitude can, however, serve as an example of what such an approach can accomplish. Foucault shows how, in the course of two hundred years, three strategies, all variations on how to identify and overcome man's essential limitations, were more or less successively explored and exhausted. The practitioners, of course, did not see themselves as restricted to a limited range of strategies that were put into play when the limitations of human beings discovered at the end of the Classical Age were defined as finitude. They did not think of themselves as playing a losing game in which they had to try to base man's ability to transcend all limitations on his ability to recognize himself as limited. From the inside, they saw themselves as at last exploring promising new research programs which would yield the truth about man. Only from the outside can these strategies be seen as governed by principles of rarity constraining the space of options open to exploration. Only the archaeologist can see that "these options are... regulated ways... of practicing the possibilities of discourse" (*AK* 70).

Foucault's discussion of the analytic of finitude also enables us to see that "the system of formation is not a stranger to time" (*AK* 74). As we have seen, the analytic of finitude sets certain boundary conditions, but the limited set of strategies this view makes possible are not all "discovered'' once man emerges as the unifying source of representation, which itself must be fully represented. Nor is there a dialectical convergence on truth in which the strategies are explored one by one, each one *aufgehoben* into a more adequate approach as it reveals its contradictions. Rather there is an overlapping series in which some strategies are gradually found to be unpromising, to lead to sterile debates, or to inaugurate infinite tasks which become boring. At the same time new twists are introduced, whose tortured complexities seem to promise new ways to organize the recalcitrant subject matter. The analytic of finitude thus sets up a space in which strategies can arise, embroil whole areas of research, and then be replaced by others as "the elements . . . undergo a number of intrinsic mutations that are ingrained into discursive practice without the general form of its regularity being altered" (*AK* 74, 75).

Once we see the way systems of formation change we realize that "definite types of discourse . . . have their own type of historicity" (*AK* 165). It is to the archaeologist's new understanding of history that we now turn to conclude our analysis of the properties of discursive formations.

HISTORICAL TRANSFORMATION: DISORDER AS A TYPE OF ORDER

Since the archaeologist describes the rules governing modern historical discourse—a discourse which takes history as meaningful progress towards the truth—the archaeologist no longer takes the teleology of history seriously, and thus no longer presupposes historical continuity. As understood by the archaeologist, serious discourse is not the gradual external expression of internal deep meaning; rather it reveals its own rules of systematic change. "It is a practice that has its own forms of sequence and succession" (*AK* 169). To the serious historian, committed to development and continuity modeled on biography, the archaeologist proclaims: "Discourse is not life; its time is not your time . . ." (*AK* 211).

What then is time and history for the archaeologist, or, better, how does *he* account for the discontinuities and transformations which are mistakenly taken to be the meaningful march of history? Do not his rules of transformation freeze all change? Foucault asserts the contrary: "Archaeology does not set out to treat as simultaneous what is given as successive; it does not try to freeze time and to substitute for its flux of events correlations that outline a motionless figure. What it suspends is the theme that succession is an absolute: a primary, indissociable sequence to which discourse is subjected by the law of its finitude . . ." (*AK* 169).

To begin with, the archaeologist is not interested in the empirical succession of events, nor is he interested in transcendental historical rules which would state the conditions of the possibility of all change. Rather the archaeologist is interested in the way one discursive formation comes to be substituted for another, that is, in how "to reveal the relations that characterize the temporality of discursive formations..." (*AK* 167). These relations would govern the succession of spaces in which, among other things, various kinds of searches for various kinds of origins, and in general, various understandings of time and history are determined. Thus "one tries to show how it is possible for there to be succession, and at what different levels distinct successions are to be found" (*AK* 169). There is no deep hermeneutic attempt to retrace succession to its source. "The role of such a discourse is not...to rediscover, in the depths of things said, ...the moment of their birth (whether this is seen as their empirical creation, or the transcendental act that gives them origin); it does not set out to be a recollection of the original or a memory of the truth. On the contrary, its task is to *make* differences: to constitute them as objects, to analyse them, and to define their concept" (*AK* 205).

But, Foucault assures us, the alternative to hermeneutics is not structuralism. The relations among differences described by the archaeologist are not ahistorical conditions of possibility which set up the space of all possible transformations. Rather they are presumably rules which determine only the conditions of existence, that is, the regularities of the transformations which actually occur. In this way Foucault would hope to have a theory of change which avoids the classical dilemma of either finally finding ahistorical rules to explain all change or leaving change completely unintelligible.

The archaeologist will "substitute for an undifferentiated reference to *change*...the analysis of *transformations*" (*AK* 172). But this still leaves open the decisive question: How systematic is this change? Do the rules of formation with their shifts and overlapping discontinuities change in a systematic way? Foucault is clear that one can and must *describe* how the different elements of a system of formation were transformed. But will this description take the form of a system of rules? If there are atemporal rules governing the historical transformations of rules and elements, these would be conditions of possibility and we would be back in structuralism.

We shall see that Foucault does not take a final stand on this point, so that the important differences between his work and that of the structuralists are, at the time of *The Archaeology of Knowledge*, left obscure. To the question, Are there metarules describing transformations? he answers that "archaeology tries to establish the *system* of transformations that constitute 'change'" (*AK* 173, our italics). But this "system" turns out to be more like a case of Wittgenstein family resemblance, where, within a family, certain similarities persist while others drop out and new ones show up, than like a rule-governed restructuring of the sort one might find in Piaget or Lévi-Strauss. "The analysis of archaeological breaks sets out...to establish, between so many different changes, analogies and differences, hierarchies, complementarities, and shifts: in short, to describe the dispersion of the discontinuities themselves" (*AK* 175).

The "systematic order" Foucault finds seems to be a meticulous description of disorder. Foucault must maintain that the tangled relationships revealed by his description of anthropological discourse are nonetheless systematizable, hence rulelike. Only if these rules can be construed as autonomous formation rules is serious discourse shielded from the influence of everyday practices.

In the last analysis, in the struggle between ultimate dispersion and discontinuity on the one hand, and the rules for systematic change that would restore order and intelligibility on the other, Foucault seems to hesitate, as if he is drawn to both alternatives and finds neither entirely satisfactory. Like a true phenomenologist, whether Husserlian or Wittgensteinian, his solution is to stick as closely as possible to the facts of dispersion and then to call the resulting description a "system of transformation." Foucault would clearly like to analyze long-term trends without recourse to humanistic teleology or structuralist metarules, and to account for discontinuities as more than random changes, but at this point he is clearer about the problems posed by the two current proposals than he is about the possibility of an alternative approach.

DISCURSIVE STRATEGIES AND THE SOCIAL BACKGROUND

A theory that would account for what actually gets said must answer one additional methodological question: Why is it, as Foucault notes in discussing strategies, that "all the possible alternatives are not in fact realized..." (*AK* 66)?[9] Why are some strategies in the human sciences, which might be taken seriously under the reigning rules, nonetheless ignored? Foucault at this point concludes from a few specific examples that the limitation at any given level of analysis must either be the result of relatively concrete segments of discourse, such as those he calls concrete models, or else of relatively abstract general discursive constellations.

9. Not that Foucault must account for every actual serious speech act. In spite of claims in an earlier sketch of the *Archaeology* that "the point is to seize the statement in the narrowness and singularity of the event . . . [and to] show why it could not have been other than it was" (*CE* 17), it seems that the *Archaeology* claims to have a theory only of the occurrence of specific *types* of statements rather than an account of how token statements are finally selected. This is presumably what Foucault means when he says rather darkly that "what are being analyzed here are certainly not the terminal states of discourse; they are the *preterminal regularities* in relation to which the ultimate state . . . is defined by its variants" (*AK* 76). This fact, that archaeology turns out to study possible types of serious speech acts rather than actual token utterances explains Foucault's at first surprising remark that the systematic relations archaeology studies can "be qualified as 'prediscursive', but only if one admits that this prediscursive is still discursive, that is, . . . that [these relations] define rules which [discourse] actualizes as a particular practice" (*AK* 76, translation modified).

It is far from obvious, however, that the only remaining possible account of the way some strategies permit or exclude others is that *discourses* systematically limit each other. Kuhn, for example, offers a different account, which also involves concrete models, and which, without taking such models to be discursive, still avoids both the transcendental and the empiricist positions. For Kuhn the most important type of concrete model, which he calls a paradigm or exemplar, is a concrete piece of research which all practitioners accept as an example of the right way to proceed. Paradigms function directly through the practices of those who have been trained to see, think, and act in terms of them. As a concrete case, an exemplar or paradigm effectively restricts possible theoretical choices. It limits the possible strategies that can be seriously envisaged, without itself being accessible to theoretical analysis. As Kuhn puts it, paradigms embody a "manner of knowing which is misconstrued if reconstructed in terms of rules that are first abstracted from exemplars and thereafter function in their stead."[10] Paradigms thus guide and restrict laboratory practice and serious discourse, yet they are not conceptual frameworks that can be analyzed in terms of transcendental rules or personal prejudices analyzable as psychological belief systems. It would seem that to admit the importance of concrete models and then to construe them as relatively specific discursive constellations preserves the primacy of discourse and its rules at the cost of ignoring the convincing evidence presented by Kuhn.

Foucault might well answer, however, that Kuhn's account only works for normal sciences such as physics where there is general agreement among those involved as to what counts as a good piece of work. The human sciences are precisely *not* normal sciences in Kuhn's sense. There are always a number of conflicting schools each with its own pseudoparadigm. Foucault contends that if we are to have a theoretical account of these conflicting schools and their conflicting strategies we must introduce a different form of intelligibility than the sort which accounts for strategic choice in the natural sciences.

Discursive strategies which are accepted cannot be the result of a generally accepted scientific paradigm since in the human sciences there is none. So Foucault proposes that in the human sciences there must be quasi-structuralist rules of formation (unknown to the practitioners) which govern a particular discourse during a particular period and thus determine the spectrum of types of strategies which can be taken seriously, that is, accepted by some schools and seriously opposed by others. We will see in chapter 9 that Foucault will later introduce a new notion, similar to a Kuhnian paradigm but not restricted to normal sciences, which will enable him to relate the question of the permission and

10. Kuhn, *Scientific Revolutions*, p. 192.

exclusion of strategies to current social practices in a more concrete and plausible way; but for the time being he has no convincing account.

Foucault seems at times to agree with Heidegger, Wittgenstein, and Kuhn that when it comes to what strategies actually get chosen and what actually gets said, the nondiscursive practices provide the horizon, background, or element in which the choice of the discursive strategy is intelligible. "Archaeological analysis individualizes and describes discursive formations. That is, it must . . . . relate them, on the basis of their specificity, to the non-discursive practices that surround them and serve as a general element for them" (*AK* 157). Moreover Foucault has a much more concrete and social notion of the nondiscursive background than that found in philosophy. Nondiscursive factors include "an institutional field, a set of events, practices and political decisions, a sequence of economic processes that also involve demographic fluctuations, techniques of public assistance, manpower needs, different levels of unemployment, etc." (*AK* 157). These nondiscursive factors, Foucault seems to be saying, sustain and surround the discursive ones. One might think that the nondiscursive factors contribute to the intelligibility of the discursive ones and supplement, if not actually influence, the laws of formation. But, as in the case of his account of primary relations, Foucault holds to the autonomy of discourse and so comes to precisely the opposite conclusion. The analysis of the external authorities which delimit choice "must show that neither . . . the processes of [discourse's] appropriation, nor its role among nondiscursive practices is extrinsic to its unity, its characterization, and the laws of its formation" (*AK* 68).

Rather than being the *element* or horizon within which the discursive practices take place, it seems that the nondiscursive practices are *elements* which discursive practices take up and transform. These external elements do not have productive powers of their own whereby they can contribute to the introduction of new objects, concepts, and strategies, nor do they just perturb in a random way what is being said. "They are . . . on the contrary [discourse's] formative elements" (*AK* 68). They act within the space allowed by the current principles of rarefaction to produce further exclusions.

In sum, archaeologists make exactly the opposite use of the social background practices than the existential-pragmatic philosophers do. For thinkers like Heidegger, Wittgenstein, Kuhn, and Searle, it is precisely the nondiscursive background practices that enable us to encounter objects and speak about them.[11] Rather than being elements which merely further rarefy the already rarefied set of acceptable statements, social practices produce and govern action and discourse and give it serious

11. The situation is really not quite so simple. Each of these thinkers, with the possible exception of Kuhn, has at one time or another been on either side of this issue and each has changed sides, although not all in the same direction. In *Being and Time* Heidegger

content. In this broadly hermeneutic view the regularities of discursive practice are influential, but are themselves explained by understanding the purposes served by specific discursive practices in everyday meaningful human activities. Contrary to Foucault, these thinkers argue, each in his own way, that practical considerations determine which theoretical strategies will be taken seriously.

These issues concerning the relation of nondiscursive practices to discursive practices are barely touched on in *The Archaeology of Knowledge*, because, as Foucault points out, strategies had not, like the other forms of unity of discursive formations, been the subject of any of his earlier books. "The place, and the implications, of the strategic choices were indicated... but I did little more than locate them, and my analysis scarcely touched on their formation" (*AK* 65).

In Foucault's subsequent books, as we shall see, strategies will come to the fore. They will no longer be restricted to theoretical options, but will be shown as truly the element which sustains discursive activity. When the character and role of strategies is thus broadened and made basic the question of the relative influence of the discursive practices vis-à-vis the nondiscursive practices is finally thematized and certain latent contradictions in the *Archaeology* are resolved. In order to see how Foucault's revised position is an important improvement over his position in the *Archaeology* we must now draw out and examine these latent contradictions.

---

held that the organized totality of everyday equipment, which he called significance, was the basis of intelligibility including speech: "In significance, (with which Dasein is always familiar): there lies the ontological condition which makes it possible for Dasein ... to disclose such things as 'significations'; upon these, in turn, is founded the being of words and language" (p. 121). Later, however, Heidegger wrote in the margin of his copy of *Being and Time* at this point: "False; language is not founded, but is the primordial essence of truth." Wittgenstein changed in the opposite direction. He started out attributing the source of all intelligibility and meaningful behavior to a shared form of life articulated by languages, but in his last book, *On Certainty,* he extended his account of meaningful behavior to babies and mammals, and said that what he was talking about was something more basic than language, from which language emerged. "Our talk gets its meaning from the rest of our proceedings" (p. 30, #229). "I want to regard man here as an animal; as a primitive being to which one grants instinct but not ratiocination. As a creature in a primitive state .... Language did not emerge from some kind of ratiocination" (p. 62, #475). Kuhn always held the view that nonlinguistic practices are basic for science, but this does not become clear until the second edition of *The Structure of Scientific Revolutions.* There he explicitly remarks that the recognition of a piece of work as similar to an exemplar (paradigm) requires a kind of nonlinguistic skill, for, although scientists can recognize this similarity, they cannot answer the question, "Similar with respect to what?" (p. 192) Searle, too, has changed his mind from the view implicit in *Speech Acts,* that linguistic behavior is autonomous and rulelike, to the view in his recent paper, *Literal Meaning,* that utterances only determine truth conditions on a background of nonlinguistic practices.

4 The Methodological Failure of Archaeology

Explanatory Power

Foucault and the hermeneuticists agree that practices "free" objects and subjects by setting up what Heidegger calls a "clearing,"[1] in which only certain objects, subjects, or possibilities for actions can be identified and individuated. They also agree that neither the primary relations of physical and social causality, nor the secondary relations of intentional mental causality can account for the way practices free entities. But they differ fundamentally in their account of how this freeing works. According to the hermeneuticists, who describe the phenomenon from the inside, nondiscursive practices "govern" human action by setting up a horizon of intelligibility in which only certain discursive practices and their objects and subjects make sense. Foucault, the archaeologist looking from outside, rejects this appeal to meaning. He contends that, viewed with external neutrality, the discursive practices themselves provide a meaningless space of rule-governed transformations in which statements, subjects, objects, concepts and so forth are taken by those involved to be meaningful. We must now ask: How, according to Foucault, do the discursive practices viewed as meaningless events in a purely external logical space form and govern speakers and the statements, subjects, and objects they take to be meaningful?

To begin with, in his account of discursive formations Foucault lucidly rejects both sides of all the pairs of possible accounts formulated in terms of the subject/object double dear to the humanistic tradition. The

1. See p. 41 for Heidegger's use of clearing. Heidegger speaks of freeing objects in *Being and Time*, for example, "Our analysis...has shown that what we encounter within-the-world has, in its very Being, been freed for our concernful circumspection, for taking account" (*Being and Time*, p. 114).

systems of formation are neither formal transcendental rules nor abstract empirical laws.

> These systems of formation must not be taken as . . . static forms that are imposed on discourse from the outside, and that define once and for all its characteristics and possibilities. They are not constraints whose origin is to be found in the thoughts of men, or in the play of their representations; but nor are they determinations which, formed at the level of institutions, or social or economic relations, transcribe themselves by force on the surface of discourses. (*AK* 73, 74).

Just what positive account Foucault himself hopes to introduce is much less clear. We have seen his apparent wavering as to whether the principles of explanation he has set forth are supposed to function as a law behind the phenomena, or as rules in the minds of performers. Indeed, "rule," "law," and "system" are used synonymously in summaries such as the following: "The characteristic relations which allow one to individualize a set of statements concerning madness are: the *rule* of simultaneous or successive appearance of the diverse objects which are named, described, analyzed, valued or judged therein; the *law* of their exclusion or of their reciprocal implication; the *system* which governs their transformation" (*CE* 22, our italics). One might hope to distinguish the rule of appearance from the law of exclusion, or the rules governing mental entities such as concepts from the physical laws governing material entities such as statements, but when Foucault attempts to lay out a general theory of discursive regularities he assimilates all the various explanatory principles that he introduced in connection with his four categories of discursive formations to *rules*.

> Groups of verbal performances are linked at the statement level . . . which implies that one can define the general set of *rules* that govern their objects, . . . the system of their referentials; . . . that one defines the general set of *rules* that govern the different modes of enunciation, the possible distribution of the subjective positions, and the systems that defines and prescribes them; . . . that one defines the set of *rules* common to all their associated domains, the forms of succession, of simultaneity . . . of which they are capable, and the system that links all these fields of coexistence together; lastly, . . . that one can define the general set of *rules* that govern the status of these statements, the way in which they are institutionalized, received, used, reused, combined together, the mode according to which they become objects of appropriation, instruments for desire or interest, elements for a strategy. (*AK* 115, our italics)

But this leads to a new difficulty. If rules that people sometimes follow account for what gets said, are these rules meant to be descriptive, so that we should say merely that people act *according to* them, or are they meant to be efficacious, so that we can say that speakers actually *follow* them. Foucault certainly does not want to say that the rules are followed by the speakers. The rules are not in the minds of those whose behavior they describe. "The field of statements is not described as a 'translation' of operations or processes that take place elsewhere (in men's thought, in their consciousness or unconscious, in the sphere of transcendental constitutions); ... it is accepted, in its empirical modesty, as the locus of particular events, regularities, relationships, modifications and systematic transformations..." (*AK* 121). One might suppose, then, that since they are not rules subjects follow, they must be rules which serve to systematize the phenomena; that statements can be given coherence according to them. And, indeed, Foucault tells us just that: "This dispersion itself—with its gaps, its discontinuities, its entanglements, its incompatibilities, its replacements, and its substitutions—can be described in its uniqueness if one is able to determine *the specific rules in accordance with which* its objects, statements, concepts, and theoretical options have been formed" (*AK* 72, our italics).

The difficulty, however, only gets deeper. Such rules would presumably have only descriptive value, yet Foucault seems to attribute to them their own causal efficacy: "If there really is a unity, it does not lie in the visible, horizontal coherence of the elements formed; it resides, well anterior to their formation, in the system that *makes possible and governs* that formation" (*AK* 72, our italics). The rules, it seems, actually operate on the phenomena: "The whole enunciative field is both regular and alerted: it never sleeps; the least statement—the most discreet or the most banal—*puts into operation* a whole set of rules in accordance with which its object, its modality, the concepts that it employs, and the strategy of which it is a part, are formed" (*AK* 146, 147, our italics).

Moreover, though they are not followed by the practitioners, the rules are nonetheless prescriptive: "By system of formation, then, I mean a complex group of relations that *function as a rule: it lays down [prescrit] what must be related,* in a particular discursive practice, for such and such an enunciation to be made, for such and such a concept to be used, for such and such a strategy to be organized" (*AK* 74, our italics). The peculiarity of this strange alliance between rules as *descriptive regularities* and as *prescriptive operative forces* becomes obvious when Foucault is led to speak of "locating the various *regularities* that [statements] *obey*" (*AK* 108, our italics).

Foucault's difficulty stems in part from the fact that he is rightly convinced that the productive and rarefying principles he has discovered are not merely descriptive, although he also sees that their mode of operation cannot be accounted for by either objective laws or subjective rules. If the archaeologist was trying to understand meaningful discourse and practices, some version of Heidegger's hermeneutic approach explaining discursive practices in terms of nondiscursive ones might have provided a third account, but since the archaeologist is committed to the reductionist project of explaining meaning in terms of "discourse-objects" (*AK* 140), no explanation in terms of horizons of intelligibility is allowed. The only strategy which remains once one has eliminated objective causal laws, subjective rules, and the horizon of meaningful practices is some modified version of structuralist theory.

The structuralist alternative is to claim a formal level of explanation which is not physical and not intentional. Formal rules define the possible permutations of objects, actions, or anything else, and these rules, along with material, social, and psychological boundary conditions, account for the phenomenon. This seems a plausible proposal if we consider the analogy to grammar. The rules of grammar are descriptive, but they do seem to govern linguistic behavior since if one wants to be understood one must conform to them. And this does not mean that one has to reflectively know and self-consciously follow the grammatical rules. Linguistic skill is picked up by acculturation. The regularities of the practice may be totally unknown to a community of speakers and hearers and yet these same regularities, reinforced by social pressure, govern and determine what types of sentences actually get uttered. Foucault seems at times to have this model in mind. He allows that "to define a system of formation in its specific individuality is therefore to characterize a discourse or a group of statements by the regularity of a practice" (*AK* 74).

But Foucault is not satisfied to accept social practices as a level of explanation. Social regularities, it seems, require a further account. In linguistics two alternative models have been proposed to explain how grammatical rules govern the formation of sentences. Either, like Chomsky and Lévi-Strauss, one can hold that grammatical rules are formal rules which govern practice by being instantiated in the brain, or else, like Heidegger and Wittgenstein, one can hold that the linguistic practices themselves have the power to sustain and perpetuate norms, and grammatical rules are just descriptive approximations made up by school teachers and linguists. In neither case can one say that the rules themselves actually "govern," "operate," "determine," or "limit" behavior. It is either the neurons or the social practices that have the causal power.

Given his commitment to history, Foucault must reject the structuralist answer to how formal laws can be causally efficacious. All-out structuralists like Chomsky and Lévi-Strauss claim causal efficacy for their transformations by grounding their rules of transformation in the laws of physics operating in the brain. But the claim that the rules of transformation have their power because they are instantiated by the laws of nature only makes sense for atemporal cross-cultural rules. Foucault's historically shifting regularities are cut off from such objective efficacy.

Without the structuralist's mechanistic explanation of their formal principles Foucault seems committed to a version of what he once called the formalist illusion, "that is, imagining that the laws of construction [of a science] are at the same time and with full legitimacy the conditions of its existence" (*CE* 38). Of course, Foucault is not making exactly this mistake. He is not reading the formal rules reconstructing a science back into the science as its conditions. He lucidly claims that the system of laws he describes operates at a deeper level than the formalization of science—a level which makes such formalization possible. "[Archaeological description] makes it possible to grasp discourses in the law of their actual development. It must be able to take account of the fact that such a discourse, at a given moment, may accept or put into operation, or, on the contrary, exclude, forget, or ignore this or that formal structure" (*AK* 128). Thus, the orthogonal archaeological description Foucault is offering is meant to explain, among other things, why at a certain period formalism became a serious strategy. For this reason "the formal *a priori* and [Foucault's] historical *a priori* neither belong to the same level nor share the same nature: if they intersect, it is because they occupy two different dimensions" (*AK* 128). Nonetheless, in his account of the causal power of the rules of discursive formations, Foucault illegitimately hypostatized the observed formal regularities which describe discursive formations into conditions of these formations' existence.

Foucault's unclearness concerning the question of causal efficacy surely shows that the archaeologist should never have raised this problem in the first place. The very claim that discourse is *governed* by rules contradicts the project of the archaeologist. As a fully consistent phenomenologist, bracketing reference and sense, he need only describe the changing discursive practices, with their apparent referent *(referentiel)* and apparent sense (plethoria of commentary), that emerge with these practices. Since such a study is situated outside of the serious meaning and truth claims of the sciences studied, it should not claim serious meaning and explanatory power for itself. Rather, to be consistent, it would have to be what Foucault is fond of reminding us it is, nothing more than "a pure description of the facts of discourse" (*CE* 16). If Foucault had restricted himself to following his own methodological principles he would have given us a valuable description of the discursive practices he set out to study. His detailed descriptions of the studies of labor, language, and life make an extremely convincing case that there are complex and regular relations between discursive practices and what counts as objects, subjects, and so forth.

But as we have followed this pure description we have found that Foucault oversteps his "modest empiricism," and although he presents his method as a Baconian quest for regularities, he cannot seem to resist giving a quasi-structuralist explanation of the phenomena he has discovered. Far from accepting a descriptive theory, he seems to want a prescriptive one: "The analysis of statements and discursive formations . . . wishes to determine the principle according to which only the 'signifying' groups that were enunciated *could appear*. It sets out to establish a law of rarity" (*AK* 118, our italics). At times he seems to go so far as to demand not merely conditions of possibility but total determination: "One must show why [a specific statement] *could not have been* other than it was" (*CE* 17, our italics). The archaeologist should discover "the play of rules which *determine* the appearance and disappearance of statements in a culture" (*CE* 19, our italics). Again and again, Foucault seems compelled to abandon the phenomenological, neutral post hoc description for some sort of explanatory a priori.

This move from an account which seeks merely descriptive adequacy to one that claims a theoretical explanation of the underlying principles that make the phenomenon possible cannot be a simple confusion. It would seem, rather, that it betrays what Heidegger would call the unthought in Foucault's early work. Is there some unthematized insight perturbing Foucault's early methodology?

One might suspect that despite his commitment to pure, double-bracketing phenomenology, Foucault is aware that discursive practices are not simply regular but that they do, indeed, have the power to form objects and subjects. Moreover, it seems clear that the regularities he describes are not simply accidental orderings which can be read off the surface of discourse, but that they must be evidence of some underlying systematic regulation. However, since at this stage he is committed to the view that discursive practices are autonomous and determine their own context, Foucault cannot look for the regulative power which seems to govern the discursive practices outside of these practices themselves. Thus, although nondiscursive influences in the form of social and institutional practices, skills, pedagogical practices, and concrete models constantly intrude into Foucault's analysis (and although one of his basic objections to the subject/object double is that it "allows us to avoid an analysis of practice" (*AK* 204)) he must locate the productive power revealed by discursive practices in the regularity of these same practices. The result is the strange notion of regularities which regulate themselves. Since the regularity of discursive practices seem to be the result of their being governed, determined, and controlled, while they are assumed to be autonomous, the archaeologist must attribute causal efficiency to the very rules which describe these practices' systematicity.

Beyond Seriousness and Meaning

What finally is the significance of Foucault's new archaeological method and the analyses it enables him to provide? It seems that in order to avoid the doubles characteristic of the analytic of finitude he has rejected serious truth and all notions of the transcendental, the cogito, and the origin which such seriousness leads one to presuppose. He is "trying to operate a decentring that leaves no privilege to any centre" (*AK* 205). But the resulting methodological purity seems to have left him in a void. He candidly admits his difficulty: "For the moment, and as far ahead as I can see, my discourse, far from determining the locus in which it speaks, is avoiding the ground on which it could find support" (*AK* 205).

For Foucault at the time of *The Archaeology of Knowledge* there seem to be only two alternatives: either a seriousness that puts such a premium on objective truth that discourse itself becomes unimportant, or, paradoxically, in the name of the importance of discourse, a position that stands outside all serious significance. And if these are the only alternatives, Foucault, who has chronicled the collapse of the double in all its forms, must choose to stand outside, despite his admiration for the poets and Sophists who knew that to speak was to move men.

The archaeologist studies mute statements and thus avoids becoming involved in the serious search for truth and meaning he describes. As we have seen, archaeology is "nothing more than a rewriting: that is, in the preserved form of exteriority, a regulated transformation of what has already been written . . . it is the systematic description of a discourse-object" (*AK* 140). The archaeologist is located in a dimension orthogonal to all discursive formations and their meaningful objects, subjects, concepts, and strategies and their attempt to discover truth. Like phenomenology, the whole enterprise rests on the notion of a pure description. But this raises a final and ultimately insurmountable series of problems for anyone wishing to assess the claims of *The Archaeology of Knowledge*. Is a pure description possible? Is there no interpretation involved in the choice of descriptive categories? Must we not be able to ask: Are these descriptions accurate or distorted? But doesn't this reintroduce truth?

The same puzzles arise with respect to meaning. The archaeologist claims he does not speak from within a horizon of intelligibility. Foucault says of his own work, "I have tried to define this blank space from which I speak, and which is slowly taking shape in a discourse that I still feel to be so precarious and so unsure" (*AK* 17). This has an advantage. The archaeologist does not have to be concerned that his interpretation might be relativized by being placed in a broader horizon. But then, if the archaeologist speaks from outside of any horizon of intelligibility how can his discourse have meaning at all? Having resolved merely to "make differences" how can the archaeological study of dispersion make any important difference? Having bracketed truth, meaning, and seriousness, there seems to be no way to get them back.

While writing *The Archaeology of Knowledge,* Foucault seems to hesitate on the brink of this precipice. Alongside the radical orthogonal phenomenological account of the archaeological method there are moments when Foucault seems to think of himself as one among many "serious workers." At such moments he strives to preserve the importance of his own discourse by asserting that he does, indeed, speak in something like the plane of meaning and truth he brackets and describes. These "lapses" point ahead to the seriousness of the genealogical method Foucault will employ in his work of the seventies.

This tendency to present his own account as one which has meaning and makes truth claims—an approach which he once found attractive and will find attractive again—comes to the fore in Foucault's discussion of his relation to the historical archive. "It is not possible for us to describe our own archive, since it is from within these rules that we speak, since it is that which gives to what we can say . . . its modes of appearance, its forms of existence and coexistence, its system of accumulation, historicity, and disappearance" (*AK* 130). The claim that it is impossible to describe one's own archive because being in it gives our discourse objects, and presumably truth and serious meaning, is familiar in hermeneutic circles, as is Foucault's use of the notion of horizon (instead of formal space of transformations): "The never completed . . . uncovering of the archive forms the general horizon to which the description of discursive formations, the analysis of positivities, the mapping of the enunciative field belong" (*AK* 131).

This view goes hand in hand with the claim that only because we are beyond the sciences of man can we now describe their system of transformation. "The description of the archive deploys its possibilities . . . on the basis of the very discourses that have just ceased to be ours; its threshold of existence is established by the discontinuity that separates us from what we can no longer say, and from that which falls outside our discursive practice" (*AK* 130, 131). This leads to the conclusion that since we are now in a different horizon, we can see that the truth of the past horizon was, like all truth, a mere epochal construction. We are thus led to abandon a certain naïve conception of truth as the correspondence of a theory to the way things are in themselves, and a naïve conception of the disciplines as engaged in the gradual approximation to this truth. The result is a kind of nihilism which emphasizes the role of interpretation.

Given Nietzsche's genealogy, Wittgenstein's linguistic relativism, Heidegger's hermeneutics, and Kuhn's description of scientific revolutions, this kind of nihilism may well be the only honest form of seriousness available in the twentieth century. Foucault evokes this break with the traditional conception of truth in his conclusion to this chapter of the *Archaeology*. Our new archive, he tells us, "deprives us of our continuities; ... it breaks the thread of transcendental teleologies; and where anthropological thought once questioned man's being or subjectivity, it now bursts open the other, and the outside.... It establishes that we are difference, that our reason is the difference of discourses, our history the difference of times, our selves the difference of masks" (*AK* 131).

But there is a more extreme nihilism lurking in these same paragraphs, a nihilism that would seek to explain, and thus explain away, all meaningful interpretation as an illusion fostered by the rule-governed rarity of statements. In this view,

> to interpret is a way of reacting to enunciative poverty, and to compensate for it by a multiplication of meaning; ... But to analyze a discursive formation is to seek the law of that poverty, ... and to determine its specific form. In one sense, therefore, it is to weigh the "value" of statements. A value that is not defined by their truth, that is not gauged by the presence of a secret content; but which characterizes their place, their capacity for circulation and exchange, their possibility of transformation, not only in the economy of discourse, but, more generally, in the administration of scarce resources. (*AK* 120)

The belief in meaning, truth, and value seems to motivate what people say, but, since we can show that what they say is determined by rules that are not in their minds at all, we also show that their belief in meaning and its efficacy is illusory. In taking the view that meaning is, in effect, epiphenomenal, the archaeologist stands outside all discursive formations. Or, to be more exact, the archaeologist, like Husserl's transcendental phenomenologist, must perform an "ego split" in order to look on as a detached spectator at the very phenomena in which, as an empirical interested ego (or in Foucault's case speaker), one can't help being involved. Foucault the archaeologist looks on, as a detached metaphenomenologist, at the historical Foucault who can't, if he thinks about human beings in a serious way, help thinking in terms of the meanings and truth claims governed by the latest discursive formation.

This combination of detachment and involvement is not merely a psychological fact about the archaeologist who can never fully overcome his tendency to take seriously the science of his own age. Nor is it, as Husserl held, that without the involvement of the phenomenologist there would be nothing to study. The archaeologist does not claim to constitute the phenomenon he is studying through his interested meaning-giving activity. Rather the archaeologist has to share the everyday context of the discourse he studies in order to practice his discipline. If all discourse was, for the archaeologist, mere meaningless noise he could not even catalogue statements.

Furthermore, it is not sufficient for the archaeologist to have an understanding of *everyday* discourse. Unless he understands the issues that concern the thinkers he studies, he will be unable to distinguish when two different utterances are the same serious speech act and when two identical utterances are different serious speech acts. To answer as Foucault might, that one can tell by observing how each statement is used, only postpones the problem. Unless the investigator has access to the meaning of the activity in question he will be unable to distinguish apparent similarity of use from the kind of similarity of use which establishes that two different utterances are, in fact, identical statements. Thus being both within and outside of the discourses he studies, sharing their meaningful truth claims while suspending them, is the archaeologist's ineluctable condition.

Even if serious discourse never really has the serious meaning it claims but is only the rule-governed transformation of meaningless objects, subjects, concepts, and strategies which archaeology reveals it to be; even if, in the last analysis, the archaeologist's monuments turn out to have been mute all along, this much still remains true: neither the serious scientist nor the archaeologist could do their work if it weren't for the illusion that there is serious meaning. Indeed, archaeology is the discipline of listening sensitively to the very monuments one treats as mute.

If, like Husserl, Foucault at the time he wrote *The Archaeology of Knowledge* identifies himself with the detached spectator and thought of the natural or involved attitude as naïve, later he will, like Merleau-Ponty, think that seriousness is not naïve but inevitable, that we are "condemned to meaning"—that we must take the involved attitude seriously—and he will come to see the idea of the detached archaeologist's position as "the thinker's privilege" and the idea that the laws of rarety make meaning superfluous as naïve, and, in fact, itself in need of explanation.

If, indeed, meaningful truth claims are the only kind of seriousness available to us, Foucault, when he is a consistent archaeologist, cuts himself off from all seriousness. In spite of his obvious concern for the issues he discusses and the labor of thought that has generated the books leading up to and including *The Archaeology of Knowledge,* Foucault is obviously tempted to make the best of the nihilistic implications of his orthogonal position. He sometimes presents himself as indistinguishable from those post-structuralists who delight in their liberation from the deadening seriousness of the past.

To the earnest critic who he imagines asks, "Are you already preparing the way out that will enable you in your next book to spring up somewhere else and to declare as you're now doing: no, no, I'm not where you are lying in wait for me, but over here, laughing at you?" (*AK* 17) he answers playfully, "What, do you imagine that I would take so much trouble and so much pleasure in writing...if I were not preparing—with a rather shaky hand—a labyrinth into which I can venture, ...in which I can lose myself and appear at last to eyes that I will never have to meet again.... Do not ask who I am and do not ask me to remain the same: leave it to our bureaucrats and our police to see that our papers are in order" (*AK* 17). Foucault is well aware that "to speak is to do something—something other than to express what one thinks; to translate what one knows, and something other than to play with the structures of a language" (*AK* 209). But at this point he can conceive of only one kind of seriousness—the seriousness gained by subservience to the rules governing some specific set of discursive practices.

There is, therefore, an important sense in which Foucault's nihilism is always a qualified nihilism. Since the archaeologist never brackets the meaning and local truth claims taken for granted in everyday discourse, he can and must share the serious concerns embodied in his cultural practices. Thus as a private, everyday person Foucault is no more or less a nihilist than anyone else in our culture. But whatever practical commitments he has must, if the archaeologist is right, remain private and personal. They can be expressed only in everyday local conversations. The archaeologist with his post-Husserlian version of the ego split, can at best take only half seriously any theory of morality or of social institutions. He can be a deeply committed private person, but in the realm of public discourse he must hide behind masks.

Freeing oneself from the bureaucrats and the discursive police is surely exhilarating, but until one finds a new position from which to speak, and a new seriousness for one's words, there is no place in archaeology for a discourse with social significance, no reason anyone should listen, and, in spite of Foucault's playful posturing, no reason anyone should write. Why spend so much effort constructing an orthogonal theory when detachment undermines any claim to meaning or seriousness that theory might have? On the other hand, if Foucault's theory is merely one more permutation of serious discourse governed by new rules that have not yet been formulated, it also hardly seems worth the prodigious labor required to write it and to read it.

Furthermore, even if one enjoys writing and unraveling complicated systems for their own sake, *The Archaeology of Knowledge* runs into the very problems it was supposed to diagnose and put behind us. As we shall attempt to show, by giving up seriousness while at the same time falling into a version of two of the doubles that plague the sciences of man, the archaeologist turns out to have the worst of both worlds.

Conclusion: Double Trouble

Now that we have described and distinguished classical, anthropological, and archaeological discourse, we are in a position to situate and evaluate Foucault's achievement—to assess its plausibility in its chosen area and on its own terms. Our question is: How radical is the difference between the discourse of the sciences of man and that of archaeology?

For Foucault the difference is the difference between dusk and dawn. Whereas for two hundred years the sciences of man contorted themselves, trying unsuccessfully to perform the acrobatic twist by which the finite knower, subject to the laws of biology, economics, and philology, frees himself "through the interplay of those very laws, to know them and to subject them to total clarification," (*OT* 310) the archaeologist by a double twist successfully catapults himself beyond serious speech acts into a position from which the changing discursive practices of the sciences of man becomes a subject for disinterested analysis. Thus, whereas the sciences of man, by trying to deal with truth, were necessarily submerged in shifting social and discursive practices from which they could not free themselves and of which they could not take account, archaeology, by dispensing with truth and meaning in a double phenomenological bracketing, was finally able to achieve the rigor of structuralist theory, that is, to set the study of human beings on the road toward that stable, autonomous theory that had eluded both the analysis of representation and the analytic of finitude.

Our detailed study of the new archaeological method has revealed, however, that it suffers from several internal strains of its own. We have seen that although it would like to be a modest empiricism describing, with double phenomenological detachment, the positivities of discursive practice, it nevertheless claims that the regularities that describe the corpus of serious discourse also regulate its production. This oscillation between description and prescription has revealed an even deeper instability concerning the status of serious meaning. Is the intense interest in the formulation and exegesis of statements explained by the fact that serious thinkers really do find meaning in them, or is the conviction that serious speech acts are meant seriously and have serious import an illusion produced by their rule-governed rarity? And where is the archaeologist situated with respect to these alternatives? It seems that an archaeologist must be a split spectator, both sharing and denying the serious meaning that motivates the production of the plethora of discourse he studies. Finally, what is the status of the laws the archaeologist discovers? Does his system allow the archaeologist to explain historical change or does it reveal history as basically contingent and unintelligible? We must ask: Is there an order and sense in the above methodological uncertainties, or are they just the "stumbling manner" Foucault admits characterizes a new enterprise, "so precarious and so unsure," (AK 17) painfully extricating itself from the self-set traps into which, in its inexperience, it constantly falls?

When viewed from this perspective, Foucault's methodological problems bear a suspicious similarity to the tensions he finds in the anthropological doubles. Of course, the archaeologist no longer shares with the students of man the belief that there is a deep truth in human beings which is constantly near and yet which constantly eludes them. He has thus freed his thought from "transcendental narcissism" (AK 203). In so doing he has situated and moved beyond an anthropological discourse which claims to possess the categories which define the field of all possible experience, and then claims to ground these conditions of possibility in the constituting activity of a transcendental subject. Foucault's analysis also dispenses with the teleology of reason that moves between a project formed in the past and its future fulfillment. All these goals which still obsessed Husserl have been left behind thanks to double bracketing. It would therefore be a serious mistake, as Foucault makes clear, "to treat archaeology as a search for the origin, for formal a prioris, for founding acts, in short, as a sort of historical phenomenology (when, on the contrary, its aim is to free history from the grip of phenomenology)" (AK 203).

Foucault quite explicitly underlines the differences between archaeology and the human sciences. "My aim was to analyse . . . history, in the discontinuity that no teleology would reduce in advance; to map it in a dispersion that no pre-established horizon would embrace; to allow it to be deployed in an anonymity on which no transcendental constitution would impose the form of the subject; to open it up to a temporality that would not promise the return of any dawn" (AK 203). The doubles which characterize the sciences of man, however, are not defined in terms of a hidden truth that man struggles in vain to possess, but simply in terms of the postulation of an identity and difference between the positive and the fundamental. Thus any discourse that seeks to establish the ground of its own possibility and that of all knowledge in itself alone is subject to the double, "that hiatus, minuscule yet invincible, which resides in the 'and' of retreat and return, of thought and unthought, of empirical and transcendental, of what belongs to the order of positivity and what belongs to the order of foundations" (OT 340). It is this identification of positivity and foundation characteristic of the human sciences, we shall now argue, which is shared by archaeology as it attempts to pass from an *analysis* of positivities into elements to an *analytic* providing the ground of the possibility of its own method and its objects. Thus archaeological discourse necessarily still suffers from a version of the transcendental/empirical, and cogito/unthought doubles. (We shall also see that, like Husserl's phenomenology, of which it is a radicalization, archaeology has not arrived at the problems which give rise to the return and retreat of the origin.)

The objects studied by the archaeologist are discursive practices. We have seen that these practices are finite and contingent yet subject to their own rules of rarefaction. They are also limited by nondiscursive practices. But this limit is not external; rather it is taken up in such a way by the discursive practices so as not to limit their autonomy. Serious discursive practices, then, have a special self-supporting finitude similar to that found in the study of man. Indeed, one can easily substitute "discourse" for "finitude" in Foucault's characterization of the double: "From one end of experience to the other, [discourse] answers itself; it is the identity and the difference of the positivities, and of their foundation, within the figure of the *Same*" (*OT* 315). One can equally substitute "discourse" for "man" in Foucault's account of the analytic of finitude: "At the foundation of all the empirical positivities, and of everything that can indicate itself as a concrete limitation of [discourse's] existence, we discover a finitude.... The limitation is expressed not as a limitation imposed upon [discourse] from outside, ... but as a fundamental finitude which rests on nothing but its own existence as fact, and opens upon the positivity of all concrete limitation" (*OT* 315).

Guided by such general substitutions, we then specifically notice, again substituting for "man," that archaeological discourse seems to embody a form of the transcendental/empirical double. "[Archaeological discourse], in the analytic of finitude, is a strange empirico-transcendental doublet, since [it] is a being such that knowledge will be attained in [it] of what renders all knowledge possible" (*OT* 318).

This should not surprise us. Serious discursive practices, we have seen, are presented as the condition of their own occurrence. Sets of discursive practices are found to reveal certain regularities. Of course, the rules describing these regularities are not presented as the conditions of the *possibility* of these ensembles since these rules do not define the total space in which all possible serious speech acts could occur. They are thus clearly differentiated from the transcendental rules of Kant and the critical philosophers. They are, however, presented as the *conditions of occurrence* of statements, so that once the archaeologist is in possession of the rules describing a discursive formation he can see that those types of speech acts which were actually uttered and taken seriously were the only ones that could have been seriously entertained at that time. The rules of formation are thus transcendental in exactly the same existentialized sense as Heidegger's existentials and Merleau-Ponty's body schemata as conditions of actuality.

In this way the archaeologist passes from post hoc positivities to a priori foundations, and one can say of archaeological discourse what Foucault says of the existential phenomenologist's discourse, viz. that it is "a discourse of mixed nature: it is directed to a specific yet ambiguous stratum, concrete enough for it to be possible to apply to it a meticulous and descriptive language, yet sufficiently removed from the positivity of things for it to be possible, from that starting-point, to escape from that naïveté, to contest it and seek foundations for it" (OT 321). Thus the move from description to prescription, from regularities to regulation, from empirical analysis to archaeological analytic, in short the claim to have discovered a "historical a priori," bears a more than superficial resemblance to what Foucault calls in his chapter on the anthropological sleep, the "Fold [in which] the transcendental function is doubled over so that it covers with its dominating network the inert, grey space of empiricity . . ." (OT 341).

There are likewise echoes in The Archaeology of Knowledge of the problems formed when one tries to ground the unthought in the cogito. Despite occasional remarks suggesting the contrary, the Archaeology generally holds that the rules governing discursive formations are not accessible to those actually making serious speech acts. The archaeologist's rules are not the rules the practitioners follow that tell them who has the right to make serious sense and what is worth saying and worth taking seriously. These internal rules are analogous to Searle's speech act rules which define (ceteris paribus—everything else being equal) what counts as a promise or an assertion. The rules that the archaeologist discovers, however, are second-order rules of rarity that determine which first-order rules, concerning what subjects, objects, concepts, and strategies can be taken seriously, are followed at a given time. Since these metarules are not applied by actual practitioners they need not be ceteris paribus rules; they can instead be regarded as strict rules which apply rigorously to types of statements. These rules are foreign to the practitioner, so it is not the task of the archaeologist, as it was of the phenomenologist, to "reawaken" "sleeping" rules and beliefs of which the speaker is the unknowing source.

Nonetheless, the unthought of the practitioners is recuperated in the theory of the archaeologist, which, like the phenomenologist's analysis of the thesis of the natural attitude ends up denying the intelligibility of the thesis it set out to explain. The discursive practices analyzed by the archaeologist are motivated by the speakers' conviction that they are uttering serious truths about man and society, or that they are helping to make explicit the implicit thoughts of those who were in possession of such truths. The analysis, however, substitutes for this "naïve" conviction as its condition of occurrence a set of meaningless strict rules.

Hermeneutic and pragmatic thinkers such as Heidegger and Wittgenstein and, more recently, Searle have argued that, indeed, all meaningful activity must be grounded in something unthought and unthinkable. All activities make sense only against a background of practices, and this common sense horizon cannot be represented or objectified. Such an account "continuously resolves itself . . . into an ontology of the unthought that automatically short-circuits the primacy of the 'I think'" (*OT* 326). But in Husserl's phenomenology, the unthought, common sense background, and in Foucault's phenomenology to end all phenomenologies the unthought background of serious discourse, is, nonetheless, made the object of study. Husserl treats the everyday background as a set of representations; Foucault treats the background of serious discourse as a space defined by formation rules. This move is typical of the human sciences which, as Foucault notes, "find themselves treating as their object what is in fact their condition of possibility. They are always animated, therefore, by a sort of transcendental mobility. . . . They proceed from that which is given to representation to that which renders representation possible, but which is still representation" (*OT* 364).

It seems that the *Archaeology* has simply transferred the problem of self-grounding from representation to objectification. Indeed, archaeology as an analysis of rules and norms not available to those who are determined by them, seems, according to Foucault's definition, to be radicalized human science. In the human sciences the *un*conscious system of significations must be recuperated by consciousness. "We shall say . . . that a 'human science' exists, not wherever man is in question, but wherever there is analysis . . . of norms, rules and signifying totalities which unveil to consciousness the conditions of its forms and contents" (*OT* 364). In archaeology this recuperation of the unthought by thought becomes the recuperation of a *non*conscious system of rules as an explicit theory. Thus, it is no longer the forms and contents of consciousness, but the forms and contents of serious discourse, whose conditions are being sought. But the structure is the same: "signifying totalities" have simply been replaced by "systems of dispersion," and transcendental rules have been replaced by transformation rules.

Instability inevitably occurs when, seeking to ground its own claims to universality, phenomenology claims to be able to represent as a belief system the everyday horizon it discovers. The same problems recur when archaeology seeks to ground its autonomy by showing that the content of the descriptive positivity it discovers is determined exclusively by formation rules.

Such self-grounding leads to a theory which inevitably asserts that the nonobjectifiable horizon which is the condition of the claim to meaning and intelligibility is an illusion generated by the involvement of the participating actors and speakers. But both phenomenology and archaeology need the natural or naïve attitude that they analyze away. In the case of archaeology the "illusion" of meaning is necessary for the production of discourse to serve as an object for analysis. The system works only as long as everyone does not share the enlightened position of the archaeologist. If everyone spoke from a position orthogonal to serious discourse, to speak orthogonally would make no sense. The dawning of freedom from the illusion of serious truth and meaning must be constantly promised but constantly postponed. If archaeology is to avoid self-elimination, it must either study only the past, or else, like therapy and phenomenology, it must see to it that its task is interminable.

One final similarity between archaeology and the cogito/unthought double now becomes understandable: the archaeologist's nihilism. The archaeologist who is necessarily immersed in the everyday practices of his age, and is both inside and outside the serious discourse of his age, cannot produce a moral theory. He may in fact share the convictions of his age, both those implicit in the everyday practices and those of the serious scientists, but as archaeologist he has become the detached observer of all serious speech acts. The double twist of bracketing both the truth and the meaning of all serious statements that has enabled him to avoid the illusions of the serious speakers also prevents him from offering any account of which social issues should be taken seriously and what might be done about them. Archaeology as the disinterested study of mute monuments can never enter the debates which rage around the monuments it studies. In fact, from the archaeological perspective the monuments were mute all along. The conflicts that produced them and were in turn produced by them are the result of a mysterious, inevitable illusion—an illusion which the archaeologist shares only to dispel—that there could ever be issues about which it would be worth arguing.

This leaves only the final double—the return and retreat of origin—without an echo in the *Archaeology*. Does it too haunt the archaeologist? Given the archaeologist's rejection of humanist history, the answer would again seem to be that it certainly could not occur in its anthropological form. Remember: "The role of [archaeological] discourse is not to dissipate oblivion, to rediscover, in the depths of things said, at the very place in which they are silent, the moment of their birth; . . . It does not set out to be a recollection of the original or a memory of the truth" (*AK* 205).

In avoiding the search for a meaningful source on the basis of which man could totally understand and thus reappropriate his historically dispersed positivity from within it, archaeological discourse avoids the search for an origin which, while producing history, constantly eludes historical study by retreating into the past and the future. As Foucault puts it in the early pages of *The Archaeology of Knowledge,* archaeological discourse must avoid the two parallel denials of the ontological importance of actual discourse characteristic of the sciences of man—that of thinking that history is the working out of the implications of an original word which is its inaccessible source but which can never be explicitly formulated, and the correlative view of thinkers who hold that there is a nonlinguistic reality, whether it be a clearing of prelinguistic practices (as in early Heidegger) or silent perception (as in Merleau-Ponty). For the archaeologist there is no deep meaning, no "concealed origin" in history or outside it, so the hermeneutic attempt to find a foundation which is before, behind, or beyond history while remaining situated in history can be rejected as one more unachievable humanistic imperative. Since it does not have serious meaning and makes no serious truth claims the archaeologist's discourse is ahistorical. The archaeologist has discovered a discourse which is not life, whose time is not the time of those who live in history and take seriously its progress, conflicts, and decline (*AK* 211).

The archaeologist is thus again beyond the version of the origin double of the sciences of man. Yet the archaeologist's enterprise begins with finitude—in this case with the archaeologist involved in his age and dispersed by the various historical fields determining both his everyday and his serious discourse—and ends with this finitude used as a ladder to a theory that is finally able to deny the validity of the original involvement. Archaeology would seem, then, to manifest the very essence of the analytic of finitude. One would expect, as with the quasi-transcendental reduplication of the empirical and the theoretical recuperation of the unthinkable, to find in the archaeologist's account of history some posthumanist variation of the return and retreat of origin. For like the human scientist the archaeologist seems paradoxically, albeit profoundly, to be trying to both affirm and deny his finitude. How can the archaeologist appear *in* history as the pure ahistorical thinker who disinterestedly catalogues the death of man and God?

Since Foucault himself would now agree that there can be no such ahistorical thinker exercising the "intellectual's privilege" and no such pure discourse as the archaeologist pretends to use, one would expect to find tensions in the treatment of history in the *Archaeology:* either implausible and unjustified claims, as in the case of the prescriptive power of description, or ingenious and self-subverting theses, such as the argument that the archaeologist shares serious discourse while explaining away its seriousness. If such strains and cracks exist in the archaeological theory of historical change, however, we have been unable to unearth them. The archaeologist who claims to have emerged in history only to have stepped outside it, and thus to have totally and definitively understood it, tells a seamless story. His own discourse poses no problem for the archaeologist, who like the phenomenologist and unlike the hermeneuticist, does not even raise the problem of his historical language. While linguists struggle with the "ancient opacity of historical language," whose origin and explanation is lost in the unreachable depths of history, and Heidegger in his later works, tries to recover the original meaning of the words he uses, the language of the archaeologist (analysis, series, system, enunciative function, element, rule, episteme), like that of the phenomenologist (analysis, synthesis, noematic system, meaning-giving activity, element, strict rule, life-world), seems to have no history but is put forward as a transparent technical terminology, invented precisely to be adequate to the phenomenon.

There are occasional slips when Foucault seems to feel obliged to justify his discourse by appealing to the possibility of an undistorted relation of discourse to being which existed in the past and is promised in a dawning new age, as if archaeological discourse had to find its legitimation in an account of the productivity of discourse that flourished before history and will flourish again at its end. But this attempt of the archaeologist to give his description a pedigree does not lead to the pursuit of an endlessly retreating past and future, but rather singles out actual historical events as evidence of the possibility of a different relation of discourse to being. These original events don't "retreat" because they are not presented as events which make history possible. Archaeology simply is an ahistorical discipline with an ahistorical technical language which is able to survey and order history precisely because it is not in history. As a radicalization of Husserlian phenomenology that dispenses with truth, meaning, and the transcendental subject, while still seeking behind the empirical practices an unthought which can be captured in an a priori system of rules, archaeology, like phenomenology, need not even raise the question of origin (or, if one asks about origins one finds them in certain factual predecessors—Plato for Husserl, the Sophists for Foucault).

In our study of the anthropological doubles we have already noted their roughly serial character. Only after one strategy is played out do thinkers take up another. Thus, only when the transcendental/empirical double as it appears in Kant no longer excites efforts at reduction of one side to the other but is stabilized and accepted can a new problem, that of recuperating the unthought in the cogito (as in Freud and Husserl), occupy men's intellectual energies and dictate what counts as worth saying.

And only after this attempt to ground knowledge in the ahistorical individual subject is seen to be fruitless (as Heidegger argued against Husserl) does the tortuous attempt to find the origin of meaning not in the clarified individual consciousness but in an interpretation of culture and history seem the only game in town. On this serial reading of the doubles, the *Archaeology,* as a repetition of the analytic of finitude without appeal to truth and man, has only gone as far as a post-humanist version of the cogito and the unthought. It thus falls into a version of the Husserlian doubles, but never arrives at the Heideggerian one. Only after the failure of double phenomenological bracketing would one expect Foucault to face the problems raised by the archaeologist's historical involvement. At that point the questions would have to be raised: Can the archaeologist avoid the search for a hidden and inaccessible origin by a radicalization of hermeneutics parallel to his radicalization of phenomenology—an interpretation to end all interpretations as it were? Would such a post-anthropological form of interpretation necessarily both affirm and deny its finitude, thus falling into some new structural variation of the return/retreat double? Or is there some way to do archaeology without detachment?

Whatever the answer to these questions, we take it to be established that the *Archaeology,* while beyond truth and deep meaning, and so beyond man, has not freed itself from two new versions of the double. That these doubles reoccur in archaeological discourse shows that Foucault's new ontology, in which after the ages of representation and of man, being is once again directly related to discourse, is still a version of the analytic of finitude. This should be no surprise since the *Archaeology* is an attempt to show the limits of the legitimacy of the knowledge claims of all finite discursive practices, while it claims that it has a clear total picture of these sets of practices as "so many science-objects" (*AK* 207) from a perspective that is free of their influence. The *Archaeology* thus affirms that all serious discourse is subject to rules which determine the production of objects, subjects, and so forth—rules which archaeological discourse claims to discover and describe. The archaeologist, indeed, aspires to contribute to a general theory of such production. "In so far as it is possible to constitute a general theory of productions, archaeology, as the analysis of the rules proper to the different discursive practices, will find what might be called its *enveloping theory*" (*AK* 207). Yet, by avoiding a claim to truth or seriousness, archaeological discourse claims to make itself exempt from the problems raised by such a total theory. It is no surprise that archaeology, by thus both affirming and denying the finitude of its own discourse, turns out to be as unstable as its precursors. In this light the promised post-modern science of human beings, far from being free of the intrinsic instabilities of modern thought, shows itself to be a new variation on an old Kantian theme.

Foucault in his modesty and foresight already entertained in *The Archaeology of Knowledge* the possibility that orthogonal archaeological discourse was not as autonomous as it claimed. In his conclusion, he reaffirms that "the archive, the discursive formations, the positivities, the statements, and their conditions of formation, [reveal] a specific domain. A domain that has not so far been made the object of any analysis (at least, of what is most specific and most irreducible to interpretations and formalizations about it)...." He adds prophetically that he "has no means of guaranteeing—at the still rudimentary stage of mapping at which I am at present—that [this domain] will remain stable and autonomous." In fact, "it may turn out that archaeology is the name given to a part of our contemporary theoretical conjuncture" (*AK* 207, 208).

We will argue in part II that, like all other discursive systems, archaeology is, indeed, a child of its times, and that therefore archaeological discourse itself has to be accounted for and relativized. Foucault's analysis of the Classical Age also reveals, in spite of his insistence on the cataclysmic break between the Age of Representation and the Age of Man, a deep continuity with the present. In the Classical Age all beings were already represented in a totalizable picture on a table, and although the representer who lays out the table had not yet emerged, the place was already awaiting him where he would appear as man, "the difficult object and sovereign subject of all possible knowledge." After man, we now see that the archaeological spectator is still both involved in and detached from the discursive systems he studies. In none of these three stages of modern thought can the various theories of human beings give a stable account of the possibility of their own allegedly autonomous discourse, nor of the positivities that are both posited by that discourse and make that discourse possible. As Foucault has shown us, all such theories of human beings must fail because the attempt to grasp the total picture requires such theories to objectify the conditions which make objectification possible.

Any enterprise which hopes to explain modern thought will itself have to avoid introducing yet another discourse that posits the world as picture and itself as not involved in what it posits. It cannot be a detached, total *theory* of representation, transcendental constitution, or discursive production, but it must be able to explain from within language and history why these three ways of picturing the world developed and were found to be illuminating sciences of human beings.

Near the end of the *Archaeology*, when Foucault considers the possibility that archaeology might not turn out to be the stable and autonomous discipline he had hoped, he notes that in such a case the problems it deals with and the tools it introduces might be "taken up later elsewhere, in a different way, at a higher level, or using different methods" (*AK* 208). These possibilities were more imminent than Foucault realized at the time. Just a few years later he himself took up this task and thus showed himself to be one of those rare thinkers, like Wittgenstein and Heidegger, whose work shows both an underlying continuity and an important reversal not because their early efforts were useless, but because in pushing one way of thinking to its limits they both recognized and overcame those limitations.

It is surely no coincidence that *The Archaeology of Knowledge* is followed by a self-imposed silence that is finally broken by two books in which the author, while still using archaeological techniques, no longer claims to speak from a position of phenomenological detachment.

II   *The Genealogy of the Modern Individual: The Interpretive Analytics of Power, Truth, and the Body*

The reversal that will provide the framework for the analyses in part II of this book is the inversion of the priority of theory to that of practice. In both his semi-structuralist and post-hermeneutic stages, that is, in the discursive theory of *The Archaeology of Knowledge* and the interpretive method of *Discipline and Punish* and *The History of Sexuality,* Foucault develops a highly original account of the relation of theory and practice. These accounts are particularly difficult to unravel because the subject matter Foucault is analyzing, and the methods he employs, have highly complicated relationships. In each stage Foucault holds that the human sciences do not provide their own intelligibility. Neither the methodological self-consciousness of the human scientists involved nor the theory they propound can explain why, at certain times, certain types of human sciences are established and survive, and why they have the objects, subjects, concepts, and strategies they do. Nor can these theories explain the institutional matrix in which the human sciences thrive and ultimately decay. Yet the surface details of these social sciences, when correctly read, provide the key to what is really going on.

In *The Archaeology of Knowledge,* as we have seen, Foucault interpreted his earlier works as studying theories in the human sciences as discourse-objects, by means of an original method we call orthogonal double bracketing. He sought to make the history of the human sciences intelligible in terms of rules which, unknown to the actors involved, regulated and governed all their serious speech acts. Social and institutional practices, whose bearing on the human sciences could not be ignored, were construed as having intelligibility and influence only insofar as they fit in with the reigning epistemic rules. (Of course, this is not to deny that primary relations such as economic forces and secondary relations such as actors' views of their own actions have a separate intelligibility and independence.) Thus the practices and the practitioners' theories of the human sciences were subordinated to a theoretical structure which governed them.

On the side of Foucault's methodology we find a similar favoring of theory over practice. The task of the archaeologist is to describe in theoretical terms the rules governing discursive practices. By bracketing truth and seriousness the archaeologist claims to operate on a level that is free of the influences of both the theories and practices he studies. Whatever intelligibility he finds, he finds among objects with which he is in no way involved. Unlike the theories he studies, his theory slips free of institutional, theoretical, and even epistemic bonds.

As we have seen in chapter 3, this twofold favoring of theory over practice leaves the relative causal contribution of the primary, secondary, and discursive relations to the discourses and practices of the human sciences unresolved and probably unresolvable. Moreover, the archaeol-

102

ogist's claim that he is totally detached from the realm of serious discourse of his day makes the meaning and relevance of his project problematic.

In Foucault's later works, practice, on all levels, is considered more fundamental than theory. Again the intelligibility of the human sciences is not to be found in their own theories. It is not to be found in some system of formation rules either; this level of rules is simply dropped. Nor is it to be found in the horizon of meaning shared by the participants. Rather, Foucault now finds the human sciences intelligible as part of a larger set of organized and organizing practices in whose spread the human sciences play a crucial role.

Foucault's account of his own position with regard to the human sciences also undergoes a radical transformation. The investigator is no longer the detached spectator of mute-discourse monuments. Foucault realizes and thematizes the fact that he himself—like any other investigator—is involved in, and to a large extent produced by, the social practices he is studying. (In his later works, he will see that the method of *The Archaeology of Knowledge* was itself heavily influenced by the seeming success of structuralism in the human sciences.) Foucault introduces genealogy as a method of diagnosing and grasping the significance of social practices from within them. As a tool for attaining a relative degree of detachment from the practices and theories of the human sciences, archaeology, while it still plays an important role, is subordinated to genealogy.

Thus Foucault opens up a new level of intelligibility of the practices, a level that cannot be captured by theory; at the same time, he introduces a new method of "deciphering" the meaning of these practices. Using this new method, theory is not only subordinated to practice but is shown to be one of the essential components through which the organizing practices operate. We will follow in detail how Foucault works out his method of genealogy, especially how he uses it to diagnose the development of what he calls bio-power, a set of historical practices which produces the human objects systematized by structuralism and the human subjects explicated by hermeneutics.

5 Interpretive Analytics

Genealogy

Without getting into a futile game of classification—early, middle, late—especially for a body of work which is still so young, we can see that from his earliest days Foucault has used variants of a strict analysis of discourse (archaeology) and paid a more general attention to that which conditions, limits, and institutionalizes discursive formations (genealogy). *There is no pre- and post-archaeology or genealogy in Foucault.* However, the weighting and conception of these approaches has changed during the development of his work.

Clearly, after May 1968 Foucault's interests began to shift away from discourse. In any case, regardless of the dynamics of Foucault's biography—a very un-Foucaultian topic—it is clear that the problem of power had not been previously thematized: "What was missing from my work was the problem of 'discursive regime', the effects of power proper on the enunciative play. I confused it too much with systematicity, the theoretical form, or something like a paradigm. Between *The History of Madness* and *The Order of Things,* there was under two different aspects, the problem of power which had not yet been well located" (*TP* 105). By the end of the 1970s, as we show in part II, the problem of power had been well-located indeed.

In his 1970 inaugural lecture at the Collège de France, "The Discourse on Language," Foucault briefly touched on the question of genealogy and its relation to archaeology. At this point Foucault was still trying to preserve his archaeological theory and to complement it with genealogy. This may explain the convoluted character of some of his remarks. He says:

Critical and genealogical descriptions are to alternate, support and complete each other. The critical side of the analysis deals with the system's enveloping discourse; attempting to mark out and distinguish the principles of ordering, exclusion and rarity in discourse. We might, to play with our words, say it practices a kind of dogged detachment [une désinvolture appliquée]. The genealogical side of analysis, by way of contrast, deals with series of effective formation of discourse: it attempts to grasp it in its power of affirmation, by which I do not mean a power opposed to that of negation, but the power of constituting a domain of objects, in relation to which one can affirm or deny true or false propositions. Let us call these domains of objects positivities, and to play on words yet again, let us say that, if the critical style is one of studied casualness [la désinvolture studieuse], then the genealogical mood is one of lighthearted positivism [un positivisme heureux]. (*DL* 234, translation modified)

Thus, Foucault poses a complementarity between the rarity of statements (for which he had given the rules in the *Archaeology*) and the effective formation of discourse by nondiscursive practices. This combination of archaeology and genealogy, which alternate, support, and complement each other is, it must be said, rather strange. On the one side, we have something, by definition meaningless, which is taken quite seriously by the archaeologist. On the other side, we have something which is meaningful and serious which is taken with lightheartedness by the genealogist. This results in a kind of double distanciation. On the archaeological side, the regularities of the discursive formation are given a kind of post hoc independence. On the genealogical side, after showing that there is no thing underlying appearances and that metaphysics is over, Foucault seems to draw the conclusion that everything is meaningless and lacks seriousness. This leads to a strange and complex attitude: one has to take the world of serious discourse seriously because it is the one we are in, and yet one can't take it seriously, first because we have arduously divorced ourselves from it, and second because it is not grounded.

In *Discipline and Punish* and in the first volume of *The History of Sexuality*, Foucault straightforwardly reverses the priority of genealogy and archaeology. Genealogy now takes precedence over archaeology. The genealogist is a diagnostician who concentrates on the relations of power, knowledge, and the body in modern society. (We will have much more to say about this later. However, here it is relevant to stress that archaeology is still an important part of this enterprise.) Underlying the longer continuities of cultural practices which the genealogist isolates, the archaeologist still has a purifying role to play. The demonstration of discontinuity and shifts of meaning remains an important task. Having begun on the inside, Foucault as archaeologist can move one step back from the discourse he is studying and treat it as a discourse-object. Archaeology still isolates and indicates the arbitrariness of the hermeneutic horizon of meaning. It shows that what seems like the continuous development of a meaning is crossed by discontinuous discursive formations. The continuities, he reminds us, reveal no finalities, no hidden underlying significations, no metaphysical certainties.

Foucault's elaboration of genealogy was the first major step toward a more satisfactory and self-consciously complex analysis of power. Foucault took this step in an essay published in 1971, entitled "Nietzsche, Genealogy, History." As we have just seen, Foucault stated in "The Discourse on Language," written at the same period, that genealogy is complemented and supported by archaeology. Hence the presentation of genealogy must not be considered to encompass all of Foucault's methodological arsenal. Yet, it would be hard to overestimate the importance of the essay for understanding the progression of the work which followed; all of the seeds of Foucault's work of the 1970s can be found in this discussion of Nietzsche.

This is not to say that Foucault is in full accord with Nietzsche—whatever that could mean for a thinker as complex, elusive, and profoundly antisystematic as Nietzsche. We plead neutrality concerning the textual accuracy of Foucault's reading. Nietzsche interpretation, a flourishing industry in France in recent years, is a field of danger and strife which we leave to others, more fully armed; our concern is with Foucault. We will use the Nietzsche essay to help present the main outlines of genealogy appearing in Foucault's major works of the 1970s, and to introduce some of his central themes—power, knowledge, and the body.

But first, what is genealogy? Genealogy opposes itself to traditional historical method; its aim is to "record the singularity of events outside of any monotonous finality" (*NGH* 139). For the genealogist there are no fixed essences, no underlying laws, no metaphysical finalities. Genealogy seeks out discontinuities where others found continuous development. It finds recurrences and play where others found progress and seriousness. It records the past of mankind to unmask the solemn hymns of progress. Genealogy avoids the search for depth. Instead, it seeks the surfaces of events, small details, minor shifts, and subtle contours. It shuns the profundity of the great thinkers our tradition has produced and revered; its archenemy is Plato. As Foucault put it in an earlier essay entitled "Nietzsche, Freud, Marx," written with a different end in mind, "Whereas the interpreter is obliged to go to the depth of things, like an excavator, the moment of interpretation [genealogy] is like an overview, from higher and higher up, which allows the depth to be laid out in front of him in a more and more profound visibility; depth is resituated as an absolutely superficial secret'' (*NFM* 187).

The interpreter as genealogist sees things from afar. He finds that the questions which were traditionally held to be the deepest and murkiest are truly and literally the most superficial. This certainly does not mean that they are either trivial or lacking in importance, only that their meaning is to be discovered in surface practices, not in mysterious depths. For example, as early as Plato's *Symposium*, eros has seemed to our civilization to be a profound and mysterious force that only poets and prophets could illuminate, yet it is a force which contains the secret springs of human motivation. Likewise, throughout the nineteenth century sex was held to be the most profound key to the meaning of a vast range of practices. Seen genealogically, this obsession with deep and hidden meaning becomes directly accessible to an observer, once he distances himself from cultural belief in deep meaning. That which seemed the most hidden (because of its supposed importance) becomes not what it seemed. Its alleged hiddenness plays an essential role that is directly visible, once it is pointed out by the genealogist. The methodological point (to be spelled out in Foucault's detailed analyses) is that, when viewed from the right distance and with the right vision, there is a profound visibility to everything.

The genealogist recognizes that the deep hidden meanings, the unreachable heights of truth, the murky interiors of consciousness are all shams. Genealogy's coat of arms might read: Oppose depth, finality, and interiority. Its banner: Mistrust identities in history; they are only masks, appeals to unity. The deepest truth that the genealogist has to reveal is "the secret that [things] have no essence or that their essence was fabricated in a piecemeal fashion from alien forms" (*NGH* 142).

For the genealogist philosophy is over. Interpretation is not the uncovering of a hidden meaning. In "Nietzsche, Freud, Marx," Foucault made a similar point: "If interpretation is a never-ending task, it is simply because there is nothing to interpret. There is nothing absolutely primary to interpret because, when all is said and done, underneath it all everything is already interpretation" (*NFM* 189). The more one interprets the more one finds not the fixed meaning of a text, or of the world, but only other interpretations. These interpretations have been created and imposed by other people, not by the nature of things. In this discovery of groundlessness the inherent arbitrariness of interpretation is revealed. For if there is nothing to interpret, then everything is open to interpretation; the only limits are those arbitrarily imposed. This insight is given further specification as Foucault's work proceeds. From a general philosophic point, he later turns it into a genealogical point. If "history is the violent and surreptitious appropriation of a system of rules, which in itself has no essential meaning, in order to impose a direction, to bend it to a new will, to force its participation in a different game, and to subject it to secondary rules, then the development of humanity is a series of interpretations" (*NGH* 151).[1] Genealogy records the history of these interpretations. The universals of our humanism are revealed as the result of the contingent emergence of imposed interpretations.

For Nietzsche, as Foucault reads him, history is the story of petty malice, of violently imposed interpretations, of vicious intentions, of high-sounding stories masking the lowest of motives. To the Nietzschean genealogist the foundation of morality, at least since Plato, is not to be found in ideal truth. It is found in *pudenda origo:* "lowly origins," catty fights, minor crudeness, ceaseless and nasty clashing of wills. The story of history is one of accidents, dispersion, chance events, lies—not the lofty development of Truth or the concrete embodiment of Freedom. For Nietzsche, the genealogist par excellence, the history of truth is the history of error and arbitrariness: "The faith on which our belief in science rests is still a metaphysical faith . . . . The Christian faith, which was also the faith of Plato, that God is Truth and truth divine . . . . But what if this equation becomes less and less credible, if the only things that may still be viewed as divine are error, blindness and lies; if God himself [the truth] turns out to be our *longest* lie?" (*GM* 288).

Foucault the genealogist is no longer outraged, as was Nietzsche, by the discovery that the claim of objectivity masks subjective motivations. Foucault is interested in how both scientific objectivity and subjective intentions emerge together in a space set up not by individuals but by social practices.

According to Foucault the task of the genealogist is to destroy the

---

1. "Rules" here clearly cannot refer to the strict formation rules Foucault thought he had found in *The Archaeology of Knowledge*. These have been definitively abandoned. In the earlier and later works, rule and principle are used in a more common sense, or at least in a typically French way, to refer to regularities, norms, constraints, conditions, conventions, and so on. Although this use of "rule" is unobjectionable and does not raise the methodological difficulties found in *The Archaeology of Knowledge,* there is still a tendency, when one uses such a vocabulary, to overemphasize those norms which *can* be made explicit at the expense of the norms picked up by apprenticeship and the sort of concrete examples Kuhn calls exemplars or paradigms, which can't.

Foucault is now interested in the use made of the norms, rules, and systems which, in *The Order of Things,* he already sees as definitive of the human sciences. Such concern is poles apart from Foucault's earlier attempt to find rules which would further "a general formalization of thought and knowledge" (*OT* 383). Foucault is no longer interested in "the question . . . of knowing whether it is possible without a play on words to employ the notion of structure; . . . a question that is central if one wishes to know . . . the conditions and limitations of a justified formalization . . ." (*OT* 382). Formal rules are precisely what Foucault does not preserve in his new combination of archaeology and genealogy.

primacy of origins, of unchanging truths. He seeks to destroy the doctrines of development and progress. Having destroyed ideal significations and original truths, he looks to the play of wills. Subjection, domination, and combat are found everywhere he looks. Whenever he hears talk of meaning and value, of virtue and goodness, he looks for strategies of domination. One important difference between Nietzsche and Foucault is that whereas Nietzsche often seems to ground morality and social institutions in the tactics of individual actors, Foucault totally depsychologizes this approach and sees all psychological motivation not as the source but as the result of strategies without strategists. Instead of origins, hidden meanings, or explicit intentionality, Foucault the genealogist finds force relations working themselves out in particular events, historical movements, and history. "Look not to the stable possession of a truth, or of power itself," Foucault would say, as if either were a result of psychological motivations; rather conceive of them as a strategy, which leads you to see "that its effects of domination are attributed not to 'appropriation', but to dispositions, manoeuvers, tactics, techniques, functionings; that one should decipher in it a network of relations, constantly in tension, in activity..." (*DP* 26).

There are many lessons to be drawn from this radical shift of perspective. The first is that "no one is responsible for an emergence; no one can glory in it, since it always occurs in the interstice" (*NGH* 150). For the genealogist, there is no subject, either individual or collective, moving history. This notion comes as no surprise. But the notion of interstice is surprising. The play of forces in any particular historical situation is made possible by the space which defines them. It is this field or clearing which is primary. As we saw, in *The Archaeology of Knowledge* Foucault already had this notion of space or clearing in which subjects and objects occur. But then he thought of the space as governed by a system of rules which emerge discontinuously and without any further intelligibility. Now, this field or clearing is understood as the result of long term practices and as the field in which those practices operate. And, of course, what takes place in the field is not simply the permutation of meaningless serious speech acts. These are social maneuvers of great consequence for those involved. The genealogist does not seek to discover substantial entities (subjects, virtues, forces) or to reveal their relationships with other such entities. Rather, he studies the emergence of a battle which defines and clears a space. Subjects do not first preexist and later enter into combat or harmony. In genealogy subjects emerge on a field of battle and play their roles, there and there alone. The world is not a play which simply masks a truer reality that exists behind the scenes. It is as it appears. This is the profundity of the genealogist's insight.

Genealogy may be opposed to hymns of progress or finalities in history, yet "in a sense, only a single drama is ever staged in this non-place, the endlessly repeated play of dominations" (*NGH* 150). But for the genealogist this drama is neither a play of meanings nor a simple locking of horns in a battle of subjects. Rather, it is an emergence of a structural field of clashes. In this field, the genealogist sees that the battle of domination is not simply the relationship of rulers and ruled, dominators and dominated: "This relationship of domination is no more a 'relationship' than the place where it occurs is a place; and, precisely for this reason, it is fixed, throughout its history, in rituals, in meticulous procedures that impose rights and obligations" (*NGH* 150). These meticulous rituals of power are not the creation of subjects, nor simply a set of relationships; nor are they easily located in specific places; nor is there an easily identifiable historical development that lies behind their emergence. The isolation of "meticulous rituals of power" is the conceptual basis for much of Foucault's later work. In *Discipline and Punish* and *The History of Sexuality* Foucault will identify specific sites in which rituals of power take place—the Panopticon of Bentham and the confessional. He will use these to localize and specify how power works, what it does and how it does it.

The rules and obligations which emerge from these rituals are inscribed in civil law, in moral codes, in the universal laws of humanity that claim to temper and prevent the violence that would supposedly exist without their civilizing constraints. But, the genealogist protests, these noble expressions are the very means by which domination advances. History is not the progress of universal reason. It is the play of rituals of power, humanity advancing from one domination to another. "Rules are empty in themselves, violent and unfinalized; they are impersonal and can be bent to any purpose" (*NGH* 151). Particular groups seize them and impose a particular interpretation on them.

The genealogist writes effective history, *wirkliche Historie*. He is opposed to a suprahistorical perspective that seeks to totalize history, to trace its internal development, to recognize ourselves in a comfortable way in the past, to offer the reassurance of an end toward which history moves. "The historian's history finds its support outside of time and pretends to base its judgments on an apocalyptic objectivity" (*NGH* 152). Effective history seeks, in contrast, to put everything in historical motion. All of our ideals of truth and beauty, our bodies, our instincts, our feelings might seem to be beyond relativity. The effective historian seeks to dissolve this comforting illusion of identity and firmness and solidity. There are no constants for the genealogist. "Nothing in man—not even his body—is sufficiently stable to serve as the basis for self-recognition or for understanding other men" (*NGH* 153).

This view, which Foucault attributes to Nietzsche, represents one possible extreme stand on the malleability of the body. In Foucault's reading, Nietzsche seems to be saying not only that the body can be used and experienced in many different ways and that desires are changed by cultural interpretations, but that every aspect of the body can be totally modified given the appropriate techniques. An even more extreme view is implied by the claim that the body cannot even serve as the basis for self-recognition. Sartre certainly held that even the body's habits can change arbitrarily and totally from day to day; it is not our task to determine whether Nietzsche held either of these views consistently or even whether he held them at all. The issues raised here are, however, of fundamental import for evaluating Foucault's project.

In spite of his brilliant analyses of the body as the place where the most minute and local social practices are linked up with the large scale organization of power (to be discussed in the next three chapters), Foucault remains elusive about how malleable the human body really is. He obviously rejects the naturalistic view that the body has a fixed structure and fixed needs, which only a limited range of cultural arrangements can express and fulfill. Considering Foucault's account of what has been done to the body and how stable this formative control has been, he would also presumably reject the Sartrian existentialist extreme; if the body were that unstable there would be no way for society to organize and control it over time. But it is harder to tell what position Foucault affirms.

An interesting alternative open to Foucault is Merleau-Ponty's notion of *le corps propre,* or lived body as distinguished from the physical body, one of the most important contributions of modern French thought. The lived body, understood as a system of correspondences between various modes of action and various sensory fields, is meant to account for the commonality of all human perception. In the *Phenomenology of Perception* Merleau-Ponty argues in detail that there are cross-cultural, ahistorical structures of the perceptual field such as size constancy, brightness constancy, up-down asymmetry, as well as social constants such as response to meaningful gestures and facial expression, and sexual signification. These he calls "intercorporeality," and asserts that they all correspond to structures in the lived body. Merleau-Ponty also projected, but never carried out, an extension of these invariant structures to cover conceptual constants and possible boundary conditions on cultural variability.

Foucault obviously is influenced by Nietzsche's account of the body, but he is also aware of the phenomenology of the body developed after the war by Merleau-Ponty. With Foucault's background in phenomenology he might well feel that Nietzsche's emphasis on the body is well-placed, but that Nietzsche allows the body too much free play. On the other hand, it seems to us that Foucault probably finds Merleau-Ponty's structural invariants too general to be useful in understanding the

111

historical specificity of body-molding techniques. Reading Merleau-Ponty one would never know that the body has a front and a back and can only cope with what is in front of it, that bodies can move forward more easily than backwards, that there is normally a right/left asymmetry, and so on. Yet such specific facts about the body no doubt have influenced those who developed disciplinary techniques. These are just the features that would interest Foucault, who is asking how the body can be divided up, reconstituted, and manipulated by society.[2]

Granted that body invariants can be described with much greater specificity than Merleau-Ponty achieved, the question still remains, What is the historical importance of such invariant structures? One would like to know to what extent they are thematized and what role they play in the successful deployment of disciplinary techniques. Are there, perhaps, other such structures whose discovery and application have important social consequences? How invariant are these structures really? Foucault is uniquely placed to address these questions raised by his work. But, so far, he has remained silent.

In any case, the task of genealogy has been to show that "the body is also directly involved in a political field.... Power relations have an immediate hold upon it; they invest it, mark it, train it, torture it, force it to carry out tasks, to perform ceremonies, to emit signs" (*DP* 25). This is directly connected to the economic system, for the body is both useful and productive. But it becomes possible to make men work efficiently and productively only after they have been "caught up in a system of subjection (in which need is also a political instrument meticulously prepared, calculated and used); the body becomes a useful force only if it is both a productive body and a subjected body" (*DP* 26).

This passage introduces the key themes we will encounter in our discussion of *Discipline and Punish* and *The History of Sexuality*. One of Foucault's major achievements has been his ability to isolate and conceptualize the way in which the body has become an essential component for the operation of power relations in modern society. Obviously, the body had been involved in political dynamics before modern times. For example, when the law was broken during the *ancien régime*, the criminal would be tortured in public. This was the "supplice" Foucault has described in agonizing detail. The sovereign's power was literally and publicly inscribed on the criminal's body in a manner as controlled, scenic, and well-attended as possible. Under our modern regimes, the body has continued to play an extremely important role. We will later

2. These features have been pointed out and discussed by Samuel Todes in *The Human Body as the Material Subject of the World*, Harvard doctoral diss., 1963. See also his "Comparative Phenomenology of Perception and Imagination, Part I: Perception": *Journal of Existentialism* (Spring 1966).

follow in detail the genealogist's exacting descriptions of how the body has been used as an integral component of the spread and localization of modern power. For the moment, however, it is important to point out the methodological—that is, genealogical—isolation of the body in Foucault's approach. He says, "There may be a knowledge of the body that is not exactly the science of its functioning, and a mastery of its forces that is more than the ability to conquer them: this knowledge and this mastery constitute what might be called the political technology of the body" (*DP* 26). Foucault has isolated a medium of great importance. In both *Madness and Civilization* and *The Birth of the Clinic,* as we have seen in chapter 1, Foucault began to analyze the interrelations of biological knowledge and modern power. He has since broadened and sharpened his approach. From the start he has been interested in the body as it has been directly investigated by scientists and in the power which resides in specialized institutions. More recently he has recognized that this potent combination of knowledge and power, localized on the body, is actually a general mechanism of power of the greatest import for Western society.

One further point of clarification is required for the moment. Part of the genius—and the difficulty—of Foucault's work is his systematic refusal to accept the usual sociological categories. The political technology of the body—the crossing of power relations, knowledge, and the body— cannot be found in one single institution nor one single apparatus of power, that is, the state. Although he is increasingly concerned with what is commonly referred to as institutional analysis, his focus is never institutions per se; it is the growth of technologies of power. The prison is an important part of that history, but it is not identical or coextensive with it. Obviously, Foucault thinks that the prison and the state play important roles in the articulation of modern power relations. But he is seeking to isolate the specific mechanisms of technology through which power is actually articulated on the body.

Foucault is attempting to write the effective history of the appearance, the articulation, and the spread of these political technologies of the body. In the course of doing this, he will describe in detail the interconnections of these technologies with the state and with specific institutions. Yet these connections are never his true locus of study. As he puts it, the political technologies of the body "cannot be localized in a particular type of institution or state apparatus. For they have recourse to it; they use, select or impose certain of its methods. But, in its mechanisms and its effects, it is situated at a quite different level. What the apparatuses and institutions operate is, in a sense, a micro-physics of power, whose field of validity is situated in a sense between these great functionings and the bodies themselves with their materiality and their forces" (*DP* 26). It would be hard to overemphasize the importance of

Foucault's originality on this point. He claims to have isolated the mechanism by which power operates: meticulous rituals of power. He claims to have found the manner in which power is localized: the political technology of the body. He also claims to have revealed the dynamics of how power works: a microphysics of power. Foucault is excessively metaphoric on this point; it remains to be seen exactly what a microphysics is and how it operates. Genealogy is still in the process of being formulated.

Foucault closes "Nietzsche, Genealogy, History" with the problem of knowledge. For the genealogist, knowledge is thoroughly enmeshed in the petty malice of the clash of dominations. Knowledge does not offer a way out; rather it increases the dangers we face. Knowledge did not "slowly detach itself from its empirical roots, the initial needs from which it arose, to become pure speculation subject only to the demands of reason.... Where religions once demanded the sacrifice of bodies, knowledge now calls for experimentation on ourselves, calls us to the sacrifice of the subject of knowledge" (*NGH* 163). All domains are now potentially open to scientific investigation. It follows that everything is potentially enmeshed in the networks of power which, as we have seen, are increasingly interconnected with the advance of knowledge. We are now on the verge of sacrificing ourselves to our own deepest lie: our belief that knowledge exists separately from power. Foucault quotes Nietzsche on "the idea of humanity sacrificing itself. It seems indisputable that if this new constellation appeared on the horizon, only the desire for truth, with its enormous prerogatives, could direct, and sustain such a sacrifice. For, to knowledge no sacrifice is too great" (*NGH* 164). In the next three chapters we will explore Foucault's detailed development of this Nietzschean idea.

If there is another theme in Foucault's recent work that holds as much importance as that of the body, it is the claim that power and knowledge are not external to one another. They operate in history in a mutually generative fashion. Neither can be explained in terms of the other, nor reduced to the other. In many ways, this is the most radical dimension of Foucault's work. Although he has unquestionably added a new complexity and refinement to our understanding of the place of the body in history, it is not something which is likely, after it is understood, to generate much resistance. In fact, it is rather more likely to generate more research, massive *thèses*. But, the internal connections between knowledge and power are, it seems clear, of a much less easily assimilable order. For it is not merely a question of changing the direction of our historical, anthropological, and sociological inquiries, but of putting the objective nature of these inquiries in question.

In *Discipline and Punish* the challenge is stated tentatively and rather coyly: "Perhaps, too, we should abandon a whole tradition that allows us to imagine that knowledge can exist only where the power relations are suspended and that knowledge can develop only outside its [power's] injunctions, its demands and its interests" (*DP* 27). It should be said immediately that this is not a simple variant of the sociology of knowledge nor a Marxist analysis of the class conditions on the production and reception of knowledge. It is more radical and far-reaching than either, although it obviously grows out of these traditions—challenged and radicalized by Foucault's reflections on Nietzsche. Thus:

> we should admit . . . that power and knowledge directly imply one another; that there is no power relation without the correlative constitution of a field of knowledge, nor any knowledge that does not presuppose and constitute at the same time power relations. These power/knowledge relations are to be analyzed, therefore, not on the basis of a subject of knowledge who is or is not free in relation to the power system, but, on the contrary, the subject who knows, the objects to be known and the modalities of knowledge must be regarded as so many effects of these fundamental implications of power/knowledge and their historical transformations. In short, it is not the activity of the subject of knowledge that produces a corpus of knowledge, useful or resistant to power, but power/knowledge, the processes and struggles that traverse it and of which it is made up, that determines the forms and possible domains of knowledge. (*DP* 27, 28)

In a sense, this internal relation of power and knowledge will be the subject of the rest of our book.

Once again, it is important to be clear about the level on which Foucault is directing his analysis, for he has been misunderstood on this point. His analysis of the political technology of the body is directed at isolating a level between the body in its biological functioning and the institutional apparatuses of force. So, too, Foucault is interested in isolating the relations which obtain between knowledge and power in particular kinds of sciences. In an interview in 1976 entitled "Truth and Power" he posed the problem in the following terms:

> If we pose to a science like theoretical physics or organic chemistry the problem of its relations with political and economic structures of the society, haven't we posed a question which is too difficult? Haven't we raised the threshold *(barre)* of explanation at too high a level? If, on the other hand, we take a science like psychiatry wouldn't the possibility of

answering the question of its relations to society be much easier to pose? The "epistemological profile" of psychiatry is low and psychiatric practice is linked to a series of institutions, immediate economic exigencies, political urgencies and social regulations. Isn't it the case that in as dubious a science as psychiatry one could seize with more certainty the intertwining of the effects of knowledge and power? (*TP* 109)

Foucault is not ruling out relations between theoretical physics and society but is suggesting that they will certainly not be direct and easily grasped if we are interested in the concepts and laws of physics per se and not merely its technological uses. Rather, Foucault has directed his attention almost entirely to those doubtful sciences, the social sciences.

As we saw in chapter 3, Foucault agrees with Nietzsche and Heidegger that at any given time cultural practices determine what will count as an object for serious investigation. But Foucault wants to make an important distinction between kinds of practices and the types of objects which each kind of practice "frees." If, with Foucault, we set aside everyday practices and their objects as outside our concerns, we are left with two distinct categories: on the one hand, the relatively stable practices and objects of those disciplines Kuhn calls normal sciences and Foucault calls sciences which have passed the threshold of scientificity (*AK* 187), and, on the other hand, the shifting practices and objects of the sciences which have not crossed this threshold. This second class includes at least some sciences like meteorology which are presumably on the way to normalization, and dubious disciplines like the human sciences which Foucault diagnoses as not even advancing towards normalcy. We saw in *The Order of Things* that, according to Foucault, the sciences of man, caught in the various doubles, simply cannot become normal. This does not foreclose the possibility, however, that some other study of human beings could, although it is clear from Foucault's recent analyses of their involvement with power that this seems highly unlikely.

Since natural science too, according to Foucault, had its birth in the practices of specific social institutions, one would like to know whether the human sciences might likewise free themselves from their involvement with power. And if not, why not? In any case, it seems incumbent on Foucault to give some account of why we can take some sciences, such as physics, as if they do in fact tell us something like the truth about how things really are, even though they are produced and used in a social context, and why we can never take the claims of the social sciences at face value. The difference cannot simply be that the natural sciences give us a great deal of power and control. Foucault's point is precisely that the social sciences also give rise to extremely effective technologies. Nor can we argue that any science which escapes the power matrix automatically gains plausibility; alchemy is no truer for being politically irrelevant. We would like to hear more from Foucault about just how he is able to distinguish the serious sciences from the dubious ones, and in what way he considers normal sciences to be capable of being true.

It is necessary, Foucault seems to be arguing, to look at the specific discursive formation, its history, and its place in the larger context of power in order to be able to evaluate its claim to describe reality. Whether we are analyzing propositions in physics or phrenology, we substitute for their apparent internal intelligibility a different intelligibility, namely their place within the discursive formation. This is the task of archaeology. But since archaeology has bracketed truth and meaning it can tell us nothing more. Archaeology is always a technique that can free us from a residual belief in our direct access to objects; in each case the "tyranny of the referent" has to be overcome. When we add genealogy, however, a third level of intelligibility and differentiation is introduced. After archaeology does its job, the genealogist can ask about the historical and political roles that these sciences play. If it is established that a particular discursive formation has not succeeded in crossing the threshold of epistemologization, then archaeology has freed us to shift to the question of what role this pseudoscience, this doubtful science, plays in the larger context. This does not prove that physics is "true" in some realist sense, or that the human sciences are "false" because of some fatal contamination by society. But it does provide a diagnostic device whereby we can begin to differentiate and locate the functions of different types of discourse.

We are then led to ask what functions these discursive formations play. This in turn leads us to pose more general questions about power and its relation to knowledge:

> Truth is not outside of power or itself lacking in power.... Truth is of this world; it is the product of multiple constraints.... Each society has its own regime of truth, its general politics of the truth.... There is a combat for the truth, or at least around the truth, as long as we understand by the truth not those true things which are waiting to be discovered but rather the ensemble of rules according to which we distinguish the true from the false, and attach special effects of power to "the truth." (*TP* 131)

For this gambit to work, Foucault owes us a radically new interpretation of both power and knowledge: one that does not see power as a possession that one group holds and another lacks; one that does not see knowledge as objective or subjective, but as a central component in the historical transformation of various regimes of power and truth. This, of course, is exactly what genealogy attempts to provide.

117

History of the Present and Interpretive Analytics

Before entering into the details of Foucault's analysis of modern power it is important to introduce one last theme. Just as Foucault employs a rather novel level of analysis, so too his practice of historical writing is cast in unorthodox terms. In order to avoid some of the possible misunderstandings of both Foucault's project and our interpretation of it, it is necessary to indicate what type of historical analysis Foucault is attempting to fashion.

In *Discipline and Punish,* Foucault says, "I would like to write the history of the prison with all the political investments of the body it gathers together in its closed architecture. Why? Simply because I am interested in the past? No, if one means by that writing a history of the past in terms of the present. Yes, if one means writing the history of the present" (*DP* 31). Foucault is making an important distinction in this Delphic pronouncement. He is not trying to capture the meaning or significance of a past epoch. He is not trying to get the whole picture of a past age, or person, or institution. He is not trying to find the underlying laws of history. Moreover, he is not reading present interests, institutions, and politics back into history, into other epochs, and claiming to discover that these institutions in earlier times had anything like their current significance. This, simply enough, would be the well-catalogued error of "presentism" in historical analysis. In the presentist fallacy, the historian takes a model or a concept, an institution, a feeling, or a symbol from his present, and attempts—almost by definition unwittingly—to find that it had a parallel meaning in the past. We might think of ethnocentrism as another common variant of this mistake. For example, if we attempted to interpret Medieval Christianity or a primitive rite entirely in terms of individual psychology, neglecting the hierarchical and cosmological reality, we would be "writing the history of the past in terms of the present."

The other side of the presentist coin might be called finalism. This is the kind of history which finds the kernel of the present at some distant point in the past and then shows the finalized necessity of the development from that point to the present. Everything that happened in between is taken up by this march forward, or else left in the backwash as the world historical spirit differentiates and individuates what is central from what is peripheral. Everything has a meaning, a place; everything is situated by the final goal history will attain. Most historians by now agree that presentism and finalism are vices to be avoided. They agree that a contemporary interest—like the environment, the family, or the prison—could well be the spur to question the past in new ways. But even this concession is traditional history. It is not what Foucault is doing.

"Writing the history of the present" is another matter. This approach explicitly and self-reflectively begins with a diagnosis of the current situation. There is an unequivocal and unabashed contemporary orientation. The historian locates the acute manifestations of a particular "meticulous ritual of power" or "political technology of the body" to see where it arose, took shape, gained importance, and so on. For example, in *The History of Sexuality*, Foucault isolates the confession as an important ritual of power in which a specific technology of the body was forged. As this is genealogy, one is not going to find a simple unity of meaning or function nor a changeless significance. The confession, as Foucault demonstrates, did not have the same meaning in the thirteenth century, the seventeenth century, or the nineteenth century as it does in the present. Even more importantly for our current purposes, Foucault is not attempting to give a complete picture of, say, seventeenth century society. He is not trying to give us a traditional history and then to pose the question: Given that history, what does confession mean to us? Rather, he is saying that confession is a vital component of modern power. He then asks: How did we get here? He can respond: "The scheme for transforming sex into discourse had been devised long before in an ascetic and monastic setting. The seventeenth century made it into a rule for everyone. It would seem in actual fact that it could scarcely have applied to any but a tiny elite. . . . An imperative was established . . . . The Christian pastoral prescribed as a fundamental duty the task of passing everything having to do with sex through the endless mill of speech" (*HS* 20, 21). Foucault is not giving us a history of the seventeenth century. He is not even claiming that this imperative was of the greatest import then. Instead he is isolating the central components of political technology today and tracing them back in time. Foucault writes the history of the confession in the seventeenth century for the purposes of writing "a history of the present."

It is important to stress two points. First, this position does not imply that any arbitrary construction will do. Foucault is most definitely trying to analyze and understand confession; he asks what it was in earlier periods and what it has become today. He is not claiming that if one is primarily interested in the seventeenth century, then one must take account of confession. Most of the topics he covers were peripheral and relatively minor in earlier epochs; in fact, that is his point. He has chosen them because of his current interests and because these topics later to some degree became enmeshed with forms of power. But he also does not want to commit the presentist fallacy of saying that because he is writing the history of the present, he is free to project current meaning back into history.

119

Second, the genealogist, having destroyed the project of writing a "true" history of the past, has no recourse to its comforts. The correspondence theory of reality is dead. The search for finalities should be over. Hence, Foucault cannot be claiming to give us a true history of the past in the sense of one that is fully adequate to the past, which represents it correctly, which gets the whole picture. Foucault's genealogical demonstration of his own involvement and his own pragmatic intent carry him away from what is for him part of the problem—traditional history.

The abandonment of objective, totalizing analysis might seem to lead to a kind of subjectivism. Foucault counters this threat by concentrating his efforts on writing the genealogy of the modern subject. As he says, "we must rid ourselves of the constituting subject, rid ourselves of the subject itself, which is to say arrive at an analysis which can account for the subject within an historical account" (*TP* 117). A major part of Foucault's efforts in the 1970s has gone to constructing an account of the place of the subject, subjectivism, and the modern individual. The central theme of Foucault's genealogy is now to show the development of power techniques oriented to individuals. "Individuality is neither the real atomistic basis of society nor an ideological illusion of liberal economics, but an effective artifact of a very long and complicated historical process" (*DP* 194). Foucault has attempted to isolate two trends (and we follow exactly this story in the following chapters): first, the genealogy of the objectifying trends in our culture; and second, that of the subjectifying practices which have been given increasing prominence and importance in recent years. In sum, Foucault is seeking to construct a mode of analysis of those cultural practices in our culture which have been instrumental in forming the modern individual as both object and subject.

Foucault concentrates his analysis on exactly those cultural practices in which power and knowledge cross, and in which our current understanding of the individual, the society, and the human sciences are themselves fabricated. Foucault's research strategy is as follows: study those doubtful sciences thoroughly enmeshed in cultural practices, which in spite of their orthodoxies show no sign of becoming normal sciences; study them with a method which reveals that truth itself is a central component of modern power. Thus Foucault, having ruled out the others, employs the only method left: a pragmatically oriented, historical interpretation.

In order to do this Foucault has introduced another technical term: *dispositif*. This troublesome term has no satisfactory English equivalent. Foucault's translators have employed "apparatus," a word that conveys Foucault's pragmatic concern that concepts be used as tools to aid in analysis, not as ends in themselves. But it remains excessively vague. Another alternative, more in keeping with our immediate aims, might be "grid of intelligibility." We acknowledge that the disadvantage of this translation is that it underestimates Foucault's attempt to reveal something about the practices themselves. But if we keep in mind that the "grid of intelligibility" is the method of the effective historian as well as the structure of the cultural practices he is examining, then we might approach a more adequate understanding of what Foucault is driving at with *dispositif*.

Although exactly what he means by the term has not been spelled out, the domain to which it points is relatively clear. *Dispositif* is distinguished from *episteme* primarily because it encompasses the nondiscursive practices as well as the discursive. It is resolutely heterogeneous, including "discourses, institutions, architectural arrangements, regulations, laws, administrative measures, scientific statements, philosophic propositions, morality, philanthropy, etc." (*CF* 194). Drawing from these disparate components, one seeks to establish a set of flexible relationships, and merge them into a single apparatus in order to isolate a specific historical problem. This apparatus brings together power and knowledge into a specific grid of analysis. Foucault defines *dispositif* by saying that when one has succeeded in isolating "strategies of relations of forces supporting types of knowledge and inversely," then one has a *dispositif*. However he has not clearly spelled out the limits of the technique: Are there certain necessary components to take into account? Is there a requirement of complexity in this grid? Are there limits to the type of practices that can be analyzed?

This *dispositif* is, of course, a grid of analysis constructed by the historian. But it is also the practices themselves, acting as an apparatus, a tool, constituting subjects and organizing them. Foucault is seeking to isolate and establish precisely the kind of intelligibility that practices have. The problem is: How to locate and understand a set of coherent practices which organize social reality when one has no recourse to a constituting subject (or a series of practitioners), to objective laws, or to the sort of rules Foucault once thought avoided these alternatives. The *dispositif* is an initial attempt on his part to name, or at least to point to the problem.

We can perhaps see what Foucault is after more clearly if we follow out an example. Freud, Foucault tells us, was an attentive student at the clinic of Charcot. Charcot was carrying out extensive medical experiments regarding sexuality, particularly that of hysterical women. The women would be given amelye nitrate to excite them and were then brought before Charcot and his interns where they would act out and speak freely about their fantasies. Under the directorship of Charcot, a whole ritual drama was enacted. Sexuality was not something hidden behind or underneath the performances that the good doctors were staging. Freud's discovery, his breakthrough, was not the sexual dimension per se; Charcot had already discovered that. Freud's originality was to take these performances seriously and symbolically. He saw that they had to be interpreted as to their sense. Hence we get *The Interpretation of Dreams* which, as Foucault says, is something very different from an etiology of neurosis. Put schematically, Charcot was searching for the objective cause of these actions; Freud saw that the actor's hidden intentions had to be interpreted if we were to understand what was going on. Foucault is taking this process one step further. "I start with the *dispositif de sexualité*, a fundamental historical given, which is the obligatory starting point for any discussion of these issues. I give it serious consideration and I take it literally *(au pied de la lettre)*, I do not place myself outside of it, because it is not possible to do this, and by so doing I am led to other things" (*CF* 218). In this example, these other things are not the objective causes of sexual neurosis, nor the hidden intentions of the hysterical women, but the organization, coherence, and intelligibility of all of the practices which make up the performances in Charcot's clinic. Foucault seeks to analyze exactly *what* these practices are doing.

Foucault calls this decipherment. But decipherment still sounds too much like the analysis of a code which, meaningless in itself, underlies the practices and gives them whatever coherence they have. We prefer to call Foucault's method interpretive analytics. Our use of *analytic* follows and develops a line that begins with Kant's transcendental analytics and is rethought in the existential analytic of *Being and Time*. Kant problematized Enlightenment thought by seeking the conditions of possibility and limitations of rational analysis. Heidegger problematized the modern attempt to find a transcendental ground in the knowing subject by investigating the ahistorical and cross-cultural existential preconditions of human self-understanding. Kant and Heidegger both took for granted the importance of studying human beings. They both wanted to provide a universal theory and to know the sources and legitimate uses of the concepts presupposed by their predecessors. Foucault accepts this project but rejects the attempts to find a universal grounding in either thought or Being. Analytics today must find a way of taking seriously the problems and conceptual tools of the past, but not the solutions and conclusions based on them. Foucault (like later Heidegger) replaces ontology with a special kind of history that focuses on the cultural practices that have made us what we are.

Our use of *interpretation* develops a line which began with Nietzsche's concept of genealogy and was rethought in Heideggerian hermeneutics. Genealogy accepts the fact that we are nothing but our history, and that therefore we will never get a total and detached picture either of who we are or of our history. Heidegger showed that Nietzsche's insight seemed to leave only the possibility of a free play of equally arbitrary interpretations. But this seems inevitable only if one forgets that it is precisely because we are nothing but our history that we can, at any time, entertain only a narrow range of possibilities; we must inevitably read our history in terms of our current practices.

The word interpretation is not ideal. It carries with it too many ambiguous and mistaken connotations. For one thing, it suggests one sense of what Foucault in *The Birth of the Clinic* called commentary. Commentary, as we use the term, paraphrases and explicates the surface meaning of the text or practices being interpreted. The most influential modern formulation of this view is Heidegger's use of the hermeneutic method in Division I of *Being and Time*. This amounts to making manifest the everyday intelligibility of the things and speech acts which people use in a shared context of meaning. Foucault's objection to this view, as stated in *The Birth of the Clinic*, was that this sort of exegesis merely adds to the proliferation of discourse without getting at what is really going on. By the time of *The Archaeology of Knowledge*, Foucault thought that a process of rarefaction and regulation of serious discourse, governed by changing systems of formation rules, was the correct level of analysis. The point was not to add more discourse, but to find the rules which determined or controlled the discourse that there was. In his recent books, Foucault still criticizes commentary for its misplaced emphasis on the meaning available to the actor. But he now sees that this overemphasis on the actor's point of view ignores the crucial importance of social practices. Not that the actors fail to understand the surface significance of what they are saying and doing. But commentary can give no reply if we ask: What is the effect of what they are doing? All commentary can do is further elaborate the background meanings shared by the actors.

Rejection of the actor's own interpretation of the meaning of his actions does *not* lead Foucault to accept the alternative form of exegesis, that which he calls interpretation and which we call, following Paul Ricoeur, the hermeneutics of suspicion. This view holds that actors do not have direct access to the meaning of their discourse and practices, that our everyday understanding of things is superficial and distorted. It is, in fact, a motivated covering-up of the way things really are. This position, worked out by Freud, and by Heidegger in Division II of *Being and Time*, still rests on the methodological assumption that there is an essential continuity between everyday intelligibility and the deeper kind of intelligibility which the everyday view works to cover up. Since the deeper intelligibility is supposedly at work causing distortions on the everyday level, one can arrive at this motivating truth by sufficiently detailed attention to these distortions. Some particular experience, whether it be a trauma or ontological anxiety, holds the key. But since the deep meaning is what motivated the distortions in the first place, the actor only gets at it when he is forced to face it by an authority; he experiences it as coming from outside. The ultimate authority still remains the actor, however, since it is his acknowledgment that establishes the truth of the deep interpretation. It is only by acknowledging this truth that the actor becomes authentic or free.

Foucault accepts certain insights of both of these forms of exegesis. We have seen in chapter 3 that he stressed, against the hermeneutic approach, that in one obvious sense of meaning, serious speakers know exactly what they mean. On the other hand, he agrees with the hermeneutics of suspicion that some surface behavior can be understood as a distortion of significances which the actor senses but is motivated to ignore. Foucault's basic objection to the hermeneutics of suspicion is that these secrets that the actor can be forced to face must not be understood as the true and deepest meaning of his surface behavior. Rather, he seeks to demonstrate that the deeper meaning, which the authority directs the actor to uncover, also hides another more important meaning, which is not directly available to the actor. This is where hermeneutics must be abandoned, since it is part of the problem, and where Foucault turns to what we are calling interpretation. The actor can come to see what his everyday behavior means; he can be led to see deeper meanings masked by this everyday behavior; but what neither he nor the authority directing the hermeneutic exegesis can see is what the exegetical situation is doing to both of them, and why. Since the hidden meaning is not the final truth about what is going on, finding it is not necessarily liberating; in fact, as Foucault points out, it can lead away from the kind of understanding which might help the actor resist the current practices of domination.

Interpretive understanding can only be obtained by someone who shares the actor's involvement, but distances himself from it. This person must undertake the hard historical work of diagnosing and analyzing the history and organization of current cultural practices. The resulting interpretation is a pragmatically guided reading of the coherence of the practices of the society. It does not claim to correspond either to the everyday meanings shared by the actors or, in any simple sense, to reveal the intrinsic meaning of the practices. This is the sense in which Foucault's method is interpretive but not hermeneutic.

Yet it is not a general method. Foucault is not trying to construct a general theory of production (like Pierre Bourdieu or many neo-Marxists). Rather, he is offering us an interpretive analytic of our current situation. It is Foucault's unique combination of genealogy and archaeology that enables him to go beyond theory and hermeneutics and yet to take problems seriously. The practitioner of interpretive analytics realizes that he himself is produced by what he is studying; consequently he can never stand outside it. The genealogist sees that cultural practices are more basic than discursive formations (or any theory) and that the seriousness of these discourses can only be understood as part oi a society's ongoing history. The archaeological step back that Foucault takes in order to see the strangeness of our society s practices no longer considers these practices meaningless. For reasons that will become clear later, he is not exhaustively involved in the productions and practices he is diagnosing. Yet Foucault is able to diagnose our problems because he shares them. We can no longer do theory. We are no longer searching for deep, hidden meaning. Yet since we still take the problems of our culture seriously, then we are drawn ineluctably to a position like Foucault's. In a sense, it is the only position left that does not regress to a tradition that is untenable nor play with trendy analyses of the "free play of signifiers" or desires.

Obviously this does not mean that one is forced to agree with Foucault's specific diagnosis of our current situation. But it does imply that some form of interpretive analytics is currently the most powerful, plausible, and honest option available. Since we share cultural practices with others, and since these practices have made us what we are, we have, perforce, some common footing from which to proceed, to understand, and to act. But that foothold is no longer one which is universal, guaranteed, verified, or grounded. We are trying to understand the practices of our culture, practices which are by definition interpretations. They quite literally and materially embody a historically constituted "form of life," to use Wittgenstein's phrase. This form of life has no essence, no fixity, no hidden underlying unity. But it nonetheless has its own specific coherence.

6   From the Repressive Hypothesis to Bio-Power

The return to an analysis of social practices is found in the lectures, interviews, and books that Foucault published in the 1970s. In *Discipline and Punish* (1975) and *The History of Sexuality* (1977), he presents important parts of a far-reaching interpretation of modernity. In this section of our book, we lay out a synoptic overview of Foucault's general story, an account which, not surprisingly, follows the broad line of argumentation used here. We should stress that Foucault has never presented his work in quite this form. His work is still very much in a process of change and refinement. There are areas of unclearness and sketchiness which can be read either as confusion or, more sympathetically, as problems he has opened up for further exploration, either by his subsequent work or by others.

The relations between the historical details Foucault chooses to emphasize and the more standard historiography also remain problematic and controversial.[1] As we are in no position to evaluate the detailed

---

1. There is obviously no simple appeal to the facts involved in evaluating Foucault's historical theses. Within the historical profession in France the evaluation of his work is sharply divided. In *L'Impossible Prison* (Paris: Editions de Seuil, 1980) a group of nineteenth century specialists discuss *Discipline and Punish*. Their reactions vary from cautious to condescending although they succeed in demonstrating very few places where Foucault is not in control of "the facts." As Foucault caustically points out, most of these historians have misunderstood his argument and hence even their minor factual corrections are simply beside the point. This was clearly an occasion missed; one would hope for a more fruitful and perceptive historical attention to detail than the one presented there. On the other hand, Paul Veyne, Professor of Roman History at the Collège de France, in an essay entitled "Foucault révolutionne l'histoire" (in *Comment on Ecrit L'Histoire,* Editions de Seuil, 1978) praises Foucault as a historian for his brilliance, his precision, and his historical acumen.

historical particulars of Foucault's account, we attempt to outline Foucault's historical material in as clear a form as seems appropriate. This entails leaving out the great quantity of minutiae and the meticulous layering by which Foucault, the genealogist, seeks to demonstrate specificity, local variation, and texture. It also omits some of the labyrinthine presentation with which Foucault covers his historical tracks. Our aim is not to resolve matters of fact but to be clear about the type of approach Foucault is pursuing. If this is made more accessible, then perhaps some of the debate about the idiosyncrasies of Foucault's presentation of events might at least take place in a context whose contours are known to participants on both sides.

Foucault clearly owes us a more explicit account of how he is proceeding in many areas. The limits and standards of evidence, refutation, and interpretation presumably exist for his interpretive analytics or his history of the present, but they can only be guessed at if one uses Foucault's own books as exemplars. This does not mean that Foucault owes us a theory of history or a manual of methodology. But as his interpretations gain more adherents and become—as they already have—stimuli to research, these problems will have to be thematized more explicitly or else they will all too likely be incorporated into empiricist historical procedures. (This latter eventuality is not something Foucault can prevent, but he obviously does not want to lend his support to this development. His silence does not help his cause. What may be an effective tactic in the intellectual field of Paris takes on a rather different function in the halls of American academia.)

The two interconnected concepts around which Foucault organizes his writing of the 1970s are the *repressive hypothesis* and *bio-technico-power* (or *bio-power*). In *The History of Sexuality,* Foucault argues against the repressive hypothesis: the view that truth is intrinsically opposed to power and therefore inevitably plays a liberating role. This position is not directly attributed to any particular individual or school. It is set up as a kind of Nietzschean parody of current received opinion—at least for French leftist circles. (As with the historical accounts Foucault gives us, there is also a form of French provincialism in his theoretical claims. Although other countries are certainly mentioned—examples are drawn from England and America, among others—the bulk of the historical material, its real frame of reference, and the theoretical opponents Foucault secretly jousts with are all French.) But it should also be understood that *The History of Sexuality* is a broad overview of a larger project that will take many years to complete. Therefore the general interpretation Foucault presents should be considered to be an interpretive exaggeration, a way of setting out markers of terrain to be covered, issues to be confronted, commonplaces to be recast, and figures to be reevaluated.

Against the foil of the repressive hypothesis, Foucault develops a striapkingly different interpretation of the relations of sex, truth, power, the body, and the individual. He calls this alternative synthesis bio-technico-power or bio-power. The juxtaposition of the repressive hypothesis and bio-power serves us here as a means of laying out the main issues one encounters in Foucault's work. Gilles Deleuze has said cryptically that Foucault should be seen not as a historian, but as a new kind of map-maker—maps made for use not to mirror the terrain.

The Repressive Hypothesis

Stated broadly, the repressive hypothesis holds that through European history we have moved from a period of relative openness about our bodies and our speech to an ever-increasing repression and hypocrisy. During the seventeenth century, or so the story goes, a lively frankness still prevailed: "It was a time of direct gestures, shameless discourse, and open transgressions, when anatomies were shown and intermingled at will, and knowing children hung about amid the laughter of adults" (*HS* 3). By the middle of the nineteenth century things had altered dramatically—and for the worse. The laughter was replaced by the "monotonous nights of the Victorian bourgeoisie." Sexuality, or what was left of it, was now confined to the home, and even there it was restricted to the parents' bedroom. A rule of silence was imposed. Censorship reigned. What sex there was became joyless and utilitarian. In the nuclear family, it was geared only to reproduction. The exclusion of all acts, speech, and desires which did not conform to a strict, repressive, and hypocritical code was strictly enforced. The law, repression, and the basest of utilities held sway. This logic obtained even at the fringes of Victorian society where concessions to licentiousness and debauchery were grudgingly made. Even there, or especially there, a policed and profitable trade was allowed to be the exception which confirmed the rule. The counter-Victorians only reaffirmed the triumph of the dour moralism represented by the unsmiling queen.

For those who hold it, the great attraction of this view of repression is that it is so easily linked with the rise of capitalism. "The minor chronicle of sex and its trials is transposed into the ceremonious history of the modes of production; its trifling aspect fades from view" (*HS* 5). Sex was repressed because it was incompatible with the work ethic demanded by the capitalist order. All energies had to be harnessed to production. The dialectic of history neatly weaves the trivial and the profound into one whole cloth. Sexuality is only an appendage to the real story of history—the rise of capitalism—but it is an important one, since repression is the general form of domination under capitalism.

Still, the tables could be turned on Foucault rather easily here. If one substituted the word "power" for the word "production" in the above quotation it would not be an unjust characterization of Foucault's project. Though Foucault is not attempting to uncover the laws of history, nor to deny the importance of capitalism, he is trying to show us the importance that sexuality has recently attained in our civilization, precisely because of its links with power. Since, as we shall see, he does not think that there is a transhistorical, cross-cultural sexuality, he will be at pains to show that our sexuality is linked to something else. This "something else" turns out, at least in part, to be specific forms of power. How to develop a view of power that does not turn into an underlying essence, a metaphysical notion, or an empty catchall is the central problem confronting Foucault's recent work.

Another inherent appeal of the repressive hypothesis is the conclusion that sexual liberation or resistance to repression would be an important battle to fight, albeit a hard one to win. (Even Freud made only minor gains in this view, for his work was quickly recuperated through its inclusion in the scientific establishment of medicine and psychiatry.) It is certainly the case that, since the nineteenth century, speaking openly and defiantly about sexuality has come to be seen in and of itself as an attack on repression, as an inherently political act. After all, sexual liberation and the overthrow of capitalism are still considered to be on the same political agenda. By this argument, when we speak of sex we are denying established power. We offer ourselves the "opportunity to speak out against the powers that be, to utter truths and promise bliss, to link together enlightenment, liberation and manifold pleasures; to pronounce a discourse that combines the fervor of knowledge, the determination to change the laws, and the longing for the garden of earthly delights" (*HS* 7). Who could resist?

The repressive hypothesis is anchored in a tradition which sees power only as constraint, negativity, and coercion. As a systematic refusal to accept reality, as a repressive instrument, as a ban on truth, the forces of power prevent or at least distort the formation of knowledge. Power does this by suppressing desire, fostering false consciousness, promoting ignorance, and using a host of other dodges. Since it fears the truth, power must suppress it.

It follows that power as repression is best opposed by the truth of discourse. When the truth is spoken, when the transgressive voice of liberation is raised, then, supposedly, repressive power is challenged. Truth itself would not be totally devoid of power, but its power is at the service of clarity, nondistortion, and one form or another of higher good, even if the higher good is nothing more substantive than clarity. Even though Foucault is presenting parodies here, they are often close to the target. Perhaps the most sophisticated counter-project available today, that of Jürgen Habermas, argues for a quasi-transcendental concept of reason as a means of criticizing and resisting the distortions of domination.

Foucault calls this view of power the "juridico-discursive" (*HS* 82). It is thoroughly negative; power and truth are entirely external to each other. Power produces nothing but "limit and lack." It lays down the law, and the juridical discourse then limits and circumscribes. Punishment for disobedience is always close at hand. Power is everywhere the same: "It operates according to the simple and endlessly reproduced mechanisms of law, taboo and censorship" (*HS* 84). Power is domination. All it can do is forbid, and all it can command is obedience. Power, ultimately, is repression; repression, ultimately, is the imposition of the law; the law, ultimately, demands submission.

Foucault offers two additional reasons why this view of power has been so readily accepted into our discourse. First, there is what he calls the "speaker's benefit" (*HS* 6). In the pose of the universal intellectual who speaks for humanity, the speaker solemnly appeals to the future which, he tells us, will surely be better. The tone of prophecy and promised pleasure neatly mesh. After all, "to utter truths and promise bliss" is a not unattractive position from which to speak. The intellectual as spokesman for conscience and consciousness locates himself in this privileged spot. He is outside of power and within the truth. His sermons—statements of oppression and promises of a new order—are pleasurable to pronounce and easy to accept. Of course, this could be taken as a description of Foucault's own privileged stance and to some extent he is not exempt from this charge. However, as genealogist he is certainly not claiming to be outside of power, nor to promise us a path to utopia or bliss.

The ease of acceptance is Foucault's second point. He argues that modern power is tolerable on the condition that it mask itself—which it has done very effectively. If truth is outside of and opposed to power, then the speaker's benefit is merely an incidental plus. But if truth and power are not external to each other, as Foucault obviously will maintain, then the speaker's benefit and associated ploys are among the essential ways in which modern power operates. It masks itself by producing a discourse, seemingly opposed to it but really part of a larger deployment of modern power. As Foucault puts it, "Power as a pure limit set on freedom is, at least in our society, the general form of its acceptability" (*HS* 86).

The root of this is historical. According to Foucault, before it took sex as a key target, power in fact acted through prohibition and restraint. The major institutions of power—the monarch and the state—arose from a sea of local and conflicting forces. Out of myriad local bonds and battles the rise of monarchy operated, *grosso modo,* to regulate, arbitrate, and demarcate. At the same time, it sought to break the bond of feudal tradition and custom. It worked to establish a more centralized order from these multilocal fiefdoms. "Faced with a myriad of clashing forces, these great forms of power functioned as a principle of right that transcended all the heterogenous claims, manifesting the triple distinction of a unitary regime, of identifying its will with the law, and of acting through mechanisms of interdiction and sanction" (*HS* 87). The power that emerged was far from unified. It operated with many weapons, but its language was that of the law. The law justified the sovereign both to himself and to his subjects. The particular historical realities of such legal legitimation of power are, of course, extraordinarily complex. Given the recent work of Georges Duby and his students on this period, and given the centrality of these themes, we expect a rich elaboration of these points in later volumes.

One of Foucault's main points is that the discourse of law as legitimation found a form which is still in use. He points out that even the opponent of a political regime speaks the same discourse regarding the law as the regime itself. During the Classical Age, criticism of the French monarchy was cast as an attack on the monarchy's abuse of the law. Later radical critiques of the state tried to demystify the way bourgeois regimes manipulated legal codes to their own advantage. What was wrong with this manipulation, presumably, was that it distorted the rule of law. In a sense, this also applies to Foucault himself, who challenges the modern institutions and discourses of power by hinting that ideals of the law are in permanent tension with the social order established by political technologies.

Foucault has clearly set up the concept of the repressive hypothesis as a deception to be revealed. He will not succeed in his attack simply by proposing the reverse, by merely changing the terms of the discourse, for the issue is not which discourse is true or even truly critical of power. Nor does he claim that the concept of the repressive hypothesis ignores the latest empirical advances, and so can be corrected by the right information. Rather, Foucault takes seriously the positions that were, at the time, taken seriously by their adherents; his aim is to give a genealogy of how the repressive hypothesis came to be and what functions it has played in our society. He reads the various components of the repressive hypothesis not as evasions, but as fundamental parts of the modern interplay of truth and power that he is seeking to diagnose. However, the analytic dimension is still undeveloped in *The History of Sexuality.* Presumably the contours will be clearer after the publication of the later volumes.

Where Foucault himself stands, in relation to his descriptions of the repressive hypothesis, is not explicitly clear. He coyly sidesteps the problem of whether he is exempt from the descriptions he is providing. It seems clear that he is presenting his analyses of power and truth because he thinks that there is something problematic about their relationship in our society. He is genealogically problematizing the way that others have related the terms as a means of showing us that these relationships are not at all absolute. This might lead to the assumption that Foucault sees himself as beyond the hold of these terms. But, as we have been arguing, Foucault considers himself, as an intellectual, to be no longer external to what he is analyzing. The archaeological method enables him to achieve a partial distancing—but only a partial one. Further, the genealogical method is one of commitment. But trying to show that the relations of truth and power have for good reasons been mistakenly held to be opposed is still a matter of applying a new and modified form of reason against a more highly complex version of power (which includes a component of truth as one of its most characteristic elements). In this, Foucault is not so terribly far from Adorno, or even from Weber.

Foucault does differentiate himself from Weber methodologically. For him, Weber's ideal type is a device which retrospectively brings together a variety of historical considerations, so as to highlight the "essence" of the historical object being studied, for example, Calvinism, capitalism, worldly asceticism. It is the ideal type which brings disparate phenomena into a meaningful model from which the historian can explain them. Foucault maintains that his approach differs in that he is interested in isolating "explicit programs" like the Panopticon, which functioned as actual programs of action and reform. There is nothing hidden about them; they are not invented by the historian to bring together an explanation. Hence, as he told a group of French historians, "discipline is not the expression of an 'ideal type' (that of the disciplined man); it is the generalisation and the connection of different techniques which are themselves responses to local objectives (apprenticeship in school, the formation of troups capable of handling rifles)" (*IP* 49). At the same time, these explicit programs were never directly and completely realized in institutions. This is not because reality never totally imitates an ideal, but rather because there were counter-programs, local conflicts, and other strategies which were perfectly analyzable, even if they were finally distinct from the initial program. Foucault's effort, as genealogist, is to stay as much as possible on the surface of things, to avoid recourse to ideal significations, general types, or essences. However, if one skips from the few methodological pronouncements Weber wrote—the several lines about ideal types have been given a vastly disproportionate attention—to his historical analyses, the gap between Foucault and Weber diminishes considerably.

Substantively, Foucault's assertion that the "problem of reason" has to be treated historically and not metaphysically is certainly something with which Weber and Adorno would agree. Foucault is clear: "I think that we must limit the sense of the word 'rationalisation' to an instrumental and relative use . . . and to see how forms of rationalisation become embodied in practices, or systems of practices" (*IP* 47). Foucault's advance over Nietzsche, Weber, and Adorno is to have taken this prescription to heart and to have produced concrete analyses of specific historical practices in which truth and power are the issue. He has isolated and identified the mechanisms of the power of rationalization with a finer grained analysis than Weber. But this should be seen as an advance, not a refutation of the Weberian project.

Finally, Foucault is not attacking reason but rather showing how a historical form of rationality has operated. As he says, "to see in this analysis a critique of reason in general is to postulate that reason can only produce the Good and that Evil can only flow from a refusal of reason. This would have little sense. The rationality of the abominable is a fact of contemporary history. But this does not give to irrationality any special rights" (*IP* 31). As we argue throughout this book, Foucault's method of interpretive analytics was constructed as a powerful and necessary tool to avoid the dilemma of value-freedom which haunted Weber or the temptation of irrationalism and despair (or a recourse to art) which was never far from the Frankfurt thinkers. Foucault is eminently reasonable; this has led him to center his work on the practical operation of "the truth" in modern regimes of power.

Bio-Power

Foucault genealogically recasts the repressive hypothesis by historically locating its components. These components extend back to the Greek polis, the Roman army, the Roman Republic, the Roman Empire, and to the Oriental bases of Christianity. However, it was only in the seventeenth century that bio-power emerged as a coherent political technology, and even then it was not actually the dominant technology during the Classical Age. Yet this was a period when the fostering of life and the growth and care of populations became a central concern of the state, when a new type of political rationality and practice found a coherent form. Foucault compares the import of the new modality of political rationality to the Gallilean revolution in the physical sciences. In the sciences of nature, the freeing of things from the traditional structures of understanding produced a successful theoretical change of the greatest magnitude. In the political realm, however, philosophers continued to espouse and take seriously traditional theories of sovereignty, natural law, and social contract. Foucault argues that this discourse helped mask the radical shifts that were in fact taking place at the level of cultural practices. Modern "power is tolerable only on condition that it mask a substantial part of itself. Its success is proportional to its ability to hide its own mechanisms" (*HS* 86).

Parallel with the persistence of earlier political theories, the Classical Age developed a new technical and political rationality. In the middle of the seventeenth century, the systematic, empirical investigation of historical, geographic, and demographic conditions engendered the modern social sciences. This new knowledge was unmoored from older ethical or prudential modes of thinking and even from Machiavellian advice to the prince. Instead, technical social science began to take form within the context of administration. This was not a general, context-independent, universal and "tending towards formalization" knowledge such as what was emerging in the physical sciences. It was instead a mode of understanding aimed at particulars. The modern social sciences branched off from traditional political theory which sought practical wisdom, and from the Hobbesian line which sought a general theory of society imitative of the physical sciences. In chapter 7 we will consider what this alliance between the sciences of man and the structures of power entails for contemporary social sciences. Here we are specifically concerned with the way in which certain social sciences came to be connected with technologies of bio-power. "Bio-power brought life and its mechanisms into the realm of explicit calculations and made knowledge/power an agent of transformation of human life . . . . Modern man is an animal whose politics places his existence in question" (*HS* 143).

In Foucault's story, bio-power coalesced around two poles at the beginning of the Classical Age. These poles remained separate until the beginning of the nineteenth century, when they combined to form the technologies of power which still recognizably characterize our current situation.

One pole was concern with the human species. For the first time in history, scientific categories—species, population, and others—rather than juridical ones became the object of political attention in a consistent and sustained fashion. Efforts to understand the processes of human regeneration were closely tied to other, more political ends. These regulative controls of the vitality of life, will be the focus of the sixth volume of Foucault's history of sexuality. We in turn will take up Foucault's present analysis of sex and sexuality in more detail in chapter 8.

The other pole of bio-power centered on the body not so much as the means for human reproduction, but as an object to be manipulated. A new science, or more accurately a technology of the body as an object of power, gradually formed in disparate, peripheral localizations. Foucault labels this "disciplinary power" and he analyzes it in detail in *Discipline and Punish* (see chapter 7). The basic goal of disciplinary power was to produce a human being who could be treated as a "docile body." This docile body also had to be a productive body. The technology of discipline developed and was perfected in workshops, barracks, prisons, and hospitals; in each of these settings the general aim was a "parallel increase in the usefulness and docility" of individuals and populations. The techniques for disciplining bodies were applied mainly to the working classes and the subproletariat, although not exclusively, as they also operated in universities and schools.

Disciplinary control and the creation of docile bodies is unquestionably connected to the rise of capitalism. But the economic changes which resulted in the accumulation of capital and the political changes which resulted in the accumulation of power are not entirely separate. The two depend on each other for their spread and their successes. For example, "the massive projection of military methods into industrial organization was an example of the modelling of the division of labor following the model laid down by the schemata of power. But this schemata did not arise in the economic sectors and it was not restricted to it" (*DP* 221). Foucault places the two major alterations in a noncausal parallelism but clearly indicates that the development of political technology, in his interpretation, preceded the economic. He contends that it was the disciplinary technologies which underlay the growth, spread, and triumph of capitalism as an economic venture. Without the insertion of disciplined, orderly individuals into the machinery of production, the new demands of capitalism would have been stymied. In a parallel manner, capitalism would have been impossible without the fixation, control, and rational distribution of populations on a large scale. These techniques of discipline, Foucault argues, supported and underlay the grander and more visible changes in the production apparatus. At least in France, the slow growth of disciplinary technology preceded the rise of capitalism—in both a temporal and a logical sense. These technologies did not cause the rise of capitalism but were the technological preconditions for its success.

As we said earlier, Foucault maintains that disciplinary technologies remained relatively hidden while they spread. They did not simply eliminate the discourse of political theory, of law, of rights and responsibilities, of justice. Practitioners of disciplinary technologies in fact used several distinct theories of the state, each of which had been elaborated at a particular time in the past. These different theories could coexist in different settings of power: in factories, in schools, in universities, in state administrative offices. This does not mean that such theories were unimportant. Rather, the intricacy and indeed even the competition between theoretical positions masked the fact that radically new practices of the time, those of bio-power, were gaining widespread acceptance. To take an example, the eighteenth-century humanist discourse of equality fired political movements of an unprecedented scale. But at the same time, in a quieter way, tighter discipline in manufacturing workshops, regimented *corvées* of vagabonds, and increased police surveillance of every member of the society assured the growth of a set of relations which were not and could not be ones of equality, fraternity, and liberty. Whereas a certain progress in terms of political representation and equality is unquestionable in the institutions of the state, the disciplines assured that all members of society were neither equal nor equally powerful: "The real, corporeal disciplines, constituted the foundation of the formal, juridical liberties. The contract may have been regarded as the ideal foundation of law; disciplinary technology constituted the technique, universally widespread of coercion and subjection" (*DP* 222, translation modified).

Although this political technology escaped from the grid of traditional political theory, it was not irrational or unthematized. Indeed it had its own distinctive political rationality. It is precisely that rationality, in association with the new technologies of bio-power, which Foucault is attempting to analyze. To understand this distinctive political body of thought, one must contrast the position that emerged during the Classical Age with earlier theories of politics and knowledge.

Traditionally in Western culture, political thinking was concerned with the just and good life. Practical reason sought to change character, as well as communal and political life, based on a larger metaphysical understanding of the ordered cosmos. Christian versions, like those of Saint Thomas, were in a line with Aristotle. Thomas was concerned with an order of virtue that was anchored in an ontotheoretical world view. Politics served a higher goal. This higher goal rested on a larger order, which could be known. Political thinking was that art which, in an imperfect world, led men toward the good life, an art which imitated God's government of nature.

A second type of political rationality emerged during the Renaissance and is usually associated with the name Machiavelli. The prince was given counsel on how best to hold onto his state. The link between the power of the prince and the type of state he ruled became the object of examination. This was, as many others have remarked, a major break from the earlier Western tradition of political thought. There were no metaphysical considerations, nor any serious attention paid to goals beyond that of the prince's power. The increase and solidarity of this power—not the freedom or virtue of the citizens, nor even their peace and tranquility—was the ultimate goal set by these treatises. Practical, technical knowledge was raised above metaphysical considerations, and strategic considerations became paramount.

A third development in political thought, usually referred to as the theory of *raison d'état*, differentiated itself from the other two. Although the earliest of these theorists appeared at the same time as Machiavelli and are often grouped together with him, Foucault sees them in a decisively different light, for he looks particularly to the authors of the police and technical manuals of the age. His point is that these men, whose names are not familiar to most of us, laid down policies for actual application. They elaborated precise techniques for ordering and disciplining individuals, while still using the mainstream Western tradition of political thought to mask their particular tactics. Yet they also represent a change in political philosophy. The tacticians of the *raison d'état* were concerned with the state as an end in itself; the state freed from a larger ethical order *and* from the fate of particular princes. Their aim, Foucault argues, was the most radical and modern of all. For them, political rationality no longer sought to achieve the good life nor merely to aid the prince, but to increase the scope of power for its own sake by bringing the bodies of the state's subjects under tighter discipline.

The first principle of this new political rationality was that the state, not the laws of men or nature, was its own end. The existence of the state and its power was the proper subject matter of the new technical and administrative knowledge, in contrast to juridical discourse, which had referred power to other ends: justice, the good, or natural law. This does not mean that the law became irrelevant or disappeared, only that it gradually came to have other functions in modern society.

The object to be understood by administrative knowledge was not the rights of people, not the nature of divine or human law, but the state itself. However, the point of this knowledge was not to develop a general theory; rather, it was to help define the specific nature of a specific historical state. And this required the gathering of information on the state's environment, its population, its resources, and its problems. As we saw earlier, a whole array of empirical methods of investigation had to be developed or advanced to generate this knowledge. The history, geography, climate, and demography of a particular country became more than mere curiosities. They were crucial elements in a new complex of power and knowledge. The government, particularly the administrative apparatus, needed knowledge that was concrete, specific, and measurable in order to operate effectively. This enabled it to ascertain precisely the state of its forces, where they were weak and how they could be shored up. The new political rationality of bio-power was therefore connected with the nascent empirical human sciences. What was first a study of population, for instance, soon became political arithmetic. One thinks here of the numerous sections in Montesquieu's *Spirit of the Laws* on climate, geography, population, and so on, sections that are often abridged or avoided by modern commentators. In Foucault's optic, these passages, and not the ones on virtue, are the most significant ones in the treatise.

It follows that the administrators would need such detailed knowledge not only about their own state, but about other states as well. If the end of this political rationality was the power of the state, then it had to be measured in terms of force. Since all other states were playing the same political game, comparison between them was crucial. Welfare and even survival were functions not of virtue, but of strength. Here too empirical knowledge, not moral theory, was the essential component.

Politics thus became bio-politics. Once the politics of life was in place, then the life of these populations, and their destruction as well, became political choices. Since these populations were nothing more or less than what the "state cares for for its own sake," the state was entitled to relocate them or to slaughter them, if it served the state's interest to do so. In sum,

> from the idea that the state has its own nature and its own
> finality, to the idea that man is the true object of the state's
> power, as far as he produces a surplus strength, as far as he is a
> living, working, speaking being, as far as he constitutes a soci-
> ety, and as far as he belongs to a population in an environment,
> we can see the increasing intervention of the state in the life of
> the individual. The importance of life for these problems of
> political power increases; a kind of animalization of man
> through the most sophisticated political techniques results.
> Both the development of the possibilities of the human and
> social sciences, and the simultaneous possibility of protecting
> life and of the holocaust make their historical appearance. (SL)

In his analysis of this new type of political rationality, Foucault isolates a new relationship between politics and history. A wise legislator could no longer bring together and relate all the elements of the state to create a situation of perfect harmony. Instead he must continually oversee a set of changing forces that are periodically strengthened or weakened by the political choices a regime makes. Since there is no longer any external principle of harmony or limit that can be imposed, so there is no inherent limit to the possible strength a state might achieve. Power, unmoored from the limitations of nature and theology, enters into a universe that is capable, at least in principle, of unbounded expansion. Expansion—or destruction—takes place on the stage of history. There are, of course, material forces acting on the course of history. The emergence of this political era is obviously related to major economic and demographic changes, above all the rise of capitalism. Yet, after more than a century of Marxist historiography, the specific importance of this particular political rationality remains relatively unanalyzed. It is the identification and analysis of these distinctive political practices which are at the center of Foucault's project.

For instance, although the new breed of administrators concerned themselves largely with populations, there was, at the same time, a concomitant administrative definition of politics and the individual. In the expanding arena of the modern state and its administrative apparatus, human beings within a given domain were considered as a resource. The individual was of interest exactly insofar as he could contribute to the strength of the state. The lives, deaths, activities, work, miseries, and joys of individuals were important to the extent that these everyday concerns became politically useful. Sometimes what the individual had to do, from the state's point of view, was to live, work, and produce in certain ways; and sometimes he had to die in order to enforce the strength of the state. The emergence of the modern individual as an object of political and scientific concern and the ramifications of this for social life now become Foucault's major problematic.

The job of the police was the articulation and administration of techniques of bio-power so as to increase the state's control over its inhabitants. While the seventeenth- and eighteenth-century French police were part of the juridical administration, they dealt with individuals not as juridical subjects but as working, trading, living human beings. (This dimension was treated archaeologically in detail in *The Order of Things*.) Through a reading of administrative manuals of the age, Foucault shows that the chief role of the police, which took more and more precedence over time, was the control of certain individuals and of the general population as they related to the state's welfare. The functions of the police were therefore very broad indeed: "Men and things envisioned as to their relationships to property, what they produce, men's coexistence on a territory, what is exchanged on the market. It also includes how they live, the diseases and the accidents which can befall them. What the police see to is a live, active, productive man. Under Louis XIV one manual says, 'the true object of the police is man'" *(SL)*. State power had previously centered on men as subjects with rights and duties. Now the police were concerned with men in their everyday activities, as the essential components of the state's strength and vitality. It was the police and its administrative adjuncts who were charged with men's welfare— and with their control.

The administrative apparatus of the state posed welfare in terms of people's needs and their happiness. Both of these were, of course, goals to which previous governments had dedicated themselves. But the relations have been reversed. Human needs were no longer conceived of as ends in themselves or as subjects of a philosophic discourse which sought to discover their essential nature. They were now seen instrumentally and empirically, as the means for the increase of the state's power. Foucault thus demonstrates the relationship between the new administrative concept of human welfare and the growth of bio-power. State administrators expressed their concepts of human welfare and state intervention in terms of biological issues such as reproduction, disease, work, or pain.

The two poles of bio-power—control of the body and control of the species—which had developed separately in the eighteenth century, were brought together in the nineteenth-century preoccupation with sex. In addition to the state, other forms of power came into play, and they too used a discourse about sexuality and new tactics for controlling sexual practices. Sex became the construction through which power linked the vitality of the body together with that of the species. Sexuality and the significance invested in it was now the principal medium through which bio-power spread.

We will discuss Foucault's important insights about the topic of sex (what he calls the deployment of sexuality) in chapter 8. At this point, we simply want to emphasize the emergence of this topic as part of the growing field of bio-power. This discourse on sexuality should not be understood in the Weberian manner as the rise of a secular asceticism. In the interpretive grid of bio-power, the deployment of sexuality led not to a decreased interest in sexuality but to an enormous explosion of discourse and concern about the vitality of the body. There was, Foucault claims, "an intensification of the body, a problematization of health and its operational terms: it was a question of techniques for maximizing life. The primary concern was . . . the body, vigor, longevity, progeniture, and descent of the classes that 'ruled' " (HS 123). Never, it seems, had so much attention been focused on every aspect of the body and every dimension of its sexuality. Sex became the object of a major investment of signifi- cation, of power, and of knowledge.

By the end of the nineteenth century the general deployment of sexuality had spread widely through the social body. Just as the middle classes had differentiated themselves at the beginning of the century from the nobility and its "symbolics of blood," they now differentiated themselves from the working classes who were being drawn into the web of sex and bio-power. At the beginning of the nineteenth century, bourgeois moralists exhorted their classmates to pay careful attention to sex, calling attention to the life hidden in it as well as the dangers it held. By the end of the century, the dangers came in for increased attention; repression and secrecy were advised. As Foucault characterizes the new discourse: "Not only is sex a formidable secret, as the directors of conscience, moralists and pedagogues, and doctors always said to former generations, not only must we search it out for the truth it conceals, but if it carries with it so many dangers, this is because—whether out of scrupulousness, an overly acute sense of sin, of hypocrisy, no matter—we have too long reduced it to silence" (*HS* 128, 129). Once the sexualization of individuals and populations had spread through the society, the differentiating mark of class could no longer be the bourgeois preoccupation with sexuality. Sex as meaning now expands to sex as administrative control.

It is at this point in the spread of bio-power that social welfare programs became professionalized. While the bourgeoisie were talking and writing about incestuous fantasies, they were now organizing social welfare programs in rural areas and in urban slums. Various reform societies sought to eradicate the actual practices of incest and other unallowable perversions among the working classes. Innumerable reports and journalistic exposés alerted the public to these ever present dangers. In addition, municipalities set up dispensaries to treat venereal disease, while an elaborate system of medical dossiers and licensed houses attempted to regulate prostitution. This extension of a disciplinary grid was carried out in the name of public hygiene and the fear of racial degeneracy. Appeals to the very fate of the race and the nation seemed to turn in large part on its sexual practices.

Shortly after, psychoanalysis entered—that is, for the bourgeoisie. It was the crown of the repressive hypothesis, the purest linking of desire and the law, of secret and wonderful signification; it was the remedy for repression, at least for some. Psychoanalysis announced that the connection between sexuality and the law as repression was absolutely universal: it was *the* basis of civilization. But the incestuous desires which founded all societies in the act of repression could, via psychoanalysis, safely be put into discourse. When the bourgeoisie gave up its exclusive hold on the discourse on sexuality, it invented another privilege for itself: the ability to talk about repressed sexuality, the deepest desires. "The task of truth was now linked to the challenging of taboos," at least for this class. Confession became linked to the command to talk about that which power forbade one to do.

Both the disciplinary and the confessional components of bio-power, although differentiated by their class applications, were unified by their common assumptions about the significance of sex. One of Foucault's examples clarifies the point. At the turn of the century, the incest taboo was scientifically pronounced as the universal law of all societies; at the same time, the administrative apparatus attempted to stamp it out in the rural and working class populations; and, through psychiatric science, intellectuals convinced themselves that by talking about this taboo they were resisting repression. The circle had been closed. The repressive hypothesis became the cornerstone for the advance of bio-power.

Thus, to return to the rhetorical question Foucault posed at the beginning of *The History of Sexuality*, the question of whether critical discourse about repression was a block to power or a part of the power mechanism it denounced, we can now answer that it was a central part. Foucault sums up this point: "Thus the law would be secure, even in the new mechanics of power. For this is the paradox of a society which, from the eighteenth century to the present, has created so many technologies of power that are foreign to the concept of the law: it fears the effects and proliferations of those technologies and attempts to recode them in forms of law" (*HS* 109).

Foucault's argument has come full circle, too. Bio-power has incorporated the repressive hypothesis. The historical conditions for the emergence of the repressive hypothesis—the cultural practices from which this theory of sexuality emerged—now dovetail with the conditions for its acceptance. In good interpretive fashion, both can only be understood when they are placed in a more comprehensive "grid of historical decipherment." Given this grid, we can now backtrack and look at these technologies and their associated rationality in more detail.

7 The Genealogy of the Modern Individual as Object

In *Discipline and Punish* Foucault presents the genealogy of the modern individual as a docile and mute body by showing the interplay of a disciplinary technology and a normative social science. As he puts it, "This book is intended as a correlative history of the modern soul and of a new power to judge; a genealogy of the present scientifico-legal complex from which the power to punish derives its basis, justifications and rules, from which it extends its effects and by which it masks its exorbitant singularity" (*DP* 23). Foucault's book is obviously not a litany of progress. Rather, it is a somber recounting of the growth of disciplinary technology within the larger historical grid of bio-power. For Foucault the rise of the modern individual and that of the concept of society (as understood in the social sciences) are joint developments. The story Foucault is telling, however, is not the triumphant scientific one of Durkheim, in which the emergence of a science of society announces the increasing autonomy of the individual and the objectivity of the social. It is rather the other way round. Foucault tells of the emergence of an objective science of society—one which treats social facts as things—and of the "mute solidity" of the modern individual, in order to show that both developments are what he calls instrument-effects of specific historical forms of power.

In *Discipline and Punish,* Foucault proposes that we approach punishment and prisons as a complex social function, not merely a set of repressive mechanisms. Punishment should be considered not as a purely juridical matter nor as a reflection of social structures nor as an indication of the spirit of the age. Rather, Foucault's approach to the prison is a way of isolating the development of a specific technique of power. Punishment is political as well as legal; it is important to be clear about this point.

Although *Discipline and Punish* is subtitled *The Birth of the Modern Prison*, its object of study is not really the prison; it is disciplinary technology. Foucault is explicit in response to his French historical critics:

What is at issue in the "birth of the prison"? French society in a given period? No. Delinquency in the eighteenth and nineteenth centuries? No. Prisons in France between 1760 and 1840? Not even. Rather something more tenuous: the reflected intentions, the type of calculation, the "ratio" which was put in place in prison reform when it was decided to introduce in a new form the old practice of incarceration. In sum, I am writing a chapter in the history of "punitive reason." (*IP* 33)

Foucault's object of study is the objectifying practices of our culture as they are embodied in a specific technology.

The broad strategic development which Foucault is analyzing is summarized by the imperative: "Make the technology of power the very principle both of the humanization of the penal system and of the knowledge of man" (*DP* 23). In this strategy, the body is the central target. So, Foucault analyzes "a political technology of the body in which might be read a common history of power relations and object relations" (*DP* 24). Clearly, these relations are complex. It is their mutual production, their historical linkages, their genealogy which Foucault describes in *Discipline and Punish*.

Prisons are nonetheless the principal figure Foucault uses to highlight the West's changing attitudes toward discipline itself. A succinct way to present this history of power relations and object relations is to summarize the three figures of punishment Foucault gives us. They are torture as a weapon of the sovereign, correct representation as a dream of humanist reformers in the Classical Age, and prison and normalizing surveillance as an embodiment of the modern technology of disciplinary power. In each case, the type of punishment illustrates the society's dealings with criminals as "objects" to be manipulated. In all three, a major goal is to shift the balance of power relations in the larger society, while a minor but related goal—at least in the second and third figures—is the transformation of the criminal. Let us recapituate the tactics and the aims of the three forms of punishment.

Three Figures of Punishment
SOVEREIGN TORTURE

In the first figure, that of the sovereign, torture was the paradigmatic form of punishment. Why, Foucault asks, were criminals put on the rack, drawn and quartered, covered in boiling oil, hacked to pieces? Why, at the moment before death, were they made to confess their crimes to "the people" in a public spectacle?

This public torture was a political ritual. The law, it was held, represented the will of the sovereign; he who violated it must answer to the wrath of the king. A breach of the law was seen as an act of war, as a violent attack on the body of the king; the sovereign must respond in kind. More precisely, he must respond with excessive force; the sheer strength and magnitude of the power underlying the law must be publicly displayed as awesome. In this ritual of violence, the criminal was physically attacked, beaten down, dismembered, in a symbolic display of the sovereign's power. Thus, the power and integrity of the law were reasserted; the affront was righted.

This excessive power found its form in the ritual of atrocity. But the same ritual also displayed its own limits: "A body effaced, reduced to dust and thrown to the winds, a body destroyed piece by piece by the infinite power of the sovereign constituted not only the ideal, but the real limit of punishment" (*DP* 50). This was a battle, albeit a ritualized one, between two people. The sovereign would almost surely triumph, but the devastated body of the challenger at the same time avenged the spent force of the sovereign, exposing its limits. Although the king's power was great, each time the law was broken, each time the power was challenged, it had to be reactivated and reapplied. Should the display fail, an even greater display of power would be necessary to reestablish the sovereign's might.

Even though the final act of punishment was this "carnival of atrocity," there were formal legal proceedings which led up to the final theatrical performance. The establishment of an accusation and the proceedings to verify the accusation were the absolute prerogative of the magistrates. They followed an extremely elaborate code of procedure, requiring evidence, proof, and so on, the details of which need not concern us here. What is important is that the accused was totally removed from these proceedings, which were held in secret. "Written, secret, subjected, in order to construct its proofs, to rigorous rules, the penal investigation was a machine that might produce the truth in the absence of the accused" (*DP* 37).

Having satisfied itself as to the truth of its accusations, the law, logically, could have stopped its proceedings at this point. However, the law demanded a confession. "The confession, an act of the criminal, responsible and speaking subject, was the complement to the written, secret preliminary investigatic ɔ" (*DP* 38). It was obtained through the ritual of public torture. Torture, Foucault points out, is not some uncontrolled act of animal rage but, quite the contrary, a controlled application of pain to the body. There were elaborate procedures developed to measure and control precisely the application of pain. "Torture rests on a whole quantitative art of pain. . . . Death-torture is the art of maintaining life in pain, by subdividing it into a 'thousand-deaths', by achieving before life ceases the most exquisite agonies'' (*DP* 33, 34). The development of this finely tuned art was directly linked with the codes of the law. Particular categories of crimes demanded particular degrees of torture; the pain of the body should fit the crime. Finally, torture was a judicial ritual. The victim had to have his punishment inscribed on his body.

But it is not only the power of the sovereign which was ritualized here. Supposedly, the truth of the accusation was demonstrated by torture leading to confession. By the eighteenth century, this production of truth had become a consistent ritual. As the criminal was tortured, he was made to confess. As the power of the law was inscribed on his body, he was made to validate the truth of the justice of the torture and the truth of the accusations. The culmination of the ritual, execution, would also be the culmination of the investigation: truth and power combined.

In sum, the figure of torture brings together a complex of power, truth, and bodies. The atrocity of torture was an enactment of power that also revealed truth. Its application on the body of the criminal was an act of revenge and an art. The power of the sovereign, however, was discontinuously applied in each of these demonstrations. The site of the application—the body—and the public place had to be retheatricalized anew with each break of power.

The ritual confession of truth which accompanied and completed the enactment of power was also vulnerable. Its particularity of technique and location suggested a specific form of resistance. In the figure of power as torture, resistance as well as power relied on the audience watching the spectacle of atrocity. Without a public assemblage the whole intent of the ceremony would be annulled. Yet the presence of large masses of people at enactments of power was double-edged. Instilling awe was the intended result, but protest and revolt were also incited at these public demonstrations. If the execution was considered unjust—either because of the accusations against the criminal or because of the art of the executioner— the criminal might be freed and the officials pursued by the mob. The criminal, in the act of confessing, might—and apparently often did—seize the occasion to proclaim his innocence and denounce the authorities. In sum, at these spectacles of atrocity, ''there was a whole aspect of the carnival, in which rules were inverted, authority mocked and criminals transformed into heroes'' (*DP* 61). The site of power could easily become the site of social disturbance, or even revolt.

This resistance is embodied in a literature of ''death speeches.'' In this curiously ambivalent genre, either the repentance of the criminal or the majesty of the crime took on epic proportions. In either case, Foucault cautions, the glorification of the criminal was neither simply the popular expression of protest nor an imposed ''moralization from above.'' Rather, it should be understood as "a sort of battleground around the crime, its punishment and its memory" (*DP* 67). Clearly, these curious orations were tolerated by the authorities, who could have blocked their publication. The funeral orations define a field of power and resistance; both justice and its violation find their glorification in them. Foucault holds that power needs resistance as one of its fundamental conditions of operation. It is through the articulation of points of resistance that power spreads through the social field. But it is also, of course, through resistance that power is disrupted. Resistance is both an element of the functioning of power and a source of its perpetual disorder. At this level of generality, Foucault is offering us little more than a provocative assertion. While his proposition is certainly compelling, in the examples he gives these historical illustrations are hardly sufficient for a general theory of power. Although Foucault claims that he is not trying to construct such a theory, others often assume him to be doing so, and he obviously is quite interested in power as a general issue. We will return to the specific place of resistance as a central component of the spread of bio-power in our last chapter.

HUMANIST REFORM

During the course of the eighteenth century, a group of humanist reformers articulated a new discourse, one which attacked the excess of violence, the flaunting of sovereign power, the glories of mob revenge. A growing legion of observers noted that public executions frightened less and incited more than they were intended. In the name of humanity, reformers condemned the "expiation of atrocity in torture" as an evil to be cured, an immoderation which must be excised in the name of a more rational distribution of power and justice. Petitions at the time of the French Revolution, summarized by the chancellery, proclaimed: "Let penalties be regulated and proportioned to the offenses, let the death sentence be passed only on those convicted of murder, and let the tortures that revolt humanity be abolished" (*DP* 73). With this discourse, we see the appearance of a new interpretation of punishment.

The humanist reformers demanded the abolition of the theater of atrocity. In their view, the essence of this ceremony was violence—excessive violence, both of the sovereign and of the people. According to the reformers, "in this violence, . . . tyranny confronts rebellion; each calls forth the other . . . . Instead of taking revenge, criminal justice should simply punish" (*DP* 74). Further, there was such excess on both sides that the system failed to function effectively. The spectacular but personal and irregular power of the sovereign showed that his ceremonies were increasingly failing to deter crime. There was also an excess of violence and illegality on the side of the people who, despite a tangled and elaborate set of legal codes, had established innumerable procedures for ignoring and circumventing them. This was particularly true when the crimes concerned property, and particularly the property of those highly placed in the social hierarchy. In the reformers' eyes, there was excess and insufficiency at every level in the old system. They proposed a new style of punishment which combined leniency with a greater efficiency of application.

Their chief theoretical justification lay in the theory of the social contract, that society is made up of individuals who have come together and through a contractual arrangement formed a society. Crime became not an attack on the body of the sovereign but a breach of contract in which the society as a whole was the victim. Society therefore had a right to redress this wrong, and punishment became the obligation of society. The standard by which justice operates was no longer the power of the sovereign and the truth of the confession but rather the "humanity" which all parties to the social contract share. Punishment, accordingly, must be modulated, made more lenient, for it is not only the criminal who is implicated in each of his actions, but the whole of society. Hence the limit of punishment—and its target—is the humanity of each subject.

The new form of punishment, then, must both redress the wrong done to society and bring the offender back to his rightful and useful place in society. This requalification of the subject relied on "a whole technology of representations" (DP 104). As we saw in chapter 1, representation in the Classical Age was the medium through which all things could be known. It follows that an art of manipulating representations could provide a technology for the correct ordering and reordering of social life.

The reformers developed a series of prescriptions based on this theory of judicial representations. First, punishment must be as unarbitrary as possible if it was to function efficiently. A perfect punishment would be "transparent to the crime it punishes" (DP 105). A representational punishment would immediately bring to mind, for those who observed it, both the nature of the crime itself and the remedy which had been imposed to correct it. Such a punishment would function as a deterrent, a recompense to society, and a lesson, all immediately intelligible to criminal and society. No longer would punishment flow from the arbitrary will of the sovereign, but henceforth it would correspond to the true order of society. New criminal legislation proposed in 1791 stated: "Exact relations are required between the nature of the offense and the nature of the punishment; he who has used violence in his crime must be subjected to physical pain; he who has been lazy must be sentenced to hard labour; he who has acted despicably will be subjected to infamy" (DP 105). Once a transparency is achieved between the act committed and the corrective procedure applied, then the punishment could be considered efficient, effective, and humane.

Second, according to the reformers, this new technology of appropriate representations should function so as to decrease the possibility of the crime being repeated. It should operate as a deterrent in society. And it should also operate on the criminal himself, so as to requalify him as a juridical subject who can be recuperated for society. The means to achieve this end were found in the application of appropriate punishments, which were adjusted to the supposed motivating root of the crime in the criminal subject. Punishment would work effectively either by attacking the wellspring of the crime itself, by making it seem less desirable to the criminal in a calculus of pleasure and pain, or by mechanistically setting the force that motivated the crime to work against itself. This would set into motion a set of representations in which the good overpowered the bad in the mind of the criminal. In sum, "the penalty that forms stable and easily legible signs must also recompose the economy of interests and dynamics of passions" (*DP* 107).

But clearly, for all this to function correctly, it had to be based on a precise knowledge. The reformers in the eighteenth century sought to construct a comprehensive table of knowledge in which each crime and its appropriate punishment would find its exact place. The remedies had to be brought together in a code of law. The various species of criminals had to be classified in great detail. It became clear from these classifications that the same crime could have substantially different effects on criminals from different social groups or with different character structures. Hence a much greater degree of individuation in the classification of criminals was demanded: "Individualization appears as the ultimate aim of a precisely adapted code" (*DP* 99). At the same time this push towards individuation led towards the objectification of crimes and criminals. The appropriate application of correct punishment required an object who was fixed as an individual and known in great detail. We have here an important step in the growth of the sciences of society and of the disciplines which will later treat men as objects.

The humanist reformers in France claimed that they applied their knowledge to the "souls" of men. They did not ignore the body, but their principal goal was to operate successfully on the soul. The correct manipulation of representations should be able to perform all the tasks demanded of it. The theory of representation, linked with the social contract view and with the imperative of efficiency (and utility), produced "a sort of general recipe for the exercise of power over men: the 'mind' as a surface of inscription for power, with semiology as its tool; the submission of bodies through the control of ideas" (*DP* 102).

The ideal form of punishment for the humanists was not public torture of the criminal or, as in the next period, incarceration. It was public works. The criminal should perform works on the roads, canals, and public squares of France. He should be visible and travel throughout the land bearing with himself the representations of his crimes. The society would benefit from his work and from his lesson. "Thus, the convict pays twice, by the labour he provides and by the signs he produces.... The convict is a focus of profit and signification" (*DP* 109). In the eyes of the reformers, the profit was good, but the morality was better. Punishment became a kind of public morality lesson. The society reinforced its system of justice by parading these convicts throughout the realm. The more perfectly the law functioned, the more appropriately constructed the remedies, the better for all. The more effectively the lesson was carried through, the better it was for the citizen gone astray, for those who might err from justice and for the society as a whole. "The publicity of punishment must not have the physical effect of terror; it must open up a book to be read" (*DP* 111).

In the process, the type of popular resistance which had turned on praise of the criminal would also be undercut. For if the criminal was himself a source of instruction, a moral lesson for all, publicly displayed, then popular discourse about his actions theoretically reinforced the lessons which were meant to be learned: "The poets of the people will at last join those who call themselves the 'missionaries of eternal reason'; they will become moralists" (*DP* 112). Through strict economy a lesson would be taught to all. The end of punishment would be the reform of souls and the moralization of society at the same time. All of society would become a theater of punishment, if only the correct representations were artfully manipulated to produce the right habits in the citizenry; for "on the soft fibres of the brain is founded the unshakable base of the soundest of Empires" (*DP* 103).

Whereas in the first figure the site of punishment was localized and only activated discontinuously, in the second the aim was the maximum circulation of signs, as continuously and widely as possible. In the first figure the power of the sovereign was inscribed directly on the body of the criminal; in the second a technique of correct manipulation of representations was applied to the mind. With torture, knowledge of the crime was acquired totally in secret by the magistrates and then displayed publicly through confession by the criminal; humanist reformers collected a vast elaboration of knowledge in order to construct a code in which all variations of criminals and punishments would be objectively, exhaustively, and publicly known. The criminal spoke his crime in his confession during torture; the juridical subject proclaimed his moral lesson by the signs society forced him to circulate throughout the country.

In the first figure resistance as social upheaval and glorification of power accompanied the theater of atrocity; in the second the stubborn refusal of the criminal to play his role with enthusiasm undermined this moral theater. More importantly, resistance to the humanist reformers never really got a chance to develop, as their myriad plans were never fully carried out. Although the period surrounding the Revolution witnessed their manifold proposals, the dramatic course of the Revolution, its aftermath, and the rise of Napoleon created a historical foreshortening in which these plans were never more than minimally implemented. All the same, elements of the humanist proposals were incorporated in the third figure of criminal punishment, that of disciplinary technology.

NORMALIZING DETENTION

The sudden emergence of the prison as the paradigmatic form of punishment is not entirely without predecessors in the Classical Age. By the middle of the eighteenth century, several Dutch correctional workhouses had incorporated a system of social and individual rehabilitation based on the rock of economic imperatives. The most famous of these institutions was the Maison de Force at Ghent. Here, criminals and vagabonds were rounded up and put to work. This served to reduce the spreading fear of criminality among the Dutch, but the political-social imperative was combined with an economic one. Prisons were expensive; therefore the prisoners should be put to work to pay for their own correction. Not only would it be economical in the short run, but from these prisons new workers would emerge, ready to contribute to the productivity and welfare of society. Recalcitrant youths would be taught the joys of labor. They would also be paid for labor done in the prison, for all work had to be remunerated in this Protestant society. In this ideal reformatory the economic and the moral, the individual and the social could all be happily combined. Yet at its time, the model found only limited application, for it seems that the humanists' distrust of detention still outweighed the utility of this northern model.

The Dutch work model was refined by English reformers, whose efforts culminated in the principles of prison reform articulated by Blackstone and Howard in 1779. To work they added isolation. The individual would discover "in the depths of his conscience the voice of good; solitary work would then become not only an apprenticeship, but also an exercise in spiritual conversion; it would rearrange not only the complex of interests proper to *homo oeconomicus,* but also the imperatives of the moral subject" (*DP* 123). The aim of such techniques, at least in these settings, was not primarily "subjective." They were considered an efficient means to bring the prisoner into a state where he would carry on the reform work on his own behavior.

In the Philadelphia model of the Quakers, the Walnut Street prison which opened in 1790, the most important lessons of the Dutch and English systems were combined into a total institution. The economic imperative was present; the prison would be supported by the work of the prisoners. Each individual would be carefully supervised, his time organized in the most efficient way possible, his day partitioned into productive segments. The moral imperative also operated: guidance and spiritual direction were provided to each prisoner. In addition the Quakers provided some new dimensions of their own. The punishment for a crime was now carried out in secret, behind prison walls. The public entrusted the right of punishment to the correct and most suitable authorities. These authorities were free to accomplish not only the transformation of the recalcitrant into the dutiful, but a complete and total rehabilitation of all aspects of a prisoner's life. Knowledge, detailed observation, complete dossiers, and scrupulous classification were the key. Detailed grilling as to the circumstances of the crime, the behavior of the criminal, his progress under detention, and an increased knowledge of the criminal and of criminality in general, combined with the economic moral reform imperatives, comprise the component elements of this new figure of punishment.

The appearance and the rapid acceptance of preventive detention as the main form of criminal punishment is striking, not because it incorporated some of the principles proposed by the Enlightenment reformers, but because it violated, reversed, or contradicted so many others. These contrasts can be summed up as follows: Punishment no longer sought significant public representation and didactic moral insight but rather attempted behavioral modification—both of the body and of the soul—through the precise application of administrative techniques of knowledge and power. Punishment would have succeeded when it produced "docile bodies." The application of punishment was once again inscribed on the body, but its aim was no longer to crush, dismember, and overpower it. Rather, the body was to be trained, exercised, and supervised. The production of a new apparatus of control was necessary, one which would carry out this program of discipline. It was to be an apparatus of total, continuous, and efficient surveillance. Whereas the ritual of torture and confession and the punitive city of the reformers were carried out in public, this new technique of punishment required secrecy. It also required an increasing autonomy of operation, free of meddling influences. "A meticulous assumption of responsibility for the body and the time of the convict, a regulation of his movements and behaviour by a system of authority and knowledge; a concerted orthopaedy applied to convicts in order to reclaim them individually; an autonomous administration of this power that is isolated both from the social body and from the judicial power in the strict sense" (*DP* 130).

Disciplinary Technology

It should be emphasized that prisons are only one example among many others of this technology of discipline, surveillance, and punishment. One of the central points Foucault is making is that the prisons themselves, as well as the tracts on the ideal form of punishment, are only the clearly articulated expressions of more generalized practices of disciplining both individuals and populations. Throughout the eighteenth century and with a vengeance in the nineteenth, these tactics extended to other sectors of the population, other places of reform, other administrations of control. The institution of the hospital or the school is not really Foucault's target, no more than the prison was. Rather, he is concerned with disciplinary procedures themselves. We can now turn to these practices and isolate their general characteristics.

Discipline is a technique, not an institution. It functions in such a way that it could be massively, almost totally appropriated in certain institutions (houses of detention, armies) or used for precise ends in others (schools, hospitals); it could be employed by preexisting authorities (disease control) or by parts of the judicial state apparatus (police). But it is not reducible or identifiable with any of these particular instances. Discipline does not simply replace other forms of power which existed in society. Rather, it "invests" or colonizes them, linking them together, extending their hold, honing their efficiency, and "above all making it possible to bring the effects of power to the most minute and distant elements" (*DP* 216).

How does it work? According to Foucault, discipline operates primarily on the body, at least in the early stages of its deployment. Of course, the imposition of a form of social control over the body is found in all societies. What is distinctive in disciplinary societies is the form that this control takes. The body is approached as an object to be analyzed and separated into its constituent parts. The aim of disciplinary technology is to forge a "docile [body] that may be subjected, used, transformed and improved" (*DP* 136).

How does this work? First, the body is divided into units, for example, the legs and arms. These are then taken up separately and subjected to a precise and calculated training. The aim is control and efficiency of operation both for the part and the whole. One thinks of the drills royal armies expend so much effort in performing. Scale is crucial; the greatest, most precise, productive, and comprehensive system of control of human beings will be built on the smallest and most precise of bases. The construction of a "micropower," starting from the body as object to be manipulated, is the key to disciplinary power.

Second, the signifying dimension is progressively ignored, minimized, and silenced. During the Classical Age, while so much attention was being devoted to the correct manipulation of representations, while the public confession still capped the rituals of sovereign power, disciplines—notably the army and the schools—were quietly developing techniques and tactics to treat human beings as objects to be molded, not subjects to be heard or signs to be circulated and read. No longer did the body seem so important as a carrier of signification. For instance, the military courage which Foucault calls "a bodily rhetoric of honour" declined; instead the focus was on the formal organization and disciplined response of the constituent parts of the body, the automatic reflex of hands, legs, or eyes. Foucault also gives the example of military exercises. While he traces back the earliest forms of such exercises to the Roman army, they were far more generalized in the eighteenth century. Exercise of bodies became an integral part of the workings of power because it concentrated primarily on the economy of internal coordination of motions of the soldiers' bodies. The rule at work here might well read: Take small units, strip them of all signifying dimensions, formalize the operations which relate these units, apply them on a large scale.

Third, micropower is directed towards a different use of time. If disciplinary power, "dressage," is to work efficiently and effectively it must operate on the bodies it seeks to reduce to docility as continuously as possible. Control must not be applied sporadically or even at regular intervals. Standardization of operation, efficiency, and the reduction of signification necessitate a constant and regular application. Moreover, the goal desired and the techniques designed to achieve it merge. To achieve this dream of total docility (and its corresponding increase of power), all dimensions of space, time, and motion must be codified and exercised incessantly. Therefore, throughout the Classical Age, disciplinary techniques were becoming more economic, analytic, technical, specific, and utilitarian. "The historical moment of the disciplines was the moment when an art of the human body was born, which was directed not only at the growth of its skills, nor at the intensification of its subjection, but at the formation of a relation that in the mechanism itself makes it more obedient as it becomes more useful, and conversely . . . . The human body was entering a machinery of power that explores it, breaks it down and rearranges it . . . . Discipline produces . . . docile bodies . . . . [It produces] an increased aptitude and an increased domination" (*DP* 137, 138).

The control of space was an essential constituent of this technology. Discipline proceeds by the organization of individuals in space, and it therefore requires a specific enclosure of space. In the hospital, the school, or the military field, we find a reliance on an orderly grid. Once established, this grid permits the sure distribution of the individuals to be disciplined and supervised; this procedure facilitates the reduction of dangerous multitudes or wandering vagabonds to fixed and docile individuals.

In disciplinary technology, the internal organization of space depends on the principle of elementary partitioning into regular units. This space is based on a principle of presences and absences. In such a simple coding, each slot in the grid is assigned a value. These slots facilitate the application of techniques of discipline to the body. Once the grid is established, the principle reads, "Each individual has a place and each place has its individual" (*DP* 143). Individuals are placed, transformed, and observed with an impressive economy of means. For the most efficient and productive operation, it is necessary to define beforehand the nature of the elements to be used; to find individuals who fit the definition proposed; to place them in the ordered space; to parallel the distribution of functions in the structure of space in which they will operate. Consequently, all of the space within a confined area must be ordered; there should be no waste, no gaps, no free margins; nothing should escape. "In discipline, the elements are interchangeable, since each is defined by the space it occupies in a series, and by the gaps that separates it from the others" (*DP* 145). The success of disciplinary space turns therefore on the coding of this "structural" organization.

One cannot help but remark that this description of spatial organization is an almost perfect analogy to the definitions of elements, transformations, and series which French structuralist thinkers were finding as universal principles. As we saw earlier, Foucault wrote *The Order of Things* as an archaeology of structuralism. We are reading *Discipline and Punish* broadly as a genealogy of structuralist discourse and associated practices.

Foucault gives two examples of this "structuralist" organization of space: a military hospital and a factory. The military hospital at Rochefort served as one of the earliest experiments in disciplinary space. Military ports were particularly appropriate locales for disciplinary experiments, since they served the most dangerous types of mixing of bodies. Here, sailors, deserters, and vagabonds came together with diseases and epidemics from all over the world. The task of the medical hospital was to regularize and control these dangerous interminglings. In such a port, rigorous partitioning of space would accomplish a number of objectives at the same time. Contagious diseases could be quarantined. Deserters could be captured. Commodities could be watched. The order of the hospital operated first on control through medicines. Then the grid extended to identify the patients and to keep them under an analytic observation. Their separation into categories was based on age, disease, and so on. "Gradually, an administrative and political space was articulated upon a therapeutic space; it tended to individualize bodies, diseases, symptoms, lives and deaths . . . . Out of discipline, a medically useful space was born" (*DP* 144).

In the factories at the end of the Classical Age the organization of space and operations was more complex. It was a question not only of controlling a population but of linking this control to production. Foucault gives the example of the Oberkampf manufactory at Jouy. The factory was divided up into a series of specialized workshops separated by function (printers, handlers, colorists, engravers, dyers). The largest building, erected in 1791, was enormous, 110 meters long and three stories high. On its ground floor there were 132 tables arranged in two rows. Each printer worked at a table with an assistant, hence 264 workers total. The finished products were carefully stacked at the end of each table. A careful supervision was possible simply by having a supervisor walk up the central aisle between the two rows of tables. The operation of the whole could be carefully watched and the specific production of each pair of workers could be easily compared to all the others. More than a hundred years before Taylorism, elementary operations were defined, each variable of this force—strength, promptness, skill constancy—was observed, compared, and assigned a particular weight. "Thus, spread out in a perfectly legible way over the whole series of individual bodies, the work force may be analysed in individual units. At the emergence of large-scale industry, one finds, beneath the division of the production process, the individualizing fragmentation of labour power; the distributions of the disciplinary space often assured both" (*DP* 145). In such a system, the individual worker, patient, or schoolboy would be precisely observed and compared to others. At the same time and by the same means, the ordering of the whole multiplicity could be successfully carried out. This control of the cell was concomitant with the order of the whole operation.

Discipline, then, operates differentially and precisely on bodies. "Discipline 'makes' individuals; it is the specific technique of a power that regards individuals both as objects and as instruments of its exercise" (*DP* 170). It does this not by crushing them or lecturing them, but by "humble" procedures of training and distribution. It operates through a combination of hierarchical observation, and normalizing judgment. These combine into a central technique of disciplinary power: the examination.

Hierarchical observation is a key element in the examination. The goal is to make surveillance an integral part of production and control. The act of looking over and being looked over will be a central means by which individuals are linked together in a disciplinary space. The control of bodies depends on an optics of power. The first model of this control through surveillance, efficiency through the gaze, order through spatial structure, was the military camp. Here total organization and observation were possible. The functions performed here were limited, but the model worked; and later it spread to the construction of grand urban schemes, working class housing projects, prisons, schools, and so forth. On a broad scale, the model of the military camp provided control through hierarchy and observation. But it first had to be refined in other settings.

Increased internal visibility, allowing for ongoing examination, became a general problematic for the architect of the Classical Age. Plans proliferated for schools, hospitals, and utopias in which visibility was increased to a maximum. For example, take the construction of the Parisian Ecole Militaire. The purpose of the Ecole was still rigor: "Train vigorous bodies, the imperative of health; obtain competent officers, the imperative of qualification; create obedient soldiers, the imperative of politics; prevent debauchery and homosexuality, the imperative of morality" (*DP* 172). The means for accomplishing this were in part architectural. The building was constructed with long halls of monastic cells. Each ten cells had an officer. Each individual was given a sealed compartment separating him from his neighbors—but with a peephole so that he could be observed. In the dining room, the tables were arranged so that the inspector's tables were higher for better observation of the recruits. The latrines had half-doors but full side walls. These and many other details seem petty, but they were an essential part of disciplinary technology. Individualization and observation were linked within this structural space.

A further degree of complication entered when these observational details were integrated into a productive apparatus. Fraud, laziness, sabotage, bad workmanship, illness, and incompetence could be extremely costly when multiplied by the increasing size of the industrial apparatus. The *Encyclopédie* article on "Manufacture" defined specialization in surveillance as an indispensable part of the means of production. Supervisors were hierarchically distinct from the workers, but internal to the new organization of production. Surveillance took on a crucial economic function, while at the same time performing its disciplinary role. Power, through the refinement of surveillance in these factories, became organized as "multiple, automatic and anonymous" (*DP* 176)—or nearly so. People, of course, carried it out, but it was the organization that made it work the way it did. "Supervisors, perpetually supervised" meant that, from an early date in industrial history, power and efficiency were joined in a system; space and production were linked through an optics of surveillance.

In order for this disciplinary system to operate, it had to have a standard that unified its operations and further solidified its punishments down to an even finer level of specification. This standard was "normalizing judgment.'' Foucault characterizes this as a kind of ''micro-penalty'' in which more and more areas of life, too trivial and local to have been included in the legal web, were now captured by power. There was ''a whole micro-penalty of time (lateness, absences, interruptions of tasks), of activity (inattention, negligence, lack of zeal), of behavior (impoliteness, disobedience), of speech (idle chatter, insolence), of the body (incorrect attitudes, irregular gestures, lack of cleanliness), of sexuality (impurity, indecency)'' (*DP* 178). Through the specification of the most detailed aspects of everyday behavior, almost anything could be potentially punishable. The nonconformist, even the temporary one, became the object of disciplinary attention.

All behavior, then, lay between two poles, the good and the bad. Between these two poles there was a precise and gradated series of steps which could be identified. One could quantify and rank a particular petty offense. The possibility of a ''penal accountancy'' was brought into play. Through these quantifiable analytic methods an objective dossier could be compiled on each individual. Hence, ''by assessing acts with precision, discipline judges individuals 'in truth'; the penality that it implements is integrated into the cycle of knowledge of individuals'' (*DP* 181). An objective hierarchy could be established by which the distribution of individuals was justified, legitimated, and made more efficient.

The effect of the normalizing judgment is complex. It proceeds from an initial premise of formal equality among individuals. This leads to an initial homogeneity from which the norm of conformity is drawn. But once the apparatus is put in motion, there is a finer and finer differentiation and individuation, which objectively separates and ranks individuals.

The procedure which brings surveillance and normalizing judgment together is what we recognize more easily as an examination. In this ritual, the modern form of power and the modern form of knowledge—that of individuals in both cases—are brought together in a single technique. At its heart, the examination ''manifests the subjection of those who are perceived as objects and the objectification of those who are subjected'' (*DP* 185). This can be, at least at first glance, a relatively benign development. Take the example of the hospital. In the seventeenth century the physician visited the hospital but had little or no say in its administration. From this he moved to a position of increasing involvement by the very nature of the kind of knowledge he sought and the methods he employed to get that knowledge. As the hospital became a locus of training and of experimental knowledge, the physician played a greater role in its operation; he had more assistants; the very form of the hospital changed to facilitate his rounds and his examinations, which had become the central focus of hospital administration. As Foucault has analyzed cogently in *The Birth of the Clinic*, the well-disciplined hospital became the physical counterpart of medical discipline. These changes were neither benign, insignificant, nor inconsequential.

The importance of the examination in the hospital or other institution is based first on a subtle but important reversal. In traditional forms of power, like that of the sovereign, power itself is made visible, brought out in the open, put constantly on display. The multitudes are kept in the shadows, appearing only at the edges of power's brilliant glow. Disciplinary power reverses these relations. Now, it is power itself which seeks invisibility and the objects of power—those on whom it operates— are made the most visible. It is this fact of surveillance, constant visibility, which is the key to disciplinary technology. "In this space of domination, disciplinary power manifests its potency, essentially, by arranging objects. The examination is, as it were, the ceremony of this objectification" (*DP* 187). It is through this reversal of visibility that power now operates.

Second, through the compilation of dossiers the examination makes each individual into a case to be known. For Foucault, this represents a major shift. The minutae of everyday life and of individual biography had previously escaped the web of the formal legal system and of any genre of writing. They are now showered with great attention. What had once been a device for lauding heroes—luminous attention to their lives, fixed in writing—is now reversed. The most mundane activities and thoughts are scrupulously recorded. The function of individualization thereby shifts its role. In regimes like the feudal one, individuality was most highly marked at the top. The more one exercised power, the more one was marked as an individual—by honors, prestige, even by the tombs in which burial takes place. In a disciplinary regime, individualization is descending. Through surveillance, constant observation, all those subject to control are individualized. The ritual of the examination produces dossiers containing minute observations. The child, the patient, the criminal are known in infinitely more detail than are the adult, the healthy individual, and the law-abiding citizen. The dossier replaces the epic.

Not only has power now introduced individuality in the field of observation, but power fixes that objective individuality in the field of writing. A vast, meticulous documentary apparatus becomes an essential component of the growth of power. The dossiers enable the authorities to fix a web of objective codification. More knowledge leads to more specification. This accumulation of individual documentation in a systematic ordering makes "possible the measurement of overall phenomena, the description of groups, the characterization of collective facts, the calculation of gaps between individuals, their distribution in a given population" (*DP* 190). The modern individual—objectified, analyzed, fixed—is a historical achievement. There is no universal person on whom power has

159

performed its operations and knowledge, its inquiries. Rather, the individual is the effect and object of a certain crossing of power and knowledge. He is the product of the complex strategic developments in the field of power and the multiple developments in the human sciences.

With the emergence of the clinical sciences of the individual, a major step was taken for the sciences of man as we know them today. This vast compilation of data, the proliferation of dossiers, and the continuous expansion of new areas of research developed concurrently with a refinement and flourishing of disciplinary techniques for observing and analyzing the body, so as to make it more available for manipulation and control. For Foucault, it was not a glorious moment: "the birth of the sciences of man . . . is probably to be found in . . . ignoble archives, where the modern play of coercion over bodies, gestures and behavior had its beginnings" (*DP* 191).

Foucault asserts that the very self-definition of the human sciences as scholarly "disciplines," as we so easily call them, is closely linked to the spread of disciplinary technologies. This is more than simply a rhetorical convergence. The social sciences (psychology, demography, statistics, criminology, social hygiene, and so on) were first situated within particular institutions of power (hospitals, prisons, administrations) where their role became one of specialization. These institutions needed new, more refined and operationalized discourses and practices. These discourses, these pseudo-sciences, these social-science disciplines developed their own rules of evidence, their own modes of recruitment and exclusion, their own disciplinary compartmentalizations, but they did so within the larger context of disciplinary technologies.

This is *not* to say that the sciences of man are a direct reflex of the prison, but only that they arose in a common historical matrix and have not separated themselves from the power/knowledge technologies which have invested the prison. The disciplinary technology of power to produce docile, useful bodies "called for a technique of overlapping subjection and objectification. . . . The carceral network constituted one of the armatures of this power/knowledge that has made the human sciences historically possible. Knowable man (soul, individuality, consciousness, conduct, whatever it is called) is the object-effect of this analytic investment, of this domination-observation" (*DP* 305).

The Objectifying Social Sciences

Foucault's account of the construction of the individual as object raises important questions about the social sciences. Once we see that the social sciences have developed in a matrix of power we are immediately led to ask: Can the social sciences separate themselves from this matrix, as did the physical sciences? But if we follow Foucault, we shift the emphasis here to two different questions: Would an autonomous and objective social science, which systematically excluded all questions concerning its own possibility, be able to come up with significant and general insights concerning human activity? And, more importantly, what is the source and the effect of this striving for autonomy and objectivity? Another question Foucault might then seem obliged to answer is: Could the social sciences recognize their dependence for their possibility upon a background of social practices, and then treat this background scientifically? Again he would turn the question around: If one could have a theory of the background practices that make specific social sciences possible, could such a theory account for the social role played by such theories themselves?

These systematic shifts in what we take to be the relevant questions might seem to be simply evasions of the fundamental philosophical issues involved, but they in fact follow from the logic of Foucault's position. To begin with, Foucault consistently refuses to become involved in a debate as to which position is true. By the time of the *Archaeology* (see chapter 3) he had radicalized phenomenology by bracketing all specific truth claims, and also all attempts to justify or ground the serious enterprise of seeking objective theory. Furthermore, from the beginning Foucault has also gone beyond phenomenology in bracketing the meaning the subject himself gives to his experiences. For the archaeologist, questions of seriousness and meaning simply cannot arise. With the addition of genealogy, however, Foucault can again raise questions concerning seriousness and meaning. The kind of seriousness involved is not the claim to objective theory, but a serious concern with the role that those theories which claim objectivity have played. We call this the analytic dimension. And the kind of meaning Foucault now finds pertains to the significance of the spread of the so called objective social sciences for our society. Spelling out this meaning requires Foucault to engage in what we call interpretation.

Returning now to our first question: Can the social sciences, like the physical sciences, free themselves from the background of social practices that makes them possible; and if they could, what would be the significance of the scientific results they could then attain? To be clear about the special role of the background practices in the study of man, we must first remember that the natural sciences too presuppose a background of techniques, shared discriminations, and a shared sense of relevance—all those skills picked up through training which form part of what Kuhn calls the "disciplinary matrix"[1] of a science.

1. Kuhn, *Scientific Revolutions*, p. 182.

161

Foucault briefly and incompletely develops a connection and a comparison between the evolution of the sciences of nature and that of the sciences of man. He draws a parallel between the growth of disciplinary techniques in the eighteenth century and the development of juridical techniques of investigation during the Middle Ages. From their roots in the newly formed courts of the twelfth and thirteenth centuries, the techniques for the independent establishment of facts have ramified in many directions. "It is perhaps true to say that, in Greece, mathematics was born from techniques of measurement; the sciences of nature, in any case, were born, to some extent, at the end of the Middle Ages, from the practices of investigation" (DP 226). It was during the Inquisition that investigation developed its operating model. Practitioners refined the procedures of investigation of natural science and separated them off from these early connections to power. Still, it was in a matrix of royal and ecclesiastical power that techniques of inquiry which observe, describe, and establish "facts" were born.

For the sciences of man, the story is different. The human sciences "which [have] so delighted our humanity for over a century, have their technical matrix in the petty, malicious minutiae of the disciplines and their investigations" (DP 226). But until now they have failed to break away from this birthplace. There has been no "Great Observer" for the social sciences comparable to Galileo for the natural ones. The procedures of examination and inscription have remained linked, if not totally, at least closely, to the disciplinary power in which they were spawned. There have been, of course, great changes, advances of technique. New disciplinary methods have seen the light of day and taken on complicated links with power. Foucault maintains, however, that these are mere refinements, not the long awaited unmooring, the crossing of the threshold into an independent science.

Why is there a historical difference in the way the disciplinary matrix functions in the natural and the social sciences?[2] To answer this question we must first look in more detail at the way background practices work in the natural sciences. Increasingly, sophisticated skills and techniques have enabled modern scientists to "work-over"[3] objects so as to fit them into a formal framework. This allows modern scientists to isolate properties from their context of human relevance, and then to take the

2. The philosophical issues involved in answering this question are dealt with in H. Dreyfus, "Holism and Hermeneutics," Review of Metaphysics, Sept. 1980.
3. According to Heidegger the objects with which science deals are produced by a special activity of refined observation which he calls bearbeitung. "Every new phenomenon emerging within an area of science is refined to such a point that it fits into the normative objective coherence of the theory." See "Science and Reflection" in The Question Concerning Technology (New York: Harper and Row, 1977), pp. 167, 169.

meaningless properties thus isolated and relate them by strict laws. Like any skills, the practices which make natural science possible involve a kind of know-how which cannot be captured by strict rules. Kuhn (as we have seen in chapter 3) stresses that these skills are acquired by working through exemplary problems, and Polanyi adds that often these skills cannot be learned from textbooks but must be acquired by apprenticeship. Moreover, these scientific skills presuppose our everyday practices and discriminations, so the skills cannot be decontextualized like the context-free physical properties they reveal. For both these reasons the practices of scientists cannot be brought under the sort of explicit laws whose formulation these practices make possible. They are, according to Kuhn, "a mode of knowing that is less systematic or less analyzable than knowledge embedded in rules, laws, or criteria of identification."[4] But the important point for the natural sciences is that natural science is successful precisely to the extent that *these background practices which make science possible can be taken for granted and ignored by the scientist.*

The human sciences constantly try to copy the natural sciences' successful exclusion from their theories of any reference to the background. Their practitioners hope that by seeking a shared agreement on what is relevant and by developing shared skills of observation, the background practices of the social scientist can be taken for granted and ignored, the way the natural scientist's background is ignored. For example, researchers now take for granted background analogies such as the computer model, and are trained in shared techniques such as programming, in the hope that they can relate by strict rules the meaningless attributes and factors which are revealed from this perspective. Given such formalizing techniques, normal social science might, indeed, establish itself; it would only do so, however, by leaving out the social skills, institutions, or power arrangements which make the isolation of features or attributes possible. However, such skills and the context of social practices they presuppose are *internal* to the human sciences, just as the laboratory skills of scientists are internal to the history and sociology of science, for *if the human sciences claim to study human activities, then the human sciences, unlike the natural sciences, must take account of those human activities which make possible their own disciplines.*

Thus, while in the natural sciences it is always possible and generally desirable that an unchallenged normal science which defines and resolves problems concerning the structure of the physical universe establish itself, in the social sciences such an unchallenged normal science would only indicate that an orthodoxy had established itself, not through scientific achievement, but by ignoring the background and eliminating all

4. Kuhn, *Scientific Revolutions,* 2d ed., p. 192.

163

competitors. It would mean that the basic job of exploring the background of practices and their meaning had been suppressed. The point is that the natural sciences can only exist as normal sciences. Of course, normal science must allow for revolutions or science would not be open to radically new ideas, but revolution means that there is a conflict of interpretations—a lack of agreement on significant questions and procedures of justification—without which normal scientific progress is impossible. On the other hand, normalcy for any particular social science would mean that it had successfully managed to ignore the social background which made its objects and disciplinary methods possible, and one might suppose that such a systematically self-limiting science would only come up with highly restricted predictive generalizations. Charles Taylor seeks to argue this point in his important paper, "Interpretation and the Sciences of Man" (1971).[5] He points out that objective political science, with its systematic grid of socioeconomic categories, itself presupposes our Western cultural practices which have produced us as isolated individuals who enter into contractual relations with other individuals to satisfy our needs and form social collectivities. Taylor argues that, because it uncritically takes for granted these background practices, objective social science is necessarily unable to predict and explain such a phenomenon as the hippie movement and the pervasive cultural agitation to which it gave partial expression. Taylor contends that only by understanding what the background cultural practices mean to the actors involved could a social science come to, if not predict, at least retroactively understand the significance of such a phenomenon.

Taylor is certainly right that a hermeneutic social science such as he advocates would have the edge over the objective social sciences in understanding movements such as those which took place in the late sixties. But, as we have seen in chapter 5, from Foucault's point of view, the hermeneutic sciences, or sciences of intersubjectivity, have intrinsic limitations as serious as those of the objective social sciences.

Indeed, if he is right, substituting the actor's point of view as to the significance of the background practices for an objective grid which excludes the background practices, while an advance, runs into equally fundamental methodological difficulties. For, from the point of view of interpretive analytics, social actors such as the hippies, even more than objective scientists, are out of touch with the progressive objectification taking place in society. The countercultural movement was no doubt correct in its self-understanding. These actors were, indeed, calling attention to and contesting a certain consensus that the rest of society and the social

---

5. Reprinted in *Interpretive Social Science,* ed. by Paul Rabinow and William Sullivan (Berkeley and Los Angeles: University of California Press, 1979).

sciences took for granted as natural and desirable. But they were quite mistaken about their own significance, and so a hermeneutics which attempted to get inside and explicate their point of view would necessarily be equally mistaken. According to Foucault's analysis, the background practices cannot be understood hermeneutically in terms of their intersubjective meaning. Just as the objects of the social sciences are products of the progressive ordering of things in the name of welfare (what Foucault calls bio-power), so too, the intersubjective or common meanings which Taylor appeals to as a basis of his analyses, are themselves products of the long-range subjectifying trends in our culture.

Taylor's hermeneutic attempt to include the background of practices in his analysis is an important corrective to the objective social sciences' attempt to exclude their own disciplinary matrix. But his overestimation of the social importance of the countercultural movement—to which his attempt to share the actor's point of view led him—shows that one cannot suppose that the actors are lucidly or even dimly aware of what their activity means—at least in Foucault's sense of "means," that is, how their activity serves to further "a complex strategical situation in a given society" (*HS* 93). Only an interpretive analytics such as Foucault's would enable one, at least retroactively, to understand how easily the counterculture movement was coopted and made to serve the very trends in the culture it opposed—those trends which produce both the objective and subjective social sciences, and which these sciences therefore inevitably fail to grasp.

Once one recognizes the importance of the background practices, the second question that arises is: Can these practices themselves be the object of a social theory? The most powerful modern answer to this question finds expression in Max Weber's attempt to develop a theoretical account of rationality and the increasing objectification of our social life. Weber saw that rationality, in the form of bureaucratization and calculative thinking, was becoming the dominant way of understanding reality in our time, and he set out to give a rational objective account of how this form of thinking had to come to dominate our practices and self-understanding. He was led, through this scientific analysis, to see that the "disenchantment of the world" that calculative thinking brings about had enormous costs. He even saw that his own theorizing was part of the same development he deplored, but, as so many commentators have pointed out, there was absolutely no way his scientific method could justify his sense that the cost of rationality was greater than any possible benefit it could bring. Given Weber's starting point, all he could do was point out the paradoxical results of his analysis and the increasing perils to our culture.

Heidegger and Adorno avoid Weber's paradoxical conclusions by asserting that one cannot have a fully objective account of the cultural background practices which make theory possible, and that therefore one does not have to contribute to objectification when doing social analysis, although, of course, one can, and most social scientists still do. Moreover, as Heidegger and Adorno saw, one is always already in a particular historical situation, which means that one's account of the significance of one's cultural practices can never be value-free, but always involves an interpretation. The knower, far from being outside of all contexts, is produced by the practices he sets out to analyze. This claim is backed up not so much by arguments as by detailed analysis: in Heidegger's case, by analyses of the general structures of the situatedness of human beings, and in Adorno's, by critical historical accounts of the production of knowledge.

In our retroactive reconstruction of Foucault's thought, the next important move was made by Merleau-Ponty, who pointed out that knowers were necessarily situated because knowledge grows out of perception, which is the work of an embodied and therefore essentially situated perceiver. However, as we have already noted, Merleau-Ponty's account of embodiment was so general that his appeal to the body as an explanation of situatedness is little more than a locating and renaming of the problem. Moreover, by approaching the question of objective knowledge from its basis in perception, Merleau-Ponty ignored, and thus was in no way able to illuminate, the historical and cultural dimensions of being a body in a situation.

Foucault, in our account, takes the best of each of these positions, while mentioning none of them, and develops them in a way that enables him to overcome some of their difficulties. From Weber he inherits a concern with rationalization and objectification as the essential trend of our culture and the most important problem of our time. But by converting Weberian science into genealogical analytics, he develops a method of rigorous analysis which has a central place for pragmatic concern, and presupposes rather than paradoxically opposes it as a necessary part of the intellectual enterprise. Like Heidegger and Adorno he emphasizes that the historical background of practices, those practices which make objective social science possible, cannot be studied by context-free, value-free, objective theory; rather, those practices produce the investigator and require an interpretation of him and his world. Having learned from Merleau-Ponty that the knower is embodied, Foucault can find the place from which to demonstrate that the investigator is inevitably situated.

This demonstration of situatedness takes the form of showing how the embodied investigator, as well as the objects he studies, have been produced by a specific technology of manipulation and formation. It also enables Foucault to account for the fact, left mysterious by Adorno, that the investigator has a position from which to criticize these practices, a position which is more than simply an irrational rejection of rationality. If the lived body is more than the result of the disciplinary technologies that have been brought to bear upon it, it would perhaps provide a position from which to criticize these practices, and maybe even a way to account for the tendency towards rationalization and the tendency of this tendency to hide itself. Merleau-Ponty already argued that the lived body was a "nascent logos" and that its attempt to get a maximum grip on the world both produced theory and objectification and hid this production. He projected a "Genealogy of Truth" based on the body. Obviously, Foucault's genealogy of truth based on the body would look quite different, but nonetheless the project is the same. Although Merleau-Ponty died before he could carry out his project, Foucault's recent work seems to be heading in this direction.

8   The Genealogy of the Modern Individual as Subject

Foucault as genealogist poses the question of sexuality in strictly historical terms; sexuality is a historical construct, not an underlying biological referent. He disputes the widely accepted notion of sex as the underlying essence, as an archaic drive, by showing that this concept, too, arose in a particular historical discourse on sexuality. He is careful to tie his choice of words and his analysis of their meaning to the course of changing policies about the body and its desires: "We have had sexuality since the eighteenth century, and sex since the nineteenth. What we had before that was no doubt the flesh" (*CF* 211).

During the eighteenth and especially the nineteenth centuries, sexuality became an object of scientific investigation, administrative control, and social concern. For physicians, reformers, and social scientists it seemed to provide the key to individual health, pathology, and identity. As we have seen (chapter 6), it was through the elaboration of a new symbolics of sexuality that the bourgeoisie demarcated themselves from the noble code of "blood" and from the working classes, carriers of various sexual dangers. In Foucault's terms, sexuality emerged as a central component in a strategy of power which successfully linked both the individual and the population into the spread of bio-power.

Foucault's thesis is that sexuality was invented as an instrument-effect in the spread of bio-power. He does not actually dispute the standard historical chronology which sees a turning in the eighteenth and especially the nineteenth century from a sexuality that is relatively free, an undifferentiated part of daily life, to one that is controlled and guarded. His point is that with these controls there came a dramatic, unprecedented rise in discussing, writing, and thinking about sex. Rather than seeing the last several centuries as a history of increasing repression of sexuality, Foucault suggests an increasing channeling, "a regulated and polymorphous incitement to discourse" (*HS* 34). This discourse posed sex as a drive so powerful and so irrational that dramatic forms of individual self-examination and collective control were imperative in order to keep these forces leashed.

Through the deployment of sexuality, bio-power spread its net down to the smallest twitches of the body and the most minute stirrings of the soul. It did this through the construction of a specific technology: the confession of the individual subject, either in self-reflection or in speech. It was through the technology of confession that several factors we have encountered in our analysis of bio-power—the body, knowledge, discourse, and power—were brought into a common localization. Broadly speaking, this technology applied primarily to the bourgeoisie, just as disciplinary technology, broadly speaking, had evolved as a means of controlling the working classes and sub-proletariat. (In both instances, this schematic simplification should be taken heuristically.) In the genealogy of the modern subject Foucault is juxtaposing the technologies of the subject and subjectification to his earlier analysis of the technologies of the object and objectification.

Foucault analyzes the particular technology and the discourse of the subject involved in the confession, just as he has analyzed those which rely on discipline. He places both within a broader grid of interpretation, that of bio-power. Therefore it is important to realize that he does not see sexual identity or sexual liberation as inherently free from or necessarily opposed to domination within our society. He has frequently been misunderstood on this point, particularly by those who claim that movements of sexual self-expression are necessarily tied to a "meaningful" political resistance to current forms of power. It is quite the opposite for Foucault, who argues that forms of domination which are tied to sexual identity are in fact characteristic of recent developments in our society and are, for that reason, harder to identify. As we saw in our discussion of the repressive hypothesis, Foucault argues that repression itself is not the most general form of domination. In fact, the belief that one is resisting repression, whether by self-knowledge or by speaking the truth, supports domination, for it hides the real working of power.

Sex and Bio-Power

The historical construction of sexuality, that is as a distinctive discourse connected to discourses and practices of power, coalesced at the beginning of the eighteenth century. A "technical incitement to talk about sex" developed as an adjunct to the administrative concern for the welfare of the population. Empirical, scientific classifications of sexual activity were carried out in the context of a concern for life. At this early stage they were still very much in the shadow of the earlier religious discourse which linked the flesh, sin, and Christian morality. But gradually demographers and police administrators began to explore empirically such issues as prostitution, population statistics, and distribution of disease. "Sex was not something one simply judged; it was a thing one administered. It was in the nature of a public potential; it called for management procedures; it had to be taken charge of by analytic discourses. In the eighteenth century, sex became a police matter" (*HS* 24).

The growing concern with statistical studies of population can serve as an example. Throughout the eighteenth century demography and its associated fields were gradually formed into disciplines. Administrators, as we have seen, approached the population as something to be known, controlled, taken care of, made to flourish: "It was necessary to analyze the birthrate, the age of marriage, the legitimate and illegitimate births, the precocity and frequency of sexual relations, the ways of making them sterile or fertile, the effects of unmarried life or of the prohibitions, the impacts of contraceptive practices" (*HS* 25, 26). From general pieties about the importance of population, French administrators in the eighteenth century gradually began to institute procedures of intervention in the sexual life of the population. Starting from these politico-economic concerns, sex became an issue involving both the state and the individual.

During the eighteenth century the link of sexuality and power had turned on matters of population. At the beginning of the nineteenth century a major shift occurred: a recasting of discourse about sexuality into medical terms. It was this change which triggered an explosion of discourse on sexuality throughout bourgeois society. The key turning point was the separation of a medicine of sex from the medicine of the body, a separation based on the isolation of "a sexual instinct capable of presenting constitutive anomalies, acquired deviations, infirmities or pathological processes" (*HS* 117). Through these "scientific" breakthroughs sexuality was linked to a powerful form of knowledge and established a link between the individual, the group, meaning, and control.

Here Foucault contrasts sex and sexuality. Sex is a family matter. "It will be granted no doubt that relations of sex gave rise, in every society, to a deployment of alliance" (*HS* 106). Up until the end of the eighteenth century the major codes of Western law centered on this deployment of alliance: a particular discourse about sex by means of articulating the religious or legal obligations of marriage together with codes for the transmission of property and the ties of kinship. These codes created statuses, permitted and forbade actions, and constituted a social system. Through marriage and procreation alliance was tied to the exchange and the transfer of wealth, property, and power.

The historical form of discourse and practice which Foucault labels "sexuality" turns on an unmooring of sex from alliance. Sexuality is an individual matter: it concerns hidden private pleasures, dangerous excesses for the body, secret fantasies; it came to be seen as the very essence of the individual human being and the core of personal identity. It was possible to know the secrets of one's body and mind through the mediation of doctors, psychiatrists, and others to whom one confessed one's private thoughts and practices. This personalization, medicalization, and signification of sex which occurred at a particular historical time is, in Foucault's terms, the deployment of sexuality.

Within the generalized spread of the production and proliferation of discourses on sexuality, Foucault isolates four "great strategic unities" in which power and knowledge combined in specific mechanisms constructed around sexuality. Each of the strategies in the deployment of sexuality began separately from the others, and each was at first relatively isolated. The details await Foucault's promised volumes of *The History of Sexuality;* however, the main themes clearly relate to the interpretation of bio-power we have been developing.

First, a hysterization of women's bodies. The body of the woman was analyzed as being fully saturated with sexuality. Through this medical "advance" the female body could be isolated "by means of a pathology intrinsic to it" and placed "in organic communication with the social body (whose regulated fecundity it was supposed to ensure)" (*HS* 104). All of the elements of the full deployment of sexuality are here: a mysterious and pervasive sexuality of the utmost importance resides somewhere and everywhere in the body; this mysterious presence is what brought the female body into the analytic discourses of medicine; through these medical discourses, both the personal identity of the woman and the future health of the population are linked in a common bond of knowledge, power, and the materiality of the body.

Second, a pedagogization of children's sex. The tactics employed in the fight against masturbation offer a clear example of the spread of bio-power as production, not restriction, of a discourse. This discourse was built on the belief that all children are endowed with a sexuality which is both natural and dangerous. Consequently, both the individual and collective interest converged in efforts to take charge of this ambiguous potential. Enfantile onanism was treated like an epidemic. "What this actually entailed, throughout this whole secular campaign that mobilized the adult world around the sex of children, was using these tenuous pleasures as a prop, constituting them as secrets (that is, forcing them into hiding so as to make possible their discovery)" (*HS* 43). Elaborate surveillance, techniques of control, innumerable traps, endless moralizing, demands for ceaseless vigilance, continual incitement to guilt, architectural reconstruction, family honor, medical advance were all mobilized in a campaign obviously doomed to failure from the start—if its goal was, in fact, the eradication of masturbation. However, if that campaign is read as the production of power and not as restriction of sexuality, it succeeded admirably: "Always relying on this support, power advanced, multiplied its relays and its effects, while its target expanded, subdivided, and branched out, penetrating further into reality at the same pace" (HS 42).

Third, a socialization of procreative behavior. In this strategy, the conjugal couple was given both medical and social responsibilities. The couple, in the eyes of the state, now had a duty to the body politic; they must protect it from pathogenic influences that a careless sexuality might increase and limit (or reinvigorate) the population by a careful attention to the regulation of procreation. Maladies or lapses in the couple's sexual vigilance would easily lead, it was held, to the production of sexual perverts and genetic mutants. The failure to monitor one's sexuality carefully could lead to the dangerous decline of health for both the individual family and for the social body. By the end of the nineteenth century, "an entire social practice, which took the exasperated but coherent form of a state-directed racism, furnished the technology of sex with a formidable power and far-reaching consequences" (HS 119).

The eugenics movements can certainly be understood in this light. However, not all the sciences that emerged to deal with human sexuality took this role of biological monitor. Foucault points out that particularly in its early days, whatever its normalizing role later on, psychoanalysis demonstrated a persistent and courageous resistance to all theories of hereditary degeneracy. Of all the medical technologies developed to normalize sex, it was the only one to vigorously resist this biologism.

Fourth, a psychiatrization of perverse pleasures. By the end of the nineteenth century sex had been isolated or, in Foucault's reading, constructed as an instinct. This instinctual drive, it was held, operated both on the biological and psychic level. It could be perverted, distorted, inverted, and warped; it could also function naturally in a healthy manner. In each case, the sexual instinct and the nature of the individual were intimately connected. Science—sexual science—constructed a vast schema of anomalies, of perversions, of species of deformed sexualities. The psychiatrists at the end of the century were particularly adroit in this species game. "There were . . . mixoscopophiles, gynecomasts, presbyophiles, sexoesthetic inverts, and dyspareunist women" (HS 43). In establishing these species on a scientific basis, the specification and detailing of individuals was supposed greatly facilitated. A whole new arena was opened for the detailed chronicling and regulation of individual life.

For the psychiatrists, sexuality penetrated every aspect of the pervert's life; hence every aspect of his life must be known. Whereas "the sodomite had been a temporary aberration; the homosexual was now a species" (*HS* 43). What had been a set of prohibited acts now turned into symptoms of a signifying mix of biology and action. Once again, "the machinery of power that focused on this whole alien strain did not aim to suppress it, but rather to give it an analytical, visible, and permanent reality" (*HS* 44). All behavior could now be classified along a scale of normalization and pathologization of this mysterious sexual instinct. Once a diagnosis of perversion was scientifically established, corrective technologies—for the good of the individual and of society—could and must be applied. A whole new "orthopedics" of sex found its justification. So, as in the other three strategies, the body, the new sexual science, and the demand for regulation and surveillance were connected. They were brought together in a cluster by the concept of a deep, omnipresent, and significant sexuality which pervaded everything it came into contact with—which was almost everything.

All of these strategies lead to a curious linking of power and pleasure. As the body was the locus of sexuality, and sexuality could no longer be ignored, science was impelled to know in minute detail all of the biological and psychic secrets which the body held. The result was, certainly, a scientific advance, but also "a sensualization of power and a gain of pleasure". Scientific advance was given an added motivation, a hidden stimulation, that became its own intrinsic pleasure. The examination, the technical heart of these new procedures, was the occasion for putting an underlying sexual discourse into acceptable medical terminology. Since the medical problem was hidden, the examination required the patient's confession. It "presupposed proximities . . . required an exchange of discourses, through questions that extorted admissions and confidences that went beyond the questions asked" (*HS* 44). Further, the person examined was also invested with a specific form of pleasure: all this careful attention, this caressing extortion of the most intimate details, these pressing explorations. "The medical examination, the psychiatric investigation, the pedagogical report, and family controls may have the overall and apparent objective of saying no to all wayward or unproductive sexualities, but the fact is that they function as mechanisms with a double impetus: pleasure and power" (*HS* 45). The medical power of penetration and the patient's pleasures of evasion seduced both parties.

Confessional Technology

For Foucault, the nineteenth-century medical examination, like other forms of circumscribed confession, exposed to figures of authority the individual's deepest sexual fantasies and hidden practices. Moreover, the individual was persuaded that through such a confession, it was possible to know himself. Sex was only one, albeit the major, theme of this confessional outpouring which has only increased in scope since the nineteenth century. "The confession has spread its effects far and wide. It plays a part in justice, medicine, education, family relationships and love relationships, in the most ordinary affairs of everyday life, and in the most solemn rites; one confesses one's crimes, one's sins, one's thoughts and desires, one's illnesses and troubles.... One admits to oneself, in pleasure and in pain, things it would be impossible to tell anyone else, the things people write books about.... Western man has become a confessing animal" (*HS* 59).

Foucault sees the confession, and especially the confession about one's sexuality, as a central component in the expanding technologies for the discipline and control of bodies, populations, and society itself. As genealogist he wants to explore the history of the confession, its ties to religion, to political power, to medical sciences. In volume I of *The History of Sexuality* he contrasts those cultures which seek to know about sex through erotic arts and our own culture, which employs a science of sex. In forthcoming volumes he will analyze the evolution of the confession, the particular techniques and types of discourse used by the Greeks, the Romans, the early Christians, and the Reformation. In this "history of the present," the aim is not to discover the moment at which the confession, and specifically the confession about one's sexuality, emerged full-blown as a technology of the self, but rather to understand the workings of this technology of the self—the particular type of discourse and the particular techniques which supposedly reveal our deepest selves. This was a promise so appealing that it enmeshed us in relations of power which are difficult to see or to break. At least in the West, even the most private self-examination is tied to powerful systems of external control: sciences and pseudosciences, religious and moral doctrines. The cultural desire to know the truth about oneself prompts the telling of truth; in confession after confession to oneself and to others, this *mise en discours* has placed the individual in a network of relations of power with those who claim to be able to extract the truth of these confessions through their possession of the keys to interpretation.

In volume I of *The History of Sexuality*, Foucault is specifically interested in the role of science in this interplay of confession, truth, and power. For one, scientific norms and a discourse of impartial scientific analysis (particularly medical discourse) have become so dominant in Western society that they seem almost sacred. In addition, through the expansion of the methods of science the individual has become an object of knowledge, both to himself and to others, an object who tells the truth about himself in order to know himself and to be known, an object who learns to effect changes on himself. These are the techniques which are tied to the scientific discourse in the technologies of the self.

Clearly, this process is similar to the technologies of discipline in which an authority effects changes on "mute and docile bodies." One clear difference is that the modern subject is not mute; he must talk. Foucault is now seeking to show the rapport between these two types of technologies, to show how they are integrated into complex structures of domination. Again, for Foucault power is not strict violence or pure coercion, but the interplay of techniques of discipline and less obvious technologies of the self. The task of the genealogist of the modern subject is to isolate the constituent components and to analyze the interplay of those components.

The key to the technology of the self is the belief that one can, with the help of experts, tell the truth about oneself. It is a central tenet not only in psychiatric sciences and medicine, but also in the law, in education, in love. The conviction that truth can be discovered through the self-examination of consciousness and the confession of one's thoughts and acts now appears so natural, so compelling, indeed so self-evident, that it seems unreasonable to posit that such self-examination is a central component in a strategy of power. This unseemliness rests on our attachment to the repressive hypothesis; if the truth is inherently opposed to power, then its uncovering would surely lead us on the path to liberation.

This conviction that confession reveals the truth finds its most powerful expression in our attention to sexuality: the belief that the body and its desires, seen through a prism of interpretation, is the deepest form of truth about a particular individual and about human beings in general. From the Christian penance to the present day, the desires of the body have held center stage in the confession. Beginning in the Middle Ages, then during the Reformation, and continuing in the present day, the language and techniques employed in religious confession have become more refined and their scope increasingly widened. Foucault will analyze the long, complex evolution of the confession in the church in the forthcoming volumes of *The History of Sexuality*. For now, it suffices to say that he characterizes that evolution as a general imperative to transform every desire of the body and the soul into discourse. "The Christian pastoral prescribed as a fundamental duty the task of passing everything having to do with sex through the endless mill of speech" (*HS* 21). The individual was incited to produce a proliferating oration on the state of his soul and the lusts of his body. This oration was elicited and then judged by the delegated representative of authority, the priest.

Both the quantity and quality of this incitement to confess have flourished. Foucault uses the example of the order given to Christians at the beginning of the thirteenth century that they must confess all of their sins at least once a year; things have changed considerably since then. He also shows that the field and locale of confession have expanded. As early as the sixteenth century, the confessional techniques unmoored themselves from a purely religious context and began to spread to other domains, first pedagogy, then to prisons and other institutions of confinement, and later, in the nineteenth century, to medicine. The details of this confessional spread await Foucault's later volumes, but the tendency he is describing is clear enough. From its Christian origins, confession became a general technology. Through it, the most particular individual pleasures, the very stirrings of the soul could be solicited, known, measured, and regulated. From the Christian concern with sex came the presupposition that sex is significant and that sexual thoughts as well as actions must be confessed in order to learn about the state of the individual soul. The major move toward placing confession, and especially sexual confession, in a power nexus occurred in the nineteenth century, when the individual was persuaded to confess to other authorities, particularly to physicians, psychiatrists, and social scientists.

However, Foucault is not claiming that an interest in sex is necessarily caught up in the technologies of the self and relations of power. There have been two wide-spread methods for dealing with sex: the erotic arts, the *ars erotica;* and a science of sex, *scientia sexualis.* In the great civilizations other than our own, sex is treated as an *ars erotica* in which "truth is drawn from pleasure itself, understood as a practice and accumulated as experience" (*HS* 57). Pleasure is its own end. It is not subordinated to utility, nor to morality, and certainly not to scientific truth. Nor is sexuality a key to the individual self, but rather a set of practices and an esoteric doctrine which a master teaches an initiate. These rituals promise "an absolute mastery of the body, a singular bliss, obliviousness to time and its limits, the elixir of life, the exile of death and its threats" (*HS* 58).

The West has followed the other path, that of the science of sexuality. Its focus is not the intensification of pleasure, but the rigorous analysis of every thought and action that related to pleasure. This exhaustive articulation of desires has produced a knowledge which supposedly holds the key to individual mental and physical health and to social well-being. The end of this analytic knowledge is either utility, morality, or truth.

In the nineteenth century the discourses on sexuality intersected with the modern sciences of man. Gradually a "great archive of pleasure" was constituted. Medicine, psychiatry, and pedagogy turned desire into a systematic scientific discourse. Systems of classification were elaborated, vast descriptions scrupulously collated, and a confessional science, one dealing with hidden and unmentionable things, came into being. The problem for these sexual scientists was how to handle the outpouring from below. There was no difficulty, it seems, in producing a discursive explosion. The problem was how to organize it into a science.

Foucault makes an important distinction at this point. He remarks that the medical sciences of sexuality branched off from the biological sciences. The sciences of sexuality were marked by a "feeble content from the standpoint of elementary rationality, nòt to mention scientificity, [which] earns them a place apart in the history of knowledge" (*HS* 54). These muddled disciplines conformed to a very different set of criteria than those operative in the biology of reproduction, which followed a more standard course of scientific development. The medicine of sex remained mired in political concerns and practices. These medical discourses on sexuality used the advances of biology as a cover, as a means of legitimation. But there was very little conceptual interpenetration: "It is as if a fundamental resistance blocked the development of a rationally formed discourse concerning human sex, its correlations, and effects. A disparity of this sort would indicate that the aim of such a discourse was not to state the truth but to prevent its very emergence" (*HS* 55).

Foucault at times sounds—and his critics frequently misread him here—as if his intention was to situate all science as a mere product of power. This is false. Instead his goal has consistently been to isolate the interconnections of knowledge and power. Throughout his intellectual itinerary it has been exactly those "pseudosciences" or "near sciences"—fundamentally the human sciences—which he has chosen as his object of study. Others, notably Georges Canguilhem and Gaston Bachelard, have devoted their attention to the "successful" sciences. Foucault has chosen another object of study, those discourses which, claiming to be advancing under the banner of legitimate science, have in fact remained intimately involved with the micropractices of power.

The medical discourses on sexuality in the nineteenth century are a perfect example of such pseudoscience. Foucault is analyzing the ways in which practitioners linked a discourse of truth with practices of power through their object of study: sex. "The truth of sex became something fundamental, useful, or dangerous, precious or formidable: in short, ... sex was constituted as a problem of truth" (*HS* 56). Sex is the alleged object which unifies our modern discussions of sexuality, making it possible to group together anatomical elements, biological functions, comportments, sensations, knowledges, and pleasures. Without this deep, hidden, and significant "something," all of these discourses would fly off in different directions. Or, more accurately, and this is the crux of Foucault's argument, they would not have been produced in anything resembling their current form. Since the nineteenth century, sex has been the hidden causal principle, the omnipotent meaning, the secret to be discovered everywhere. "It is the name that can be given to a historical construct; not a furtive reality that is difficult to grasp, but a great surface network in which the stimulation of bodies, the intensification of pleasures, the incitement to discourse, the formation of special knowledges, the strengthening of controls and resistances, are linked to one another in accordance with a few major strategies of power and knowledge" (*HS* 105, 106).

Sex is the historical fiction which provides the link between the biological sciences and the normative practices of bio-power. When sex was categorized as an essentially natural function that could be disoperative, it followed that this drive had to be contained, controlled, and channeled. Being natural, sex was supposedly external to power. But, Foucault counters, it is exactly the successful cultural construction of sex as a biological force which enabled it to link up with the micropractices of bio-power. "Sex is the most speculative, most ideal, and most internal element in a deployment of sexuality organized by power in its grip on bodies and their materiality, their forces, energies, sensations and pleasures" (*HS* 155).

The Subjectifying Social Sciences

At the end of the discussion on disciplinary technology (chapter 7), we saw a range of objectifying social sciences which emerged with the spread of the disciplines. In a parallel fashion, a wide range of interpretive sciences emerged with the spread of confessional technology. The aims and techniques of the two kinds of science are quite distinct. The construction of sex as the deepest underlying meaning and of sexuality as a web of concepts and practices is associated with—in fact, needs—a series of subjectifying methods and procedures to interpret confessions, rather than an objectifying set of procedures to control bodies.

The examination and the confession are the principal technologies for the subjectifying sciences. It was through the clinical methods of examining and listening that sexuality became a field of signification and the specific technologies developed. As opposed to other forms of medical examination which continued in a parallel but separate development of medical science, certain nineteenth-century medical and psychiatric examinations required the subject to speak and a duly recognized authority to interpret what the subject said. Hence, in a fundamental way, these procedures were hermeneutic.

The first requirement was a change of locale for the confession. In a clinical setting the doctor could combine the discussion of confession with the techniques of examination. These techniques, as we saw earlier, had already produced results on the "object" side. The task was now to elaborate procedures of examination which could code and control the signifying discourse of the subject. While the interventions enacted on the mute and docile bodies were essentially corrective, the interventions on the side of the subject were essentially therapeutic. Sexuality was now a medical question: "Spoken in time, to the proper party and by the person who was both the hearer of it and the one responsible for it, the truth healed" (*HS* 67).

Still, there were theoretical dilemmas about what to do with these techniques for confessions: How should one treat the material gained through introspection? What kind of evidence did experience provide? How does one treat consciousness as the object of empirical investigation? In short, was a science of the subject possible? Posed in Foucault's terms, the problem was, "Can one articulate the production of truth according to the old juridico-religious model of confession and the extortion of confidential evidence according to the rules of scientific discourse?" (*HS* 64). How could all this talk be incorporated into a science, even a bastard one?

The need to create a scientific structure to explain sex in turn meant that only the trained scientist, not the individual subject, could understand what was being said. In the confessional paradigm, the more the subject talks (or is forced to talk), the more science knows; the more the scope of legitimate examination of consciousness grows, the finer and wider the web of confessional technology. As this power spread, it became clear that the subject himself could not be the final arbiter of his own discourse. Since sex was a secret, the subject himself was not simply hiding it because of reserve, moralism, or fear; the subject did not and could not know the secrets of his own sexuality.

The significance of sexuality, extracted in a clinical setting, ultimately could only be brought to its full importance by an active, forceful Other. The clinician who listened to this discourse had the imperative to decipher it. The Other became a specialist in meaning. He became adept at the art of interpretation. The one who listens became a "master of the truth." What had originally been a judgmental, moralizing role was transformed into an analytic, hermeneutic one. "With regard to the confession, his power was not only to demand it before it was made, or to decide what was to follow it, but also to constitute a discourse of truth on the basis of its decipherment, and by making sexuality something to be interpreted the nineteenth century gave itself the possibility of causing the procedures of confession to operate within the regular formation of a scientific discourse" (*HS* 67). Hermeneutics—that discipline which deals with deep meaning, meaning necessarily hidden from the subject, but nonetheless accessible to interpretation—now occupied one pole of the sciences of man.

For Foucault, the modern development of these hermeneutic sciences passed, *grosso modo,* through two stages. In the first, the subject was capable, through confession, of putting his desires into an appropriate discourse. The listener provoked, judged, or consoled the subject, but the essential intelligibility of the discourse was still accessible, at least in principle, to the subject himself. Foucault gives the example of a mid-nineteenth-century psychiatrist, Luria, who used the technique of cold showers; not only confessions of madness, but also the patient's own recognition of madness were the essential dimension of the cure. In the second stage, roughly contemporary with Freud, the subject was no longer considered capable of making his own desires fully intelligible to himself, although he still had to confess them in speech. Their essential meaning was hidden from him, either because of their unconscious nature or because of deep bodily opacities which only a specialist could interpret. The subject now needed an interpretive Other to listen to his discourse and also to bring it to fruition, to master it. Yet despite this fundamental detour, the subject still had to acknowledge, and thus establish for himself, the truth of this expert interpretation. Individuality, discourse, truth, and coercion were thereby given a common localization.

Interpretation and the modern subject imply each other. The interpretive sciences proceed from the assumption that there is a deep truth which is both known and hidden. It is the job of interpretation to bring this truth to discourse. This is obviously *not* to say that all of the interpretive sciences can be accounted for by this schematic account of confessional technology in the deployment of sexuality. Just as Foucault was not claiming that the role of the objective social sciences was a simple reflex of the prisons, so too he is not reducing the arts and sciences of interpretation, which had such a prominent role in nineteenth- and twentieth-century thought, to psychiatric examination. It would be an important and rewarding task to analyze the growth of other interpretive practices and to show their relations with and differences from those Foucault has discussed. (One only has to think of the sudden importance given to participant observation in anthropology at roughly the same period. But one could not simply transfer Foucault's scheme.)

Nonetheless, part of the power of these interpretive sciences is that they claim to be able to reveal the truth about our psyches, our culture, our society—truths that can only be understood by expert interpreters. Foucault ends *The History of Sexuality* by saying, "The irony of this deployment is in having us believe that our liberation is in the balance" (*HS* 159). As long as the interpretive sciences continue to search for a deep truth, that is, to practice a hermeneutics of suspicion, as long as they proceed on the assumption that it is the Great Interpreter who has privileged access to meaning, while insisting that the truths they uncover lie outside the sphere of power, these sciences seem fated to contribute to the strategies of power. They claim a privileged externality, but they actually are part of the deployment of power.

There is a striking parallel here between the methodological problems raised by the hermeneutic study of the subject and the would-be objective and social sciences. In both cases we find a "superficial" kind of social science which takes human beings uncritically, simply as subjects or objects, and studies their self-interpretations or their objective properties as if these gave the investigator access to what was really going on in the social world. In both cases too, there is a critical perspective which points out that one cannot take at face value the subject's account of what his behavior means, or the objective social scientist's account of the social world. Critical reflection consequently leads, on the one hand, to a deep interpretation of the subject which attempts to get at what his behavior really means, a meaning unknown to him; and, on the other, to the attempt to develop an objective theory of the historical background practices which make objectification and theory possible.

In both cases, this attempt to save subjective and objective social science by going "deeper" runs into problems. As Nietzsche and Foucault have pointed out, the very project of finding a deep meaning underlying appearances may itself be an illusion, to the extent that it thinks it is capturing what is really going on. The hermeneutics of suspicion rightly has the uneasy suspicion that it has not been suspicious enough. The objective social sciences, insofar as they want to have a theory of the whole, run into the problem that the meaning of the practices they study seems to be part of the whole story but falls outside their domain. This forces them to treat the actor's point of view and, more importantly, the meaning of the background practices themselves, as if they were objectively graspable. This leads to programmatic assertions that all this "meaning" will eventually be taken into account in terms of "belief systems," "genetically based programs," or "quasi-transcendental constitutive rules." We have seen in our discussion (chapter 4) how Foucault's *Archaeology*, one of the most sophisticated versions of this third alternative, fails; the other two alternatives (cognitive science and sociobiology, respectively) have their serious problems as well.[1] Not that these fundamental methodological problems in any way diminish the output and impact of all forms of the social scientific enterprise, but the truth of their assertions is not what keeps them going.

1. For a criticism of the cognitive sciences see H. Dreyfus, *What Computers Can't Do* (New York: Harper and Row, 1979). For a critique of sociobiology see several of the essays in *Sociobiology and Human Nature,* ed. by Anita Silvers et al. (San Francisco: Jossey-Bass Press, 1978).

There are also definite limits for the interpretive social sciences, even within their own terms of supposedly being outside the matrix of power. The objective social sciences cannot account for their own possibility, legitimacy, and access to their objects because the practices which make objectification possible fall out of their range of investigation. So too, the "subject" social sciences must remain unstable, and can never become normal, because they attribute the final explanatory power either to everyday meaning or to deep meaning, while that which makes subjectivity and meaning possible escapes them. Both surface meaning and deep significance are produced within a particular set of historical practices and therefore can only be understood in terms of those practices.

The cultural practices which tend toward objectification are not at all necessarily doomed to failure, however. This leads us back to bio-power. As we have seen, one of the distinctive characteristics of modern power is the portrayal of knowledge as external to power. Again, the repressive hypothesis—the lynchpin of bio-power—rests on this assumption of externality and difference. The conditions of the rise of the objectifying human sciences were such that it seems that the only logical way to achieve a fully objective science of human beings would be with the totally successful production of human beings as objects. Foucault does not foreclose this possibility. But even if this were to occur (and there are good reasons to think it hasn't and won't), even then such a theory would still mask the practices that had produced its very actuality.

Each type of social science develops an important partial insight. Individual subjects in their everyday affairs do know, with an appropriate pragmatic degree of accuracy, what they are saying and what they are doing. But (and this is the insight of the hermeneutics of suspicion) this same behavior may have another significance of which the actor is unaware. On the objective side, many aspects of social life are indeed mechanically regimented, and are therefore appropriately treated by objective social science. But—here those social scientists who want to have a theoretical account of the overall pattern, including the background practices, have a point—the particular objective characteristics studied by "naïve" objective social science is part of a larger organized and structured pattern.

Finally, if Foucault is right, the very difficulties which plague the social sciences are a rich source of anomalies. The promise that these anomalies will eventually yield to their procedures justifies the grant proposals, enlarged research facilities, and government agencies by which the social sciences nourish themselves and spread. As in the case of prisons, their failure to fulfill their promises does not discredit them; in fact, the failure itself provides the argument they use for further expansion. The inverse relationship between their cognitive advances and their social success can only be understood when one sees the role of social sciences in our society and the way that role is made necessary and significant by the long term development of confessional and disciplinary background practices.

But the parallel between the object side and the subject side of Foucault's story stops there. In *Discipline and Punish* Foucault holds out no promise of a better objective social science. What he does offer in *The History of Sexuality* is an incisive example of what a better interpretation looks like. By taking the story of the historical construction of the interpretive sciences as a component of bio-power—one in which their function is to construct a nonexistent object, sex, which they then proceed to discover—Foucault is offering us an interpretation of these events which is not a theory, nor is it an interpretation based on deep meaning, a unified subject, signification rooted in nature, privileged access of the interpreter. If we label the misguided kind of interpretive method "hermeneutics," then we can call Foucault's current method "interpretive analytics." Interpretive analytics avoids the pitfalls of structuralism or hermeneutics by proceeding to analyze human seriousness and meaning without resort to theory or deep hidden significance. Just as Foucault attempted in *The Archaeology of Knowledge* to reflect on the method in his earlier works and to give us a theoretical description of the right way to do theory, he now owes us an interpretive description of his own right way to do interpretation. He has not provided one yet, although *The History of Sexuality* and *Discipline and Punish* are certainly examples of what such a method could produce. While waiting for Foucault to produce this interpretation of interpretation, in the sections which follow we sketch the contours of the questions it would have to confront, and the kind of positions it would have to articulate.

9 Power and Truth

We have highlighted three methodological themes in Foucault's inquiries. The first is his shift from an exclusive emphasis on discursive formations during the mid-1960s to a broadening of analytic concerns to include once again nondiscursive issues: the move to cultural practices and power. Second is his focus on meticulous rituals of power, centering on certain cultural practices which combined knowledge and power. Third is his isolation of bio-power, a concept which links the various political technologies of the body, the discourses of the human sciences, and the structures of domination which have been articulated over the last two hundred and fifty years (and particularly since the beginning of the nineteenth century). Each of these themes, and particularly the third, raises questions about the nature of this articulation, its significance, and its implications. What is power? How does it relate to truth? What implications does Foucault's position have for thinking and acting?

Power

Foucault's account of power is not intended as a theory. That is, it is not meant as a context-free, ahistorical, objective description. Nor does it apply as a generalization to all of history. Rather, Foucault is proposing what he calls an analytics of power, which he opposes to theory. He says, "If one tries to erect a theory of power one will always be obliged to view it as emerging at a given place and time and hence to deduce it, to reconstruct its genesis. But if power is in reality an open, more-or-less coordinated (in the event, no doubt, ill-coordinated) cluster of relations, then the only problem is to provide oneself with a grid of analysis which makes possible an analytic of relations of power" (*CF* 199).

Toward this end Foucault presents a series of propositions about power in *The History of Sexuality,* and he has extended some of these ideas in his afterword to our book. These propositions are really cautionary rules of thumb, rather than theses which have been spelled out. First, power relations are "nonegalitarian and mobile." Power is not a commodity, a position, a prize, or a plot; it is the operation of the political technologies throughout the social body. The *functioning* of these political rituals of power is exactly what sets up the nonegalitarian, asymmetrical relations. It is the spread of these technologies and their everyday operation, localized spatially and temporally, that Foucault is referring to when he describes them as "mobile." If power is not a thing, or the control of a set of institutions, or the hidden rationality to history, then the task for the analyst is to identify how it operates. The aim, for Foucault, "is to move less toward a theory of power than toward an analytics of power: that is, toward a definition of a specific domain formed by power relations and toward a determination of the instruments that will make possible its analysis" (*HS* 82).

Foucault's aim is to isolate, identify, and analyze the web of unequal relationships set up by political technologies which underlies and undercuts the theoretical equality posited by the law and political philosophers. Bio-power escapes from the representation of power as law and advances under its protection. Its "rationality" is not captured by the political languages we still speak. To understand power in its materiality, its day to day operation, we must go to the level of the micropractices, the political technologies in which our practices are formed.

Foucault's next proposals follow from this first one. Power is not restricted to political institutions. Power plays a "directly productive role;" "it comes from below;" it is multidirectional, operating from the top down and also from the bottom up. We have seen that political technologies cannot be identified with particular institutions. But we have also seen that it is precisely when these technologies find a localization within specific institutions (schools, hospitals, prisons), when they "invest" these institutions, that bio-power really begins its take-off. When the disciplinary technologies establish links between these institutional settings, then disciplinary technology is truly effective. It is in this sense that Foucault says power is productive; it is not in a position of exteriority to other types of relationships. Although relationships of power are imminent to institutions, power and institutions are not identical. But neither are their relationships merely pasted-on, superstructural detail. For example, the school cannot be reduced to its disciplinary function. The content of Euclid's geometry is not changed by the architecture of the school building. However, many other aspects of school life are changed by the introduction of disciplinary technology (rigid scheduling, separation of pupils, surveillance of sexuality, ranking, individuation and so on).

Power is a general matrix of force relations at a given time, in a given society. In the prison, both the guardians and the prisoners are located within the same specific operations of discipline and surveillance, within the concrete restrictions of the prison's architecture. Though Foucault is saying that power comes from below and we are all enmeshed in it, he is not suggesting that there is no domination. The guards in Mettray prison had undeniable advantages in these arrangements; those who constructed the prison had others; both groups used these advantages to their own ends. Foucault is not denying this. He is affirming, however, that all of these groups were involved in power relations, however unequal and hierarchical, which they did not control in any simple sense. For Foucault, unless these unequal relations of power are traced down to their actual material functioning, they escape our analysis and continue to operate with unquestioned autonomy, maintaining the illusion that power is only applied by those at the top to those at the bottom.

Domination, then, is not the essence of power. When questioned about class domination, Foucault gives the example of social-welfare legislation in France at the end of the nineteenth century. Obviously he does not deny the realities of class domination. Rather, his point is that power is exercised upon the dominant as well as on the dominated; there is a process of self-formation or autocolonization involved. In order for the bourgeoisie to establish its position of class domination during the nineteenth century, it had to form itself as a class. As we have seen, there was first a dynamic exercising of strict controls primarily on its own members. The technologies of confession and the associated concern with life, sex, and health were initially applied by the bourgeoisie to itself. Bio-power was one of the central strategies of the self-constitution of the bourgeoisie. It was only at the end of the century that these technologies were applied to the working class. Foucault says,

> One could say that the strategy of moralisation (health campaigns, workers' housing, clinics, etc.) of the working class was that of the bourgeoisie. One could even say that it is this strategy which defined them as a class and enabled them to exercise their domination. But, to say that the bourgeoisie at the level of its ideology and its projects for economic reform, acting as a sort of real and yet fictive subject, invented and imposed by force this strategy of domination, that simply cannot be said. (*CF* 203)

Unless the political technologies had already successfully taken hold at the local level, there would have been no class domination. Unless the political technologies had succeeded in forming the bourgeoisie in the first place, there would not have been the same pattern of class domination. It is in this sense that Foucault views power as operating throughout society.

This leads us to what is probably Foucault's most provocative proposal about power. Power relations, he claims, are "intentional and non-subjective." Their intelligibility derives from this intentionality. "They are imbued, through and through, with calculation: there is no power that is exercised without a series of aims and objectives" (*HS* 95). At the local level there is often a high degree of conscious decision making, planning, plotting and coordination of political activity. Foucault refers to this as "the local cynicism of power." This recognition of volitional activity enables him to take local level political action fairly literally; he is not pushed to ferret out the secret motivations lying behind the actors' actions. He does not have to see political actors as essentially hypocrites or pawns of power. Actors more or less know what they are doing when they do it and can often be quite clear in articulating it. But it does not follow that the broader consequences of these local actions are coordinated. The fact that individuals make decisions about specific policies or particular groups jockey for their own advantage does not mean that the overall activation and directionality of power relations in a society implies a subject. When we analyze a political situation, "the logic is perfectly clear, the aims decipherable, and yet it is often the case that no one is there to have invented them, and few who can be said to have formulated them" (*HS* 95).

This is the insight, and this is the problem. How to talk about intentionality without a subject, a strategy without a strategist? The answer must lie in the practices themselves. For it is the practices, focused in technologies and innumerable separate localizations, which literally embody what the analyst is seeking to understand. In order to arrive at "a grid of intelligibility of the social order . . . one needs to be nominalistic, no doubt: power is not an institution, and not a structure; neither is it a certain strength we are endowed with; it is the name that one attributes to a complex strategical relationship in a particular society" (*HS* 93). There is a logic to the practices. There is a push towards a strategic objective, but no one is pushing. The objective emerged historically, taking particular forms and encountering specific obstacles, conditions and resistances. Will and calculation were involved. The overall effect, however, escaped the actors' intentions, as well as those of anybody else. As Foucault phrased it, "People know what they do; they frequently know why they do what they do; but what they don't know is what what they do does" (personal communication).

This is not a new form of functionalism. The system is not in any way in equilibrium; nor is it, except in the most extended of senses, a system. There is no inherent logic of stability. Rather, at the level of the practices there is a directionality produced from petty calculations, clashes of wills, meshing of minor interests. These are shaped and given a direction by the political technologies of power. This directionality has nothing inherent about it and hence it cannot be deduced. It is not a suitable object for a theory. It can, however, be analyzed, and this is Foucault's project.

Foucault's refusal to elaborate a theory of power follows from his insight that theory only exists and is only intelligible when it is set against and among particular cultural practices. This is perhaps why he so often restricts his general comments on power. Instead he has presented a systematic analysis of technologies of power for which he claims a certain significance and generality, although as a characterization these comments still appear to be rather all-encompassing and mysterious. Let us therefore return to Foucault's analysis of disciplinary technology as exemplified in Bentham's Panopticon, to see how this normalizing power works and what general inferences can be drawn from this analysis.

Meticulous Rituals of Power

Foucault picks out Jeremy Bentham's plan for the Panopticon (1791) as the paradigmatic example of a disciplinary technology. It is not the essence of power, as some have taken it to be, but a clear example of how power operates. There are other technologies which function in similar ways and could have served Foucault as illustrations. The Panopticon, Foucault tells us, is "a generalizable model of functioning; a way of defining power relations in terms of the everyday life of men . . . . It is the diagram of a mechanism of power reduced to its ideal form . . . . It is in fact a figure of political technology that may and must be detached from any specific use . . . . It is polyvalent in its applications" (*DP* 205).

Bentham's Panopticon might appear to be simply a minor individual scheme or an idealistic proposal for the reform and perfection of society. However, this viewpoint would not be quite accurate. Bentham was not the first to explore the techniques he used, although his was the most perfected, and the best known version. His Panopticon was not a utopian setting, located nowhere, meant as a total critique and reformulation of all aspects of society, but a plan for a specific mechanism of power. Bentham presented this instrument as a closed and perfect design, not for the satisfaction of designing an ideal form, but precisely for its applicability to a large number of diverse institutions and problems. The very genius of the Panopticon lies in its combination of abstract schematization and very concrete applications. It is, above all, flexible.

Let us briefly review the architectural functioning of the Panopticon. It consists of a large courtyard with a tower in the center and a set of buildings, divided into levels and cells, on the periphery. In each cell, there are two windows: one brings in light and the other faces the tower, where large observatory windows allow for the surveillance of the cells. The cells are like "small theatres in which each actor is alone, perfectly individualized and constantly visible" (*DP* 200). The inmate is not only visible to the supervisor, he is only visible to the supervisor; he is cut off from any contact with those in adjoining cells. "He is the object of information, never a subject in communication" (*DP* 200). The major benefit Bentham claimed for his Panopticon was a maximum of efficient organization. Foucault stresses that it did this by inducing in the inmate a state of objectivity, a permanent visibility. The inmate cannot see if the guardian is in the tower or not, so he must behave as if surveillance is constant, unending, and total. The architectural perfection is such that even if there is no guardian present the apparatus of power is still operative.

This new power is continuous, disciplinary, and anonymous. Anyone could operate it as long as he were in the correct position and anyone could be subjected to its mechanisms. The design is multipurpose. The surveillant in the tower could easily be observing a criminal, a madman, a worker, or a schoolboy. If the Panopticon functioned perfectly, almost all internal violence would be eliminated. For if the prisoner is never sure when he was being observed, he becomes his own guardian. And, as the final step, through the use of this mechanism one could also control the controllers. Those who occupy the central position in the Panopticon are themselves thoroughly enmeshed in a localization and ordering of their behavior. They observe, but in the process of so doing, they are also fixed, regulated, and subject to administrative control.

The Panopticon is not merely a highly efficient and clever technique for the control of individuals; it is also a laboratory for their eventual transformation. Experiments could easily be carried out in each of the cells and the results observed and tabulated from the tower. In factories, schools or hospitals, the surveillant could observe with great clarity the encoded and differentiated grid which lay before his gaze.

In Foucault's terms, the Panopticon brings together knowledge, power, the control of the body, and the control of space into an integrated technology of discipline. It is a mechanism for the location of bodies in space, for the distribution of individuals in relation to one another, for hierarchical organization, for the efficient disposition of centers and channels of power. The Panopticon is an adaptable and neutral technology for the ordering and individuating of groups. Whenever the imperative is to set individuals or populations in a grid where they can be made productive and observable, then Panoptic technology can be used.

The Panopticon effects its control over bodies in part through its efficient organization of space. An important distinction must be made here. This is not so much an architectural model which represents or embodies power, but a means for the operation of power in space. It is the techniques for the use of the structure, more than the architecture itself, that allows for an efficient expansion of power.

A digression to another of Foucault's examples may help clarify this point about space and architecture. The leper colony and the quarantined city were two ancient European methods for controlling individuals in space. In the seventeenth century, the quarantine as a method of plague control proceeded through a strict spatial partitioning. Officials divided the entire town and the surrounding countryside into administrative quarters. Under penalty of death no movement beyond the house was allowed; only the officials and those wretched enough to be assigned the duty of moving the bodies were allowed to circulate through the streets. There was a constant alert, a daily surveillance down to each of the houses and its occupants; those who did not appear had to be accounted for. The information collected was passed up through a hierarchy of officials. They even had the right to appropriate private property in the case of death: procedures of purification entailed evacuation of a contaminated dwelling, followed by fumigation. All medical care was carefully supervised; all pathologies had to be known by the central authorities; all space was controlled by them; all movement was regulated.

This was a disciplinary mechanism carried out in space. It entailed the analysis of a geographical area; the supervision of its inhabitants; the control of individuals; a hierarchy of information, decision making, and movement down to the regulation of the smallest details of everyday life. "The plague as a form, at once real and imaginary, of disorder had as its medical and political correlative discipline. Behind the disciplinary mechanisms can be read the haunting memory of contagions, of the plague, of rebellions, crimes, vagabondage, desertions, people who appear and disappear, live and die in disorder" (*DP* 198). The ordering of space in the quarantined city was a technology which claimed to contain such disorder.

The leper colony offers the counterimage of population control through spatial enforcement of power. The leper was excluded from society, separated out and stigmatized. He was thrown with his suffering brothers into an undifferentiated mass. The authority to locate and exile lepers into separate communities where they were required to live and die was an act of "massive, binary division between one set of people and another" (*DP* 198). The point here is the authority's right to exclude lepers from one space and restrict them to another, for the ordering of space within the leper colony itself was never very rigorous, even if

190

Foucault links it with the political dream of "a pure community" (*DP* 198).

Taken together, the discipline through space in the quarantine model joins the exclusion developed for the leper colony to provide insights into new "Panoptic" technologies of control. These technologies exercised power through space. The resulting spatial forms included temporary emergency laws on movements and property, strictly differentiated boundaries between populations, architectural prototypes like the Panopticon, and institutional settings that were in fact built and used. Each legal definition of space and each architectural model provided increasingly sophisticated and complex ways of exercising power. They were also the evidence that power was being enforced and hence the basis for the expansion of that enforcement.

> Treat lepers as plague victims, project the subtle segmentations of discipline onto the confused space of internment, combine it with the methods of analytic distribution proper to power, individualize the excluded, but use procedures of individualization to mark exclusion—this is what was operated regularly by the disciplinary power from the beginning of the nineteenth century in the psychiatric asylum, the penitentiary, the reformatory, the approved school, and to some extent, the hospital. (*DP* 199)

When the fear of the plague had been successfully transferred to the fear of the abnormal and the techniques for isolation of abnormalities had been developed, then the disciplinary paradigm had triumphed.

To return to the Panopticon as a schema of power, we can see it as a place perfectly designed for its purpose: that of constant surveillance of its inhabitants. It operates through a reversal of visibility, one of the principal components of modern power that is perfectly expressed in its form. Whereas in monarchical regimes it was the sovereign who had the greatest visibility, under the institutions of bio-power it is those who are to be disciplined, observed, and understood who are made the most visible. Bentham's Panopticon captures and manifests this reversal of visibility in its organization of space. The architecture itself is a means for that visibility and the subtle forms of control it entails. The Panopticon is not a symbol of power; it doesn't refer to anything else. Nor does it have any deep, hidden meaning. It carries within itself its own interpretation, a certain transparency. Its function is to increase control. Its very form, its materiality, every aspect down to the smallest detail (here Bentham is totally explicit, carrying on for many pages about numerous petty details of construction) yields the interpretation of what it does. The mechanism itself is neutral and, in its own fashion, universal. It is a perfect technology. It is only when it "invests" and undermines other institutions that it takes on its own momentum.

The Panopticon presents us with a precise connection between the control of bodies and spaces, while it makes clear that this control was exercised in the interest of increasing power. At this point, let us recapitulate the fundamental components of power which Foucault has drawn from the example of the Panopticon. His major insight is that power is exercised, not simply held. The tendency for power to be depersonalized, diffused, relational, and anonymous, while at the same time totalizing more and more dimensions of social life, is captured, made possible, and summed up in the Panoptic technology. Bentham observed that in the Panopticon, "each comrade becomes a guardian." As Foucault puts it, "Such is perhaps the most diabolical aspect of the idea and of all the applications it brought about. In this form of management, power is not totally entrusted to someone who would exercise it alone, over others, in an absolute fashion; rather this machine is one in which everyone is caught, those who exercise this power as well as those who are subjected to it" (EP 156).

The Panopticon then is an exemplary technology for disciplinary power. Its chief characteristics are its ability to make the spread of power efficient; to make possible the exercise of power with limited manpower at the least cost; to discipline individuals with the least exertion of overt force by operating on their souls; to increase to a maximum the visibility of those subjected; to involve in its functioning all those who come in contact with the apparatus. In sum, Panopticism is a perfect example of a meticulous ritual of power which, by its mode of operation, establishes a site where a political technology of the body can operate; here rights and obligations are established and imposed.

The final component in Panopticism is the connection between bodies, space, power, and knowledge. The widespread interest in the Panopticon provided the mechanism for the insertion and activation of a new form of continuous administration and control of everyday life. The Panopticon itself must be understood as "the diagram of a mechanism of power reduced to its ideal form; its functioning abstracted from any obstacle, resistance or friction, must be represented as a pure architectural or optical system; it is in fact a figure of political technology that may and must be detached from any specific use" (DP 205). Even if, as Foucault himself points out, the Panopticon was never actually constructed, the numerous discussions about its operations and its potentialities served to formulate ideas about correction and control. It therefore represents for us the schematization of modern disciplinary technology: "The automatic functioning of power, mechanical operation is absolutely not the thesis of Discipline and Punish. Rather it is the idea, in the eighteenth century, that such a form of power is possible and desirable. It is the theoretical and practical search for such mechanisms, the will, constantly attested, to organize this kind of mechanism which constitutes the object of my analysis" (*IP* 37).

Panoptic technology was designed to generalize the various disciplines which had emerged during the seventeenth and eighteenth centuries. At first highly localized and isolated in functionally specific settings, disciplinary technology now gradually overflowed its institutional bounds. The techniques of the Panopticon were applied, in admittedly less fully articulated form, in numerous kinds of institutions, and these institutions in turn kept close surveillance not only on the individuals within their walls but on those outside as well. The hospital, for example, not only organized the care of its own inmates; it became a center for observing and organizing the general population. As we have seen, disciplinary measures had their most impressive successes in those sectors of society concerned with the integration of production, utility, and control: "factory production, the transmission of knowledge, the diffusion of aptitude and skills, the war machine" (*DP* 211). Here, too, authorities came to see workers as individuals who needed to be studied, trained, and disciplined, first where they worked and later in their homes and schools and clinics, too. The technology of discipline linked the production of useful and docile individuals with the production of controlled and efficient populations.

There is a particular rationality, too, which goes along with the Panoptic technology, one which is self-contained, nontheoretical, efficient, and productive. The Panopticon seemed to pose no standard of judgment, only an efficient technique for distributing individuals, knowing them, ordering them along a graded scale in any of a number of institutional settings. Therefore the Panopticon had the effect of focusing the practices of the culture: it provided a paradigmatic form for their visibility. People—or at least educated reformers—could agree: a factory, school, prison, or even a harem (think of the Fouerierists, or Bentham) should be run efficiently, without overt violence, with as much individuation as possible, scientifically and successfully. "The Panopticon arrangement provides the formula for this generalization. Its programs, at the level of an elementary and easily transferable mechanism, the basic functioning of a society penetrated through and through with disciplinary mechanisms" (*DP* 209).

As disciplinary technology undermined and advanced beyond its mask of neutrality, it imposed its own standard of normalization as the only acceptable one. Gradually the law and other standards outside of power were sacrificed to normalization. We see this tendency most clearly in the prisons. "The theme of the Panopticon—at once surveillance and observation, security and knowledge, individualization and totalization, isolation and transparency—found in the prison its privileged locus of realization'' (*DP* 249). This concentration of Panoptic procedures in turn allowed for the emergence of particular intellectual disciplines that were successfully applied in the prisons. The new penitentiary system that suddenly appeared in Europe at the beginning of the nineteenth century served, among other things, as a laboratory for the constitution of a body of knowledge about the criminal and his crimes. Following the twin imperatives of the newly emergent episteme of man and the technological ''take-off'' of disciplinary power, this was the ideal locale for a subject who was simultaneously the object of new scientific research and the object of disciplinary power. Scientific psychology was born, and it was quickly taken up in the prisons. ''The supervision of normality was firmly encased in a medicine or a psychiatry that provided it with a sort of 'scientificity'; it was supported by a judicial apparatus which, directly or indirectly, gave it legal justification'' (*DP* 296). It was between these two impeccable guardians that the ''normalization of the power of normalization'' advanced.

Foucault is not reductionistic about the relations of knowledge and power. Sometimes, as we have seen in the case of the natural sciences, knowledge separates itself from the practices in which it was formed. Combinations must be analyzed in each instance, not assumed beforehand. He explains: ''I am not saying that the human sciences emerged from the prison. But, if they have been able to be formed and to produce so many profound changes in the episteme, it is because they have been conveyed by a specific and new modality of power . . . [which] required definite relations of knowledge in relations of power. . . . Knowable man (soul, individuality, consciousness, conduct, whatever it is called) is the object-effect of this analytic investment, of this domination-observation'' (*DP* 305). This is not to say, obviously, that each aspect of each social science has a direct disciplinary effect—and Foucault never takes such a position. Yet, in the case of many human sciences there was a continuous, mutual, and prolonged interplay and reinforcement of these relationships.

In just such an instance, hybrid fertilization produced the delinquent: ''The delinquent is to be distinguished from the offender by the fact that it is not so much his act as his life that is relevant in characterizing him'' (*DP* 251). The criminal became a quasi-natural species, identified, isolated, and known by the newly emergent human sciences of psychiatry and criminology. Hence, it was no longer sufficient merely to punish his crime; the criminal had to be rehabilitated. To be rehabilitated, he had to be understood and known in his individuality, as well as classified as a certain type of criminal. Under the banner of normalization, knowledge was brought foursquare into the fray. It was through this tactic that crime, which had been primarily a legal and political matter, became invested with new dimensions of scientific knowledge and normalizing intent.

The delinquent and the new penitentiary system appeared together; they complemented and extended one another. "The delinquent makes it possible to join [moral and political monsters and juridical subjects] and to constitute under the authority of medicine, psychology or criminology, an individual in whom the offender of the law and the object of scientific technique are superimposed" (*DP* 256). Modern power and the sciences of man found their common point of articulation; there would be many others to follow. The truly effective spread of normalizing power began with this coupling.

However, an extremely important dimension of the functioning of the prison system is that it never succeeded in living up to its promises. From its very inception through the present, prisons have not worked. Foucault's recounting of the numbers of recidivists and the uniformity of reform rhetoric is compelling. They have not done what their advocates claimed they were uniquely qualified to do: produce normal citizens out of hardened criminals. Yet this does not mean that prison reformers necessarily failed to achieve their goals. During the last century and a half, spokesmen have consistently offered the prison system as the remedy for its own ills. The question, therefore, is not, Why have the prisons failed? It is rather, What other ends are served by this failure, which is perhaps not a failure after all? Foucault's answer is direct: "One would be forced to suppose that the prison, and no doubt punishment in general, is not intended to eliminate offenses, but rather to distinguish them, to distribute them, to use them: that it is not so much that they render docile those who are liable to transgress the law but that they tend to assimilate the transgression of the laws in a general tactic of subjection" (*DP* 272). Penitentiaries, and perhaps all normalizing power, succeed when they are only partially successful.

An essential component of technologies of normalization is that they are themselves an integral part of the systematic creation, classification, and control of anomalies in the social body. Their *raison d'être* comes from their claim to have isolated such anomalies and their promises to normalize them. As Foucault has shown in great detail in *Discipline and Punish* and *The History of Sexuality,* the advance of bio-power is contemporary with the appearance and proliferation of the very categories of anomalies—the delinquent, the pervert, and so on—that technologies of power and knowledge were supposedly designed to eliminate. The spread of normalization operates through the creation of abnormalities which it then must treat and reform. By identifying the anomalies scientifically, the technologies of bio-power are in a perfect position to supervise and administer them.

This effectively transforms into a technical problem—and thence into a field for expanding power—what might otherwise be construed as a failure of the whole system of operation. Political technologies advance by taking what is essentially a political problem, removing it from the realm of political discourse, and recasting it in the neutral language of science.[1] Once this is accomplished the problems have become technical ones for specialists to debate. In fact, the language of reform is, from the outset, an essential component of these political technologies. Bio-power spread under the banner of making people healthy and protecting them. When there was resistance, or failure to achieve its stated aims, this was construed as further proof of the need to reinforce and extend the power of the experts. A technical matrix was established. By definition, there ought to be a way of solving any technical problem. Once this matrix was established, the spread of bio-power was assured, for there was nothing else to appeal to; any other standards could be shown to be abnormal or to present merely technical problems. We are promised normalization and happiness through science and law. When they fail, this only justifies the need for more of the same.

Once the hold of bio-power is secure, what we get is not a true conflict of interpretations about the ultimate worth or meaning of efficiency, productivity, or normalization, but rather what might be called a conflict of implementations. The problem bio-power has succeeded in establishing is how to make the welfare institutions work; it does not ask, What do they mean? or, as Foucault would put it, What do they do?

Foucault gives a perfect example of this conflict of implementations when he discusses the early nineteenth-century debates about which of the American model prison systems—Auburn or Philadelphia—provided a better solution to the problems of isolating prisoners. The Auburn model drew on the monastery and the factory for elements of its solution. Hence, prisoners were assigned to sleep in separate individual cells but were allowed to eat and work together, although in both situations they were strictly forbidden to speak to one another. The advantage of the system, according to the Auburn reformers, was that it duplicated in a pure form the conditions of society—hierarchy and surveillance in the name of order—and hence prepared the criminal's return to social life. In contrast, the Philadelphia model of the Quakers stressed individual reform of conscience through isolation and self-reflection. Kept in continual

1. Habermas and many others have addressed this point. Their general analytic framework is more systematically presented than is Foucault's. Foucault, however, has been more successful in pinpointing the concrete mechanisms by which this process works.

confinement, the criminal would supposedly undergo a deep and pervasive change in character, rather than a superficial alteration of surface habits and attitudes. The Quakers believed he would discover his moral conscience through the elimination of sociality.

Foucault has isolated two different models of implementation; two different models of society and the individual; two different models of subjection. Each is based on an implicit acceptance of disciplinary technology per se. Advocates of either system agreed that there should be isolation and individualization of prisoners. The only conflict was how this individualization and isolation should be carried out.

> A whole series of different conflicts stemmed from the opposition between two models: religious (must conversion be the principle element of correction?), economic (which methods cost less?), medical (does total isolation drive convicts insane?), architectural and administrative (which form guarantees the best surveillance?). This, no doubt, was why the argument lasted so long. But, at the heart of the debate, and making it possible, was this primary objective of carceral action: coercive individualization by the termination of any relation that is not supervised by authority or arranged according to hierarchy. (*DP* 239)

The project itself was not a topic of dispute. It was the unquestioned acceptance of hierarchical, coercive individualization which made possible a wide range of techniques of implementation. Through these differences and these agreements (however tacit and embedded in the practices), under the guidance of science and the law, normalization and discipline advanced.

Paradigms and Practices

Readers familiar with Kuhn's account of how sciences are established and proceed will recognize a striking similarity between Kuhn's account of normal science and Foucault's account of normalizing society. According to Kuhn a science becomes normal when the practitioners in a certain area all agree that a particular piece of work identifies the important problems in a field and demonstrates how certain of these problems can be successfully solved. Kuhn calls such an agreed-upon achievement a paradigm or exemplar, and points to Newton's *Principia* as a perspicuous example. Paradigms set up normal science as the activity of finding certain puzzling phenomena which seem at first to resist incorporation into the theory, but which normal science, by its very definition, must ultimately account for in its own terms. The ideal of normal science is that all these anomalies will eventually be shown to be compatible with the theory. Kuhn notes that "perhaps the most striking feature

197

of . . . normal research problems . . . is how little they aim to produce major novelties, conceptual or phenomenal. . . . To scientists, at least, the results gained in normal research are significant because they add to the scope and precision with which the paradigm can be applied."[2]

Normalizing technologies have an almost identical structure. They operate by establishing a common definition of goals and procedures, which take the form of manifestos and, even more forceful, agreed-upon examples of how a well-ordered domain of human activity should be organized. These exemplars, such as the Panopticon and the confessional, immediately define what is normal; at the same time, they define practices which fall outside their system as deviant behavior in need of normalization. Thus, although neither the scientific nor the social paradigm has any intrinsic validity, by determining what counts as a problem to be solved and what counts as a solution, they set up normal science and normal society as totalizing fields of activity which continually extend their range of prediction and control. There is, however, a major difference between the operation of normal science and that of normalizing technologies; whereas normal science aims in principle at the final assimilation of all anomalies, disciplinary technology works to set up and preserve an increasingly differentiated set of anomalies, which is the very way it extends its knowledge and power into wider and wider domains.

Of course, the really important difference between the two is political. Whereas normal science has turned out to be an effective means of accumulating knowledge about the natural world (where knowledge means accuracy of prediction, number of different problems solved, and so on, not truths about how things are in themselves), normalizing society has turned out to be a powerful and insidious form of domination.

Given Foucault's persuasive story of the deleterious effect of normalizing paradigms, the question remains: Could there be other kinds of paradigms which set up other kinds of societies? Foucault does not explicitly thematize, let alone generalize, his insight into the central role of shared exemplars in taking up scattered practices, focusing them, and giving a direction to the strategies implicit in them. Yet this discovery is highly provocative and seems worthy of further attention. It would be interesting to investigate whether there have been in our past, and whether there might be in our future, paradigms which function in such a way as to focus important concerns for the culture, without preordaining, in a normalizing way, what responses would count as appropriate. We could then ask: Would such social paradigms be superior to the Panopticon and confessional simply by virtue of being nonnormalizing, or would we then need some other standards by which to evaluate them?

2. Kuhn, *Scientific Revolutions*, pp. 35–36.

In any case, once one sees the importance of paradigms for a culture, one also sees their methodological importance for understanding society. One can use them hermeneutically, as we have seen Kuhn do, as a way of getting inside the serious meanings of the investigators whose behavior makes sense in terms of the paradigm. But one can also use them, as Kuhn also does, to reveal a certain aspect of the scientist's behavior, of which he is neither directly nor even dimly aware, and yet one that is essential to understanding the meaning of his activity. Thus natural scientists do not believe, and are even resistant to discussing the possibility, that the validity of their work is a matter of consensus rather than correspondence. Yet, if Kuhn is right, the whole significance of normal natural science consists in the way paradigms direct and produce the behavior of the scientists who operate in terms of those paradigms. Kuhn does not confuse the two kinds of accounts. He calls the attempt to get inside the thought of a school of thought hermeneutics. As far as we know, he had no name for the analysis of the structure of scientific normalcy and revolution, even though it is his most original and important contribution. We think that this second method is very close to the analytical dimension of what we call interpretive analytics.

Just as Foucault has not thematized his substantive insights into the functioning of paradigms, so he has not drawn this methodological moral about their importance for interpretive analytics. Yet his current work clearly follows a course that uses these insights, if not the words themselves. He is now proceeding through a description of discourse as the historical articulation of a paradigm, and approaching analytics in a manner that is heavily dependent on the isolation and description of social paradigms and their practical applications. For Foucault the analysis of discourse is no longer systematized in terms of the formation rules of the episteme. Allowing for differences in their interests and fields of investigation, Foucault would presumably agree with Kuhn's remark that "Rules . . . derive from paradigms, but paradigms can guide research even in the absence of rules."[3] Moreover, as opposed to the analysis in *The Order of Things* and *The Archaeology of Knowledge,* where discourse and the abstract systemic structure which regulates it were taken to be methodologically privileged, Foucault in his later writings sees discourse as part of a larger field of power and practice whose relations are articulated in different ways by different paradigms. The rigorous establishment of these relations is the analytic dimension Foucault's work shares with Kuhn.

Foucault's interest in society, however, requires him to introduce an interpretive dimension which has no place in Kuhn's work. It is not a

3. Kuhn, *Scientific Revolutions,* p. 42.

matter of interpretation when Kuhn contends that for several centuries Newton's work served as an exemplar for natural scientists. Nor is it Kuhn's job *qua* historian of science to decide whether the general effect of the rise of natural science in the West carries with it consequences which should be supported or resisted. The study of social phenomena, however, requires an interpretive dimension. First, there is no obvious consensus about the central organizing paradigms of our current culture and, second, even if we were to agree on the centrality of certain paradigms, the question of how to evaluate their effect is still open.

This interpretive contribution is not a superfluous moralizing indulgence, nor can it be a matter of personal preference. It rests on three independent but mutually supporting moves. First, the interpreter must take up a pragmatic stance on the basis of some socially shared sense of how things are going. This means he cannot speak out of mere arbitrary personal feeling, whether of distress or euphoria. But, of course, in any given society at any given time, there will be different groups with different shared senses of the state of things. Thus, for example, although almost all of the intellectuals in France have felt, since the revolution, that society is in a major crisis which puts it in peril, there is presumably a consensus among administrators, expressed in their memos to each other, that things are basically in hand and that the general welfare and productivity of the population is constantly improving. It should be obvious that, even if there were a general consensus as to the state of the society, this would only prove that an orthodoxy had taken hold, not that the sense of things had assumed the status of objective truth.

Second, the investigator must produce a disciplined diagnosis of what has gone on and is going on in the social body to account for the shared sense of distress or well-being. It is here that detailed, "grey, meticulous labor" in the archives and laboratories takes place in order to establish what was and is being said and done, by whom to whom, and to what effect. This research is subject to its own canons of rigor, but Foucault has so far remained relatively silent about them. Of course, most practitioners in the human sciences spend most of their effort in this aspect of the enterprise, which, like normal science, is largely puzzle-solving, with its own internal value, even though it ignores the disciplinary matrix and the larger social context it takes for granted. If an institutionalized sort of Foucaultian study of human beings were to become widespread, most researchers would still carry on this "positivist" labor.

To complete this self-supporting "circular project" (*HS* 90) which Foucault acknowledges all interpretation requires, the investigator owes the reader an account of why the practices he describes should produce the shared malaise or contentment which gave rise to the investigation. It

200

goes without saying that it would contradict the whole point of such an analysis to appeal to an objective theory of human nature in order to say what sort of social arrangement can produce well-being and what sort can produce disorder and distress. Nor can one legitimize one's discourse by appealing to a past golden age, or to the principles which would govern an ideal future community. The only possibility left seems to be that something in our historical practices has defined us, for the time being at least, as the sort of beings who, when sensitive, resist submitting to and furthering the sort of totalizing ordering which Foucault's analysis has shown to be characteristic of our current practices. This is not an appeal to a golden age since there is no claim that everything was fine at some point in the past, nor does the appeal to these historical practices involve a nostalgia for their resuscitation. Rather, some concrete paradigm of health would seem to be required, if one claims to have a concrete diagnosis of how things have gone wrong.

There are some provocative hints, scattered in Foucault's work, that he sees this problem. For example, he points to the emergence of theoretical knowing among the Greeks as the great turning point in our history. He says that the pragmatic and poetic discourse of early Greek civilization was destroyed by the rise of theory: "The Sophists were routed.... From the time of the great Platonic division onwards, the [Platonic] will to truth has had its own history...[one which] relies on institutional support" (*DL* 218, 219). This change altered all aspects of Greek social life: "When Hippocrates had reduced medicine to a system, observation was abandoned and philosophy was introduced into medicine" (*BC* 56); or "The West has managed... to annex sex to a field of rationality.... We are accustomed to such conquests since the Greeks" (*HS* 78). Presumably we have something to learn in the social field from studying what society was like in the time of the Sophists, before metaphysics and technology reigned. But obviously Foucault is not seeking to draw directly from pre-Socratic Greece. This is a historical fiction. Perhaps it can be used as a diagnostic aid to see the beginnings of the totalizing ordering of things, and perhaps it can help us look for those social practices which have still escaped technological totalization.

Foucault is faced with a dilemma concerning the status of those practices which have escaped or successfully resisted the spread of bio-power. While dispersed, these practices escape disciplinary totalization but offer little resistance to its further spread. However, if Foucault were to advocate directly focusing on them in an ordered way, even in the name of countertradition or resistance, he would risk their takeover and normalization. Short of offering us an answer to this extremely thorny problem, it would seem incumbent on Foucault to use his work to locate the endangered species of resistant practices and to consider how they could be strengthened in nontotalizing, nontheoretical and non-normalizing ways. If truth is to operate in society so as to resist techno-logical power, we must find a way to make it positive and productive. Whether such a possibility exists remains an open question.

One way of summing up the three mutually supporting aspects of interpretive analytics is to note a parallel with medical diagnosis. The doctor starts from his patient's sense of how well or ill he feels, although he cannot trust this sense completely. The diagnosis must then give a technical explanation of why the patient feels the way he does, which in turn requires an appeal to examples of what everyone agrees to be a healthy body. Foucault paraphrases and presumably agrees with Nietzsche when he says, "Historical sense has more in common with medicine than philosophy . . . . Its task is to become a curative science" (*NGH* 156).

Power and Truth

A doctor can stand outside a patient and treat him objectively, but a practitioner of interpretive analytics has no such external position. The disease he seeks to cure is part of an epidemic which has also affected him. Hence, we must return again, one last time, to the problem of the analyst. For surely these dramatically new characterizations of power relations must put the analyst in a different position from that of the traditional intellectual or philosopher. Foucault has provided some in-dications of how he sees the problem. He has systematically criticized the self-proclaimed master of truth and justice, the intellectual who claimed to speak truth to power and thereby to resist power's supposed repressive effect. The "speaker's benefit" was revealed as a component in the ad-vance of bio-power.

Foucault generalizes this point. He advises intellectuals to abandon their universal prophetic voice. He urges them to drop their pretensions about predicting the future and, even more, their self-proclaimed legisla-tive role. "The Greek wise man, the Jewish prophet, the Roman legislator are still models that haunt those, who today, practice the profession of speaking and writing" (*Telos* 161). In more recent times, our model of the intellectual has been the writer-jurist who claims to be outside of partisan interest, to speak in the universal voice, to represent either God's law or that of the state, to make known the universal dictates of reason. The exemplary figure in the Classical Age was perhaps Voltaire—proclaiming the rights of humanity, unveiling deceit and hypocrisy, attacking des-potism and false hierarchies, combating injustices and inequalities. The function of the modern intellectual is to bring the truth to articulate clarity.

Today the supposedly free subject, the universal intellectual, can offer us little guidance. But this does not mean that those who seek to understand human beings and to change society are either outside of power or powerless. Rather, as Foucault's account of the rise and spread of bio-power makes clear, knowledge is one of the defining components for the operation of power in the modern world.

Knowledge is not in a superstructural relationship to power; it is an essential condition for the formation and further growth of industrial, technological society. To take only the example we most recently discussed, that of the prisons, the categorizing and individualizing of prisoners was an essential component for the operation of this field of power; this disciplinary technology could not have taken the form it had, achieved the spread it did, or produced delinquents in the way it did, if power and knowledge were merely external to one another. But power and knowledge are not *identical* with each other either. Foucault does not seek to reduce knowledge to a hypothetical base in power nor to conceptualize power as an always coherent strategy. He attempts to show the specificity and materiality of their interconnections. They have a correlative, not a causal relationship, which must be determined in its historical specificity. This mutual production of power and knowledge is one of Foucault's major contributions. The universal intellectual plays power's game because he fails to see this point.

Foucault is not claiming to be outside of these practices of power; at the same time, he is not identical to them. First, when he shows that the practices of our culture have produced both objectification and subjectification, he has already loosened the grip, the seeming naturalness and necessity these practices have. The force of bio-power lies in defining reality as well as producing it. This reality takes the world to be composed of subjects and objects and their totalizing normalization. Any solution that takes these terms for granted—even if it is to oppose them—will contribute to the hold of bio-power. Through interpretive analytics, Foucault has been able to reveal the concrete, material mechanisms which have been producing this reality, while he describes with minute detail the transparent masks behind which these mechanisms are hidden.

This leads us to our second point. Foucault has been able to diagnose our current situation because he shares it. He offers us, from the inside, pragmatically guided accounts. He offers us a genealogy of the organizing trends in our culture. Clearly Foucault is not saying that all of the practices of our culture are disciplinary or confessional, or that every production of knowledge functions immediately as a power-effect. The trend towards normalization has not succeeded in totalizing all of the practices. In fact, given this trend, and given Foucault's position that truth is not external to power, he draws the conclusion that "philosophy's question ... is the question as to what we ourselves are. That is why contemporary philosophy is entirely political and entirely historical. It is the politics immanent in history and the history indispensable to policies" (*Telos* 159). We have no recourse to objective laws, no recourse to pure subjectivity, no recourse to totalizations of theory. We have only the cultural practices which have made us what we are. To know what that is, we have to grapple with the history of the present.

The additional conclusion that Foucault draws is that the job to be done is *not* to free truth from power. In the human sciences all such attempts only seem to provide energy to disciplinary and technological trends in our society. The job is rather to make this pragmatic account function differently within a field of power.

> I am fully aware that I have never written anything other than fictions. For all that, I would not want to say that they were outside the truth. It seems plausible to me to make fictions work within truth, to introduce truth-effects within a fictional discourse, and in some way to make discourse arouse, "fabricate," something which does not yet exist, thus to fiction something. One "fictions" history starting from a political reality that renders it true, one "fictions" a politics that does not yet exist starting from a historical truth. (*ILF* 75)

Taken together, interpretation and analytics protect the practitioner of fictive history from traditional philosophy's *esprit sérieux* and from contemporary playfulness. Analytics respects established problems and concepts, recognizing that they are concerned with something important; it does so in a way that reveals more about society and its practices than about ultimate reality. Interpretation starts from current society and its problems. It gives them a genealogical history, without claiming to capture what the past really was. The concepts that people used in their efforts to understand themselves provide archaeological ballast; taking current problems seriously keeps one from playing intellectual games with these concepts from our past.

Conclusion

The work of Michel Foucault is still very much "in progress." Although the major contours are clear, his future writing is sure to contain unexpected twists and turns. Consequently, in lieu of a definitive conclusion, we have decided to pose a series of questions which have arisen in the course of our investigations. We feel that these questions help to situate the major themes and major uncertainties of Michel Foucault's current corpus, and also raise the most general problems which contemporary thought must address.

We pose these questions as a series of dilemmas. In each set there is a seeming contradiction between a return to the traditional philosophic view that description and interpretation ultimately must correspond to the way things really are, and a nihilist view that physical reality, the body, and history are whatever we take them to be. We have constructed these questions—and this book—so as to demonstrate how Foucault has sought to avoid embracing either or both of these formulations. His project has been an adroit demarcation of the course to be pursued and a skillful avoidance of the responses traditionally or currently given to these problems. His "concrete demonstrations" have marked out a terrain. But they cannot be accepted as a fully satisfactory map. Foucault himself has described his tactic as a "slalom" (personal communication) between the traditional philosophy and an abandonment of all seriousness. Yet, Foucault's ascetic refusal to go beyond his concrete demonstrations, while consistent and even admirable, does not make the questions disappear; nor does it fully satisfy our perhaps still traditional desire to have a picture of the course. Therefore, let us pose these questions as markers on the course that modern thinkers must follow.

Questions

TRUTH

A) Is there a place for the nondubious sciences (physics, biology, and so forth) between the correspondence theory of truth and an approach that treats every discipline as a discursive formation? How autonomous and free of the social relations are they? In what sense are they true? Has Kuhn opened the way to answering these questions? If not, what direction would provide a better answer? Or are philosophical questions such as these passé?

B) Is the main philosophic task to give a content to Merleau-Ponty's analysis of *le corps propre?* Or is such an attempt which finds ahistorical and cross-cultural structures in the body misdirected? If there are such structures can one appeal to them without returning to naturalism? Is one of the bases of resistance to bio-power to be found in the body? Can the body be totally transformed by disciplinary techniques? Merleau-Ponty sees the body as having a *telos* towards rationality and explicitness; if he is correct how is it that power and organizational rationality are so infrequently linked in other cultures? If, on the other hand, power and rationality are not grounded in the body's need to get a maximum grip on the world, what is the relation between the body's capacities and power?

C) To what extent and how should the history of the present be responsible to the facts of the past? Is every analysis which grows out of a pragmatic concern equally valid or are there other criteria of validity? What is the relation of analysis and truth? What is the role of empirical confirmation and disconfirmation?

RESISTANCE

A) What is wrong with carceral society? Genealogy undermines a stance which opposes it on the grounds of natural law or human dignity, both of which presuppose the assumptions of traditional philosophy. Genealogy also undermines opposing carceral society on the basis of subjective preferences and intuitions (or posing certain groups as carriers of human values capable of opposing carceral society). What are the resources which enable us to sustain a critical stance?

B) How is the resistance to bio-power to be strengthened? Dialectical arguments which appeal to the correct theoretical understanding of human beings and society are hardly sufficient to move large numbers of people and, following Foucault's analysis, are part of the current problem. Clearly, the rhetorical dimension is crucial here. Granted that the Platonic conception of truth is "our longest lie," must we be reduced to a Platonic conception of rhetorical and pragmatic discourse as mere manipulation? Or is there an art of interpretation which draws on other resources and opens up the possibility of using discourse to opposed domination?

C) Is there any way to resist the disciplinary society other than to understand how it works and to thwart it whenever possible? Is there a way to make resistance positive, that is, to move toward a "new economy of bodies and pleasures?"

POWER

A) Power in Foucault's work functions as a concept which attempts to understand how social practices work, without falling into a traditional theory of history. But the status of this concept is highly problematic. Clearly power, for Foucault, is not meant to function as a metaphysical ground. But if power is "nominalized," in what ways is it explanatory?

B) The genealogy of truth and of the body are now extended far back into our cultural history. Is power to be extended equally far back? If so, how? If not, why not?

C) What is power? It cannot be a merely external force organizing local interactions; nor can it be reduced to the totality of individual interactions, since in an important way it produces interaction and individuals. And yet, if it is to be a useful notion, something specific has to be said about its status. How can power be, at the same time, a productive principle in the practices themselves, and a merely heuristic principle used for giving the practices a retroactive intelligibility?

Afterword
The Subject and Power
MICHEL FOUCAULT

Why Study Power: The Question of the Subject

The ideas which I would like to discuss here represent neither a theory nor a methodology.

I would like to say, first of all, what has been the goal of my work during the last twenty years. It has not been to analyze the phenomena of power, nor to elaborate the foundations of such an analysis.

My objective, instead, has been to create a history of the different modes by which, in our culture, human beings are made subjects. My work has dealt with three modes of objectification which transform human beings into subjects.

The first is the modes of inquiry which try to give themselves the status of sciences; for example, the objectivizing of the speaking subject in *grammaire générale*, philology, and linguistics. Or again, in this first mode, the objectivizing of the productive subject, the subject who labors, in the analysis of wealth and of economics. Or, a third example, the objectivizing of the sheer fact of being alive in natural history or biology.

In the second part of my work, I have studied the objectivizing of the subject in what I shall call "dividing practices." The subject is either divided inside himself or divided from others. This process objectivizes him. Examples are the mad and the sane, the sick and the healthy, the criminals and the "good boys."

Finally, I have sought to study—it is my current work—the way a human being turns him- or herself into a subject. For example, I have chosen the domain of sexuality—how men have learned to recognize themselves as subjects of "sexuality."

"Why Study Power: The Question of the Subject" was written in English by Michel Foucault; "How is Power Exercised?" was translated from the French by Leslie Sawyer.

208

Thus it is not power, but the subject, which is the general theme of my research.

It is true that I became quite involved with the question of power. It soon appeared to me that, while the human subject is placed in relations of production and of signification, he is equally placed in power relations which are very complex. Now, it seemed to me that economic history and theory provided a good instrument for relations of production; that linguistics and semiotics offered instruments for studying relations of signification; but for power relations we had no tools of study. We had recourse only to ways of thinking about power based on legal models, that is: What legitimates power? Or we had recourse to ways of thinking about power based on institutional models, that is: What is the state?

It was therefore necessary to expand the dimensions of a definition of power if one wanted to use this definition in studying the objectivizing of the subject.

Do we need a theory of power? Since a theory assumes a prior objectification, it cannot be asserted as a basis for analytical work. But this analytical work cannot proceed without an ongoing conceptualization. And this conceptualization implies critical thought—a constant checking.

The first thing to check is what I should call the "conceptual needs." I mean that the conceptualization should not be founded on a theory of the object—the conceptualized object is not the single criterion of a good conceptualization. We have to know the historical conditions which motivate our conceptualization. We need a historical awareness of our present circumstance.

The second thing to check is the type of reality with which we are dealing.

A writer in a well-known French newspaper once expressed his surprise: "Why is the notion of power raised by so many people today? Is it such an important subject? Is it so independent that it can be discussed without taking into account other problems?"

This writer's surprise amazes me. I feel skeptical about the assumption that this question has been raised for the first time in the twentieth century. Anyway, for us it is not only a theoretical question, but a part of our experience. I'd like to mention only two "pathological forms"—those two "diseases of power"—fascism and Stalinism. One of the numerous reasons why they are, for us, so puzzling, is that in spite of their historical uniqueness they are not quite original. They used and extended mechanisms already present in most other societies. More than that: in spite of their own internal madness, they used to a large extent the ideas and the devices of our political rationality.

What we need is a new economy of power relations—the word *economy* being used in its theoretical and practical sense. To put it in other words: since Kant, the role of philosophy is to prevent reason from going beyond the limits of what is given in experience; but from the same moment—that is, since the development of the modern state and the political management of society—the role of philosophy is also to keep watch over the excessive powers of political rationality. Which is a rather high expectation.

Everybody is aware of such banal facts. But the fact that they're banal does not mean they don't exist. What we have to do with banal facts is to discover—or try to discover—which specific and perhaps original problem is connected with them.

The relationship between rationalization and excesses of political power is evident. And we should not need to wait for bureaucracy or concentration camps to recognize the existence of such relations. But the problem is: What to do with such an evident fact?

Shall we try reason? To my mind, nothing would be more sterile. First, because the field has nothing to do with guilt or innocence. Second, because it is senseless to refer to reason as the contrary entity to nonreason. Lastly, because such a trial would trap us into playing the arbitrary and boring part of either the rationalist or the irrationalist.

Shall we investigate this kind of rationalism which seems to be specific to our modern culture and which originates in *Aufklärung?* I think that was the approach of some of the members of the Frankfurt School. My purpose, however, is not to start a discussion of their works, although they are most important and valuable. Rather, I would suggest another way of investigating the links between rationalization and power.

It may be wise not to take as a whole the rationalization of society or of culture, but to analyze such a process in several fields, each with reference to a fundamental experience: madness, illness, death, crime, sexuality, and so forth.

I think that the word *rationalization* is dangerous. What we have to do is analyze specific rationalities rather than always invoking the progress of rationalization in general.

Even if the *Aufklärung* has been a very important phase in our history and in the development of political technology, I think we have to refer to much more remote processes if we want to understand how we have been trapped in our own history.

I would like to suggest another way to go further towards a new economy of power relations, a way which is more empirical, more directly related to our present situation, and which implies more relations between theory and practice. It consists of taking the forms of resistance against different forms of power as a starting point. To use another metaphor, it consists of using this resistance as a chemical catalyst so as to bring to light power relations, locate their position, find out their point of application and the methods used. Rather than analyzing power from the point of view of its internal rationality, it consists of analyzing power relations through the antagonism of strategies.

For example, to find out what our society means by sanity, perhaps we should investigate what is happening in the field of insanity.

And what we mean by legality in the field of illegality.

And, in order to understand what power relations are about, perhaps we should investigate the forms of resistance and attempts made to dissociate these relations.

As a starting point, let us take a series of oppositions which have developed over the last few years: opposition to the power of men over women, of parents over children, of psychiatry over the mentally ill, of medicine over the population, of administration over the ways people live.

It is not enough to say that these are antiauthority struggles; we must try to define more precisely what they have in common.

1) They are "transversal" struggles; that is, they are not limited to one country. Of course, they develop more easily and to a greater extent in certain countries, but they are not confined to a particular political or economic form of government.

2) The aim of these struggles is the power effects as such. For example, the medical profession is not criticized primarily because it is a profit-making concern, but because it exercises an uncontrolled power over people's bodies, their health and their life and death.

3) These are "immediate" struggles for two reasons. In such struggles people criticize instances of power which are the closest to them, those which exercise their action on individuals. They do not look for the "chief enemy," but for the immediate enemy. Nor do they expect to find a solution to their problem at a future date (that is, liberations, revolutions, end of class struggle). In comparison with a theoretical scale of explanations or a revolutionary order which polarizes the historian, they are anarchistic struggles.

But these are not their most original points. The following seem to me to be more specific.

4) They are struggles which question the status of the individual: on the one hand, they assert the right to be different and they underline everything which makes individuals truly individual. On the other hand, they attack everything which separates the individual, breaks his links

with others, splits up community life, forces the individual back on himself and ties him to his own identity in a constraining way.

These struggles are not exactly for or against the "individual," but rather they are struggles against the "government of individualization."

5) They are an opposition to the effects of power which are linked with knowledge, competence, and qualification: struggles against the privileges of knowledge. But they are also an opposition against secrecy, deformation, and mystifying representations imposed on people.

There is nothing "scientistic" in this (that is, a dogmatic belief in the value of scientific knowledge), but neither is it a skeptical or relativistic refusal of all verified truth. What is questioned is the way in which knowledge circulates and functions, its relations to power. In short, the *régime du savoir*.

6) Finally, all these present struggles revolve around the question: Who are we? They are a refusal of these abstractions, of economic and ideological state violence which ignore who we are individually, and also a refusal of a scientific or administrative inquisition which determines who one is.

To sum up, the main objective of these struggles is to attack not so much "such or such" an institution of power, or group, or elite, or class, but rather a technique, a form of power.

This form of power applies itself to immediate everyday life which categorizes the individual, marks him by his own individuality, attaches him to his own identity, imposes a law of truth on him which he must recognize and which others have to recognize in him. It is a form of power which makes individuals subjects. There are two meanings of the word *subject:* subject to someone else by control and dependence, and tied to his own identity by a conscience or self-knowledge. Both meanings suggest a form of power which subjugates and makes subject to.

Generally, it can be said that there are three types of struggles: either against forms of domination (ethnic, social, and religious); against forms of exploitation which separate individuals from what they produce; or against that which ties the individual to himself and submits him to others in this way (struggles against subjection, against forms of subjectivity and submission).

I think that in history, you can find a lot of examples of these three kinds of social struggles, either isolated from each other, or mixed together. But even when they are mixed, one of them, most of the time, prevails. For instance, in the feudal societies, the struggles against the forms of ethnic or social domination were prevalent, even though economic exploitation could have been very important among the revolt's causes.

The Subject and Power

In the nineteenth century, the struggle against exploitation came into the foreground.

And nowadays, the struggle against the forms of subjection—against the submission of subjectivity—is becoming more and more important, even though the struggles against forms of domination and exploitation have not disappeared. Quite the contrary.

I suspect that it is not the first time that our society has been confronted with this kind of struggle. All those movements which took place in the fifteenth and sixteenth centuries and which had the Reformation as their main expression and result should be analyzed as a great crisis of the Western experience of subjectivity and a revolt against the kind of religious and moral power which gave form, during the Middle Ages, to this subjectivity. The need to take a direct part in spiritual life, in the work of salvation, in the truth which lies in the Book—all that was a struggle for a new subjectivity.

I know what objections can be made. We can say that all types of subjection are derived phenomena, that they are merely the consequences of other economic and social processes: forces of production, class struggle, and ideological structures which determine the form of subjectivity.

It is certain that the mechanisms of subjection cannot be studied outside their relation to the mechanisms of exploitation and domination. But they do not merely constitute the "terminal" of more fundamental mechanisms. They entertain complex and circular relations with other forms.

The reason this kind of struggle tends to prevail in our society is due to the fact that since the sixteenth century, a new political form of power has been continuously developing. This new political structure, as everybody knows, is the state. But most of the time, the state is envisioned as a kind of political power which ignores individuals, looking only at the interests of the totality or, I should say, of a class or a group among the citizens.

That's quite true. But I'd like to underline the fact that the state's power (and that's one of the reasons for its strength) is both an individualizing and a totalizing form of power. Never, I think, in the history of human societies—even in the old Chinese society—has there been such a tricky combination in the same political structures of individualization techniques, and of totalization procedures.

This is due to the fact that the modern Western state has integrated in a new political shape, an old power technique which originated in Christian institutions. We can call this power technique the pastoral power.

First of all, a few words about this pastoral power.

213

It has often been said that Christianity brought into being a code of ethics fundamentally different from that of the ancient world. Less emphasis is usually placed on the fact that it proposed and spread new power relations throughout the ancient world.

Christianity is the only religion which has organized itself as a Church. And as such, it postulates in principle that certain individuals can, by their religious quality, serve others not as princes, magistrates, prophets, fortune-tellers, benefactors, educationalists, and so on, but as pastors. However, this word designates a very special form of power.

1) It is a form of power whose ultimate aim is to assure individual salvation in the next world.

2) Pastoral power is not merely a form of power which commands; it must also be prepared to sacrifice itself for the life and salvation of the flock. Therefore, it is different from royal power, which demands a sacrifice from its subjects to save the throne.

3) It is a form of power which does not look after just the whole community, but each individual in particular, during his entire life.

4) Finally, this form of power cannot be exercised without knowing the inside of people's minds, without exploring their souls, without making them reveal their innermost secrets. It implies a knowledge of the conscience and an ability to direct it.

This form of power is salvation oriented (as opposed to political power). It is oblative (as opposed to the principle of sovereignty); it is individualizing (as opposed to legal power); it is coextensive and continuous with life; it is linked with a production of truth—the truth of the individual himself.

But all this is part of history, you will say; the pastorate has, if not disappeared, at least lost the main part of its efficiency.

This is true, but I think we should distinguish between two aspects of pastoral power—between the ecclesiastical institutionalization which has ceased or at least lost its vitality since the eighteenth century, and its function, which has spread and multiplied outside the ecclesiastical institution.

An important phenomenon took place around the eighteenth century—it was a new distribution, a new organization of this kind of individualizing power.

I don't think that we should consider the "modern state" as an entity which was developed above individuals, ignoring what they are and even their very existence, but on the contrary as a very sophisticated structure, in which individuals can be integrated, under one condition: that this individuality would be shaped in a new form, and submitted to a set of very specific patterns.

In a way, we can see the state as a modern matrix of individualization, or a new form of pastoral power.

A few more words about this new pastoral power.

1) We may observe a change in its objective. It was no longer a question of leading people to their salvation in the next world, but rather ensuring it in this world. And in this context, the word *salvation* takes on different meanings: health, well-being (that is, sufficient wealth, standard of living), security, protection against accidents. A series of "worldly" aims took the place of the religious aims of the traditional pastorate, all the more easily because the latter, for various reasons, had followed in an accessory way a certain number of these aims; we only have to think of the role of medicine and its welfare function assured for a long time by the Catholic and Protestant churches.

2) Concurrently the officials of pastoral power increased. Sometimes this form of power was exerted by state apparatus or, in any case, by a public institution such as the police. (We should not forget that in the eighteenth century the police force was not invented only for maintaining law and order, nor for assisting governments in their struggle against their enemies, but for assuring urban supplies, hygiene, health and standards considered necessary for handicrafts and commerce.) Sometimes the power was exercised by private ventures, welfare societies, benefactors and generally by philanthropists. But ancient institutions, for example the family, were also mobilized at this time to take on pastoral functions. It was also exercised by complex structures such as medicine, which included private initiatives with the sale of services on market economy principles, but which also included public institutions such as hospitals.

3) Finally, the multiplication of the aims and agents of pastoral power focused the development of knowledge of man around two roles: one, globalizing and quantitative, concerning the population; the other, analytical, concerning the individual.

And this implies that power of a pastoral type, which over centuries—for more than a millennium—had been linked to a defined religious institution, suddenly spread out into the whole social body; it found support in a multitude of institutions. And, instead of a pastoral power and a political power, more or less linked to each other, more or less rival, there was an individualizing "tactic" which characterized a series of powers: those of the family, medicine, psychiatry, education, and employers.

At the end of the eighteenth century Kant wrote, in a German newspaper—the *Berliner Monatschrift*—a short text. The title was *Was heisst Aufklärung?* It was for a long time, and it is still, considered a work of relatively small importance.

But I can't help finding it very interesting and puzzling because it was the first time a philosopher proposed as a philosophical task to investigate not only the metaphysical system or the foundations of scientific knowledge, but a historical event—a recent, even a contemporary event.

When in 1784 Kant asked, Was heisst Aufklärung?, he meant, What's going on just now? What's happening to us? What is this world, this period, this precise moment in which we are living?

Or in other words: What are we? as *Aufklärer,* as part of the Enlightenment? Compare this with the Cartesian question: Who am I? I, as a unique but universal and unhistorical subject? I, for Descartes is everyone, anywhere at any moment?

But Kant asks something else: What are we? in a very precise moment of history. Kant's question appears as an analysis of both us and our present.

I think that this aspect of philosophy took on more and more importance. Hegel, Nietzsche . . . .

The other aspect of "universal philosophy" didn't disappear. But the task of philosophy as a critical analysis of our world is something which is more and more important. Maybe the most certain of all philosophical problems is the problem of the present time, and of what we are, in this very moment.

Maybe the target nowadays is not to discover what we are, but to refuse what we are. We have to imagine and to build up what we could be to get rid of this kind of political "double bind," which is the simultaneous individualization and totalization of modern power structures.

The conclusion would be that the political, ethical, social, philosophical problem of our days is not to try to liberate the individual from the state, and from the state's institutions, but to liberate us both from the state and from the type of individualization which is linked to the state. We have to promote new forms of subjectivity through the refusal of this kind of individuality which has been imposed on us for several centuries.

How is Power Exercised?

For some people, asking questions about the "how" of power would limit them to describing its effects without ever relating those effects either to causes or to a basic nature. It would make this power a mysterious substance which they might hesitate to interrogate in itself, no doubt because they would prefer *not* to call it into question. By proceeding this way, which is never explicitly justified, they seem to suspect the presence of a kind of fatalism. But does not their very distrust indicate a presupposition that power is something which exists with three distinct qualities: its origin, it basic nature, and its manifestations?

If, for the time being, I grant a certain privileged position to the question of "how" it is not because I would wish to eliminate the questions of "what" and "why." Rather it is that I wish to present these questions in a different way; better still, to know if it is legitimate to imagine a power which unites in itself a what, a why, and a how. To put it bluntly, I would say that to begin the analysis with a "how" is to suggest that power as such does not exist. At the very least it is to ask oneself what contents one has in mind when using this all-embracing and reifying term; it is to suspect that an extremely complex configuration of realities is allowed to escape when one treads endlessly in the double question: What is power? and Where does power come from? The little question, What happens? although flat and empirical, once it is scrutinized is seen to avoid accusing a metaphysics or an ontology of power of being fraudulent; rather it attempts a critical investigation into the thematics of power.

"How," not in the sense of "How does it manifest itself?" but "By what means is it exercised?" and "What happens when individuals exert (as they say) power over others?"

As far as this power is concerned, it is first necessary to distinguish that which is exerted over things and gives the ability to modify, use, consume, or destroy them—a power which stems from aptitudes directly inherent in the body or relayed by external instruments. Let us say that here it is a question of "capacity." On the other hand, what characterizes the power we are analyzing is that it brings into play relations between individuals (or between groups). For let us not deceive ourselves; if we speak of the structures or the mechanisms of power, it is only insofar as we suppose that certain persons exercise power over others. The term "power" designates relationships between partners (and by that I am not thinking of a zero-sum game, but simply, and for the moment staying in the most general terms, of an ensemble of actions which induce others and follow from one another).

It is necessary also to distinguish power relations from relationships of communication which transmit information by means of a language, a system of signs, or any other symbolic medium. No doubt communicating is always a certain way of acting upon another person or persons. But the production and circulation of elements of meaning can have as their objective or as their consequence certain results in the realm of power; the latter are not simply an aspect of the former. Whether or not they pass through systems of communication, power relations have a specific nature. Power relations, relationships of communication, objective capacities should not therefore be confused. This is not to say that there is a question of three separate domains. Nor that there is on one hand the field of things, of perfected technique, work, and the transformation of the real; on the other that of signs, communication, reciprocity, and the production of meaning; finally that of the domination of the means of constraint, of inequality and the action of men upon other men.[1] It is a question of three types of relationships which in fact always overlap one another, support one another reciprocally, and use each other mutually as means to an end. The application of objective capacities in their most elementary forms implies relationships of communication (whether in the form of previously acquired information or of shared work); it is tied also to power relations (whether they consist of obligatory tasks, of gestures imposed by tradition or apprenticeship, of subdivisions and the more or less obligatory distribution of labor). Relationships of communication imply finalized activities (even if only the correct putting into operation of elements of meaning) and, by virtue of the modifying the field of information between partners, produce effects of power. They can scarcely be dissociated from activities brought to their final term, be they those which permit the exercise of this power (such as training techniques, processes of domination, the means by which obedience is obtained) or those which in order to develop their potential call upon relations of power (the division of labor and the hierarchy of tasks).

Of course the coordination between these three types of relationships is neither uniform nor constant. In a given society there is no general type of equilibrium between finalized activities, systems of communication, and power relations. Rather there are diverse forms, diverse places, diverse circumstances or occasions in which these interrelationships establish themselves according to a specific model. But there are also "blocks" in which the adjustment of abilities, the resources of communication, and power relations constitute regulated and concerted systems. Take for example an educational institution: the disposal of its space, the meticulous regulations which govern its internal life, the different activities which are organized there, the diverse persons who live there or meet one another, each with his own function, his well-defined character—all these things constitute a block of capacity-communication-power. The activity which ensures apprenticeship and the acquisition of aptitudes or types of behavior is developed there by means of a whole ensemble of regulated communications (lessons, questions and answers, orders, exhortations, coded signs of obedience, differentiation marks of the "value" of each person and of the levels of knowledge) and

1. When Habermas distinguishes between domination, communication, and finalized activity, I do not think that he sees in them three separate domains, but rather three "transcendentals."

by the means of a whole series of power processes (enclosure, surveillance, reward and punishment, the pyramidal hierarchy).

These blocks, in which the putting into operation of technical capacities, the game of communications, and the relationships of power are adjusted to one another according to considered formulae, constitute what one might call, enlarging a little the sense of the word, disciplines. The empirical analysis of certain disciplines as they have been historically constituted presents for this very reason a certain interest. This is so because the disciplines show, first, according to artificially clear and decanted systems, the manner in which systems of objective finality and systems of communication and power can be welded together. They also display different models of articulation, sometimes giving preeminence to power relations and obedience (as in those disciplines of a monastic or penitential type), sometimes to finalize activities (as in the disciplines of workshops or hospitals), sometimes to relationships of communication (as in the disciplines of apprenticeship), sometimes also to a saturation of the three types of relationship (as perhaps in military discipline, where a plethora of signs indicates, to the point of redundancy, tightly knit power relations calculated with care to produce a certain number of technical effects).

What is to be understood by the disciplining of societies in Europe since the eighteenth century is not, of course, that the individuals who are part of them become more and more obedient, nor that they set about assembling in barracks, schools, or prisons; rather that an increasingly better invigilated process of adjustment has been sought after—more and more rational and economic—between productive activities, resources of communication, and the play of power relations.

To approach the theme of power by an analysis of "how" is therefore to introduce several critical shifts in relation to the supposition of a fundamental power. It is to give oneself as the object of analysis power relations and not power itself—power relations which are distinct from objective abilities as well as from relations of communication. This is as much as saying that power relations can be grasped in the diversity of their logical sequence, their abilities, and their interrelationships.

What constitutes the specific nature of power?

The exercise of power is not simply a relationship between partners, individual or collective; it is a way in which certain actions modify others. Which is to say, of course, that something called Power, with or without a capital letter, which is assumed to exist universally in a concentrated or diffused form, does not exist. Power exists only when it is put into action, even if, of course, it is integrated into a disparate field of possibilities brought to bear upon permanent structures. This also means that power is

219

not a function of consent. In itself it is not a renunciation of freedom, a transference of rights, the power of each and all delegated to a few (which does not prevent the possibility that consent may be a condition for the existence or the maintenance of power); the relationship of power can be the result of a prior or permanent consent, but it is not by nature the manifestation of a consensus.

Is this to say that one must seek the character proper to power relations in the violence which must have been its primitive form, its permanent secret and its last resource, that which in the final analysis appears as its real nature when it is forced to throw aside its mask and to show itself as it really is? In effect, what defines a relationship of power is that it is a mode of action which does not act directly and immediately on others. Instead it acts upon their actions: an action upon an action, on existing actions or on those which may arise in the present or the future. A relationship of violence acts upon a body or upon things; it forces, it bends, it breaks on the wheel, it destroys, or it closes the door on all possibilities. Its opposite pole can only be passivity, and if it comes up against any resistance it has no other option but to try to minimize it. On the other hand a power relationship can only be articulated on the basis of two elements which are each indispensable if it is really to be a power relationship: that "the other" (the one over whom power is exercised) be thoroughly recognized and maintained to the very end as a person who acts; and that, faced with a relationship of power, a whole field of responses, reactions, results, and possible inventions may open up.

Obviously the bringing into play of power relations does not exclude the use of violence any more than it does the obtaining of consent; no doubt the exercise of power can never do without one or the other, often both at the same time. But even though consensus and violence are the instruments or the results, they do not constitute the principle or the basic nature of power. The exercise of power can produce as much acceptance as may be wished for: it can pile up the dead and shelter itself behind whatever threats it can imagine. In itself the exercise of power is not violence; nor is it a consent which, implicitly, is renewable. It is a total structure of actions brought to bear upon possible actions; it incites, it induces, it seduces, it makes easier or more difficult; in the extreme it constrains or forbids absolutely; it is nevertheless always a way of acting upon an acting subject or acting subjects by virtue of their acting or being capable of action. A set of actions upon other actions.

Perhaps the equivocal nature of the term *conduct* is one of the best aids for coming to terms with the specificity of power relations. For to "conduct" is at the same time to "lead" others (according to mechanisms of coercion which are, to varying degrees, strict) and a way of behaving within a more or less open field of possibilities.[2] The exercise of power consists in guiding the possibility of conduct and putting in order the possible outcome. Basically power is less a confrontation between two adversaries or the linking of one to the other than a question of government. This word must be allowed the very broad meaning which it had in the sixteenth century. "Government" did not refer only to political structures or to the management of states; rather it designated the way in which the conduct of individuals or of groups might be directed: the government of children, of souls, of communities, of families, of the sick. It did not only cover the legitimately constituted forms of political or economic subjection, but also modes of action, more or less considered and calculated, which were destined to act upon the possibilities of action of other people. To govern, in this sense, is to structure the possible field of action of others. The relationship proper to power would not therefore be sought on the side of violence or of struggle, nor on that of voluntary linking (all of which can, at best, only be the instruments of power), but rather in the area of the singular mode of action, neither warlike nor juridical, which is government.

When one defines the exercise of power as a mode of action upon the actions of others, when one characterizes these actions by the government of men by other men—in the broadest sense of the term—one includes an important element: freedom. Power is exercised only over free subjects, and only insofar as they are free. By this we mean individual or collective subjects who are faced with a field of possibilities in which several ways of behaving, several reactions and diverse comportments may be realized. Where the determining factors saturate the whole there is no relationship of power; slavery is not a power relationship when man is in chains. (In this case it is a question of a physical relationship of constraint.) Consequently there is no face to face confrontation of power and freedom which is mutually exclusive (freedom disappears everywhere power is exercised), but a much more complicated interplay. In this game freedom may well appear as the condition for the exercise of power (at the same time its precondition, since freedom must exist for power to be exerted, and also its permanent support, since without the possibility of recalcitrance, power would be equivalent to a physical determination).

The relationship between power and freedom's refusal to submit cannot therefore be separated. The crucial problem of power is not that of voluntary servitude (how could we seek to be slaves?). At the very heart of the power relationship, and constantly provoking it, are the re-

---

2. Foucault is playing on the double meaning in French of the verb *conduire*—to lead or to drive, and *se conduire*—to behave or conduct oneself, whence *la conduite,* conduct or behavior. (Translator's note)

calcitrance of the will and the intransigence of freedom. Rather than speaking of an essential freedom, it would be better to speak of an "agonism"[3]—of a relationship which is at the same time reciprocal incitation and struggle; less of a face-to-face confrontation which paralyzes both sides than a permanent provocation.

How is one to analyze the power relationship?

One can analyze such relationships, or rather I should say that it is perfectly legitimate to do so, by focusing on carefully defined institutions. The latter constitute a privileged point of observation, diversified, concentrated, put in order, and carried through to the highest point of their efficacity. It is here that, as a first approximation, one might expect to see the appearance of the form and logic of their elementary mechanisms. However, the analysis of power relations as one finds them in certain circumscribed institutions presents a certain number of problems. First, the fact that an important part of the mechanisms put into operation by an institution are designed to ensure its own preservation brings with it the risk of deciphering functions which are essentially reproductive, especially in power relations between institutions. Second, in analyzing power relations from the standpoint of institutions one lays oneself open to seeking the explanation and the origin of the former in the latter, that is to say finally, to explain power to power. Finally, insofar as institutions act essentially by bringing into play two elements, explicit or tacit regulations and an apparatus, one risks giving to one or the other an exaggerated privilege in the relations of power and hence to see in the latter only modulations of the law and of coercion.

This does not deny the importance of institutions on the establishment of power relations. Instead I wish to suggest that one must analyze institutions from the standpoint of power relations, rather than vice versa, and that the fundamental point of anchorage of the relationships, even if they are embodied and crystallized in an institution, is to be found outside the institution.

Let us come back to the definition of the exercise of power as a way in which certain actions may structure the field of other possible actions. What therefore would be proper to a relationship of power is that it be a mode of action upon actions. That is to say, power relations are rooted deep in the social nexus, not reconstituted "above" society as a supplementary structure whose radical effacement one could perhaps dream of. In any case, to live in society is to live in such a way that action upon other actions is possible—and in fact ongoing. A society without power

3. Foucault's neologism is based on the Greek ἀγώνισμα meaning "a combat." The term would hence imply a physical contest in which the opponents develop a strategy of reaction and of mutual taunting, as in a wrestling match. (Translator's note)

relations can only be an abstraction. Which, be it said in passing, makes all the more politically necessary the analysis of power relations in a given society, their historical formation, the source of their strength or fragility, the conditions which are necessary to transform some or to abolish others. For to say that there cannot be a society without power relations is not to say either that those which are established are necessary, or, in any case, that power constitutes a fatality at the heart of societies, such that it cannot be undermined. Instead I would say that the analysis, elaboration, and bringing into question of power relations and the "agonism" between power relations and the intransitivity of freedom is a permanent political task inherent in all social existence.

Concretely the analysis of power relations demands that a certain number of points be established:

1) *The system of differentiations* which permits one to act upon the actions of others: differentiations determined by the law or by traditions of status and privilege; economic differences in the appropriation of riches and goods, shifts in the processes of production, linguistic or cultural differences, differences in know-how and competence, and so forth. Every relationship of power puts into operation differentiations which are at the same time its conditions and its results.

2) *The types of objectives* pursued by those who act upon the actions of others: the maintenance of privileges, the accumulation of profits, the bringing into operation of statutory authority, the exercise of a function or of a trade.

3) *The means of bringing power relations into being:* according to whether power is exercised by the threat of arms, by the effects of the word, by means of economic disparities, by more or less complex means of control, by systems of surveillance, with or without archives, according to rules which are or are not explicit, fixed or modifiable, with or without the technological means to put all these things into action.

4) *Forms of institutionalization:* these may mix traditional pre-dispositions, legal structures, phenomena relating to custom or to fashion (such as one sees in the institution of the family); they can also take the form of an apparatus closed in upon itself, with its specific *loci*, its own regulations, its hierarchical structures which are carefully defined, a relative autonomy in its functioning (such as scholastic or military institutions); they can also form very complex systems endowed with multiple apparatuses, as in the case of the state, whose function is the taking of everything under its wing, the bringing into being of general surveillance, the principle of regulation and, to a certain extent also, the distribution of all power relations in a given social ensemble.

5) *The degrees of rationalization:* the bringing into play of power relations as action in a field of possibilities may be more or less elaborate

in relation to the effectiveness of the instruments and the certainty of the results (greater or lesser technological refinements employed in the exercise of power) or again in proportion to the possible cost (be it the economic cost of the means brought into operation, or the cost in terms of reaction constituted by the resistance which is encountered). The exercise of power is not a naked fact, an institutional right, nor is it a structure which holds out or is smashed: it is elaborated, transformed, organized; it endows itself with processes which are more or less adjusted to the situation.

One sees why the analysis of power relations within a society cannot be reduced to the study of a series of institutions, not even to the study of all those institutions which would merit the name "political." Power relations are rooted in the system of social networks. This is not to say, however, that there is a primary and fundamental principle of power which dominates society down to the smallest detail; but, taking as point of departure the possibility of action upon the action of others (which is coextensive with every social relationship), multiple forms of individual disparity, of objectives, of the given application of power over ourselves or others, of, in varying degrees, partial or universal institutionalization, of more or less deliberate organization, one can define different forms of power. The forms and the specific situations of the government of men by one another in a given society are multiple; they are superimposed, they cross, impose their own limits, sometimes cancel one another out, sometimes reinforce one another. It is certain that in contemporary societies the state is not simply one of the forms or specific situations of the exercise of power—even if it is the most important—but that in a certain way all other forms of power relation must refer to it. But this is not because they are derived from it; it is rather because power relations have come more and more under state control (although this state control has not taken the same form in pedagogical, judicial, economic, or family systems). In referring here to the restricted sense of the word *government*, one could say that power relations have been progressively governmentalized, that is to say, elaborated, rationalized, and centralized in the form of, or under the auspices of, state institutions.

Relations of power and relations of strategy

The word *strategy* is currently employed in three ways. First, to designate the means employed to attain a certain end; it is a question of rationality functioning to arrive at an objective. Second, to designate the manner in which a partner in a certain game acts with regard to what he thinks should be the action of the others and what he considers the others think to be his own; it is the way in which one seeks to have the advantage over others. Third, to designate the procedures used in a situation of confrontation to deprive the opponent of his means of combat and to reduce him to giving up the struggle; it is a question therefore of the means destined to obtain victory. These three meanings come together in situations of confrontation—war or games—where the objective is to act upon an adversary in such a manner as to render the struggle impossible for him. So strategy is defined by the choice of winning solutions. But it must be borne in mind that this is a very special type of situation and that there are others in which the distinctions between the different senses of the word *strategy* must be maintained.

Referring to the first sense I have indicated, one may call power strategy the totality of the means put into operation to implement power effectively or to maintain it. One may also speak of a strategy proper to power relations insofar as they constitute modes of action upon possible action, the action of others. One can therefore interpret the mechanisms brought into play in power relations in terms of strategies. But most important is obviously the relationship between power relations and confrontation strategies. For, if it is true that at the heart of power relations and as a permanent condition of their existence there is an insubordination and a certain essential obstinacy on the part of the principles of freedom, then there is no relationship of power without the means of escape or possible flight. Every power relationship implies, at least *in potentia*, a strategy of struggle, in which the two forces are not superimposed, do not lose their specific nature, or do not finally become confused. Each constitutes for the other a kind of permanent limit, a point of possible reversal. A relationship of confrontation reaches its term, its final moment (and the victory of one of the two adversaries) when stable mechanisms replace the free play of antagonistic reactions. Through such mechanisms one can direct, in a fairly constant manner and with reasonable certainty, the conduct of others. For a relationship of confrontation, from the moment it is not a struggle to the death, the fixing of a power relationship becomes a target—at one and the same time its fulfillment and its suspension. And in return the strategy of struggle also constitutes a frontier for the relationship of power, the line at which, instead of manipulating and inducing actions in a calculated manner, one must be content with reacting to them after the event. It would not be possible for power relations to exist without points of insubordination which, by definition, are means of escape. Accordingly, every intensification, every extension of power relations to make the insubordinate submit can only result in the limits of power. The latter reaches its final term either in a type of action which reduces the other to total impotence (in which case victory over the adversary replaces the exercise of power) or by a confrontation with those whom one governs and their transformation into adversaries. Which is to say that every strategy of confrontation dreams of becoming a relationship of power and every relationship of power leans toward the idea that, if it follows its own line of development and comes up against direct confrontation, it may become the winning strategy.

In effect, between a relationship of power and a strategy of struggle there is a reciprocal appeal, a perpetual linking and a perpetual reversal. At every moment the relationship of power may become a confrontation between two adversaries. Equally, the relationship between adversaries in society may, at every moment, give place to the putting into operation of mechanisms of power. The consequence of this instability is the ability to decipher the same events and the same transformations either from inside the history of struggle or from the standpoint of the power relationships. The interpretations which result will not consist of the same elements of meaning or the same links or the same types of intelligibility, although they refer to the same historical fabric and each of the two analyses must have reference to the other. In fact it is precisely the disparities between the two readings which make visible those fundamental phenomena of "domination" which are present in a large number of human societies.

Domination is in fact a general structure of power whose ramifications and consequences can sometimes be found descending to the most incalcitrant fibers of society. But at the same time it is a strategic situation more or less taken for granted and consolidated by means of a long-term confrontation between adversaries. It can certainly happen that the fact of domination may only be the transcription of a mechanism of power resulting from confrontation and its consequences (a political structure stemming from invasion); it may also be that a relationship of struggle between two adversaries is the result of power relations with the conflicts and cleavages which ensue. But what makes the domination of a group, a caste, or a class, together with the resistance and revolts which that domination comes up against, a central phenomenon in the history of societies is that they manifest in a massive and universalizing form, at the level of the whole social body, the locking together of power relations with relations of strategy and the results proceeding from their interaction.

Afterword (1983)

On the Genealogy of Ethics:
An Overview of Work in Progress

The following is the result of a series of working sessions with Michel Foucault conducted at Berkeley in April 1983. Although we have retained the interview form, the material has been jointly re-edited. We should emphasize that Foucault has generously allowed us to publish these preliminary formulations, which are the product of oral interviews and free conversations in English and therefore lack the precision and supporting scholarship found in Foucault's written texts.

History of the Project

Q: The first volume of *The History of Sexuality* was published in 1976, and none have appeared since. Do you still think that understanding sexuality is central for understanding who we are?

A: I must confess that I am much more interested in problems about techniques of the self and things like that rather than sex . . . sex is boring.

Q: It sounds like the Greeks were not too interested either.

A: No, they were not much interested in sex. It was not a great issue. Compare, for instance, what they say about the place of food and diet. I think it is very, very interesting to see the move, the very slow move, from the privileging of food which was overwhelming in Greece, to interest in sex. Food was still much more important during the early Christian days than sex. For instance, in the rules for monks, the problem was food, food, food. Then you can see a very slow shift during the Middle Ages when they were in a kind of equilibrium . . . and after the seventeenth century it was sex.

Q: Yet, volume 2 of *The History of Sexuality, L'Usage des plaisirs* is concerned almost exclusively with, not to put too fine a point on it, sex.

229

A: Yes. One of the numerous reasons I had so much trouble with that book was that I first wrote a book about sex, which I put aside. Then I wrote a book about the self and the techniques of the self, sex disappeared, and for the third time I was obliged to rewrite a book in which I tried to keep the equilibrium between one and the other.

You see, what I wanted to do in volume 2 of *The History of Sexuality* was to show that you have nearly the same restrictive, the same prohibition code in the fourth century B.C. and in the moralists and doctors at the beginning of the empire. But I think that the way they integrate those prohibitions in relation to oneself is completely different. I don't think one can find any normalization in, for instance, the Stoic ethics. The reason is, I think, that the principal aim, the principal target of this kind of ethics was an aesthetic one. First, this kind of ethics was only a problem of personal choice. Second, it was reserved for a few people in the population; it was not a question of giving a pattern of behavior for everybody. It was a personal choice for a small elite. The reason for making this choice was the will to live a beautiful life, and to leave to others memories of a beautiful existence. I don't think that we can say that this kind of ethics was an attempt to normalize the population.

The continuity of the themes of this ethics is something very striking, but I think that behind, below this continuity there were some changes, which I have tried to acknowledge.

Q: So, the equilibrium in your work has shifted from sex to techniques of the self?

A: I wondered what the technology of the self before Christianity was, or where the Christian technology of the self came from, and what kind of sexual ethics was characteristic of the ancient culture. And then I was obliged after I finished *Les Aveux de la chair,* the book about Christianity, to re-examine what I said in the introduction of *L'Usage des plaisirs* about the supposed pagan ethics, because what I had said about pagan ethics was only clichés borrowed from secondary texts. And then I discovered, first, that this pagan ethics was not at all as liberal, tolerant, and so on, as it was supposed to be; second, that most of the themes of Christian austerity were very clearly present nearly from the beginning, but that also in pagan culture the main problem was not the rules for austerity but much more the techniques of the self.

Reading Seneca, Plutarch, and all those people, I discovered that there were a very great number of problems about the self, the ethics of the self, the technology of the self, and I had the idea of writing a book composed of a set of separate studies, papers about such and such aspects of ancient, pagan technology of the self.

Q: What is the title?

A: *Le Souci de soi.* So, in the series about sexuality: the first one is *L'Usage des plaisirs,* and in this book there is a chapter about the technology of the self, since I think it's not possible to understand clearly what Greek sexual ethics was without relating it to this technology of the self. Then, a second volume in the same sex series, *Les Aveux de la chair,* deals with Christain technologies of the self. And, then, *Le Souci de soi,* a book separate from the sex series, is composed of different papers about the self—for instance, a commemtary on Plato's *Alcibiades* in which you find the first elaboration of the notion of *epimeleia heautou,* "care of the self," about the role of reading and writing in constituting the self, maybe the problem of the medical experience of the self, and so on . . .

Q: And what will come next? Will there be more on the Christians when you finish these three?

A: Well, I am going to take care of myself! . . . I have more than a draft of a book about sexual ethics in the sixteenth century, in which also the problem of the techniques of the self, self-examination, the cure of souls is very important, both in the Protestant and Catholic churches.

What strikes me is that in Greek ethics people were concerned with their moral conduct, their ethics, their relations to themselves and to others much more than with religious problems. For instance, what happens to us after death? What are the gods? Do they intervene or not?—these are very, very unimportant problems for them, and they are not directly related to ethics, to conduct. The second thing is that ethics was not related to any social—or at least to any legal—institutional system. For instance, the laws against sexual misbehavior were very few and not very compeling. The third thing is that what they were worried about, their theme, was to constitute a kind of ethics which was an aesthetics of existence.

Well, I wonder if our problem nowadays is not, in a way, similar to this one, since most of us no longer believe that ethics is founded in religion, nor do we want a legal system to intervene in our moral, personal, private life. Recent liberation movements suffer from the fact that they cannot find any principle on which to base the elaboration of a new ethics. They need an ethics, but they cannot find any other ethics than an ethics founded on so-called scientific knowledge of what the self is, what desire is, what the unconscious is, and so on. I am struck by this similarity of problems.

Q: Do you think that the Greeks offer an attractive and plausible alternative?

A: No! I am not looking for an alternative; you can't find the solution of a problem in the solution of another problem raised at another moment by other people. You see, what I want to do is not the history of solutions, and that's the reason why I don't accept the word "alternative." I would like to do genealogy of problems, of *problématiques.* My point is not that everything is bad, but that everything is dangerous, which is not exactly the same as bad. If everything is dangerous, then we always have something to do. So my position leads not to apathy but to a hyper- and pessimistic activism.

I think that the ethico-political choice we have to make every day is to determine which is the main danger. Take as an example Robert Castel's analysis of the history of the antipsychiatry movement *(La Gestion des risques)*. I agree completely with what Castel says, but that does not mean, as some people suppose, that the mental hospitals were better than antipsychiatry; that does not mean that we were not right to criticize those mental hospitals. I think it was good to do that, because *they* were the danger. And now it's quite clear that the danger has changed. For instances, in Italy they have closed all the mental hospitals, and there are more free clinics, and so on—and they have new problems.

Q: Isn't it logical, given these concerns, that you should be writing a genealogy of bio-power?

A: I have no time for that now, but it could be done. In fact, I have to do it.

Why the Ancient World Was Not a Golden Age, but What We Can Learn from It Anyway

Q: So, Greek life may not have been altogether perfect; still it seems an attractive alternative to endless Christian self-analysis.

A: The Greek ethics was linked to a purely virile society with slaves, in which the women were underdogs whose pleasure had no importance, whose sexual life had to be only oriented toward, determined by their status as wives, and so on.

Q: So, the women were dominated, but surely homosexual love was better than now.

A: It might look that way. Since there is an important and large literature about loving boys in Greek culture, some historians say, "Well, that's the proof that they loved boys." But I say that proves that loving boys was a problem. Because if there were no problem, they would speak of this kind of love in the same terms as love between men and women. The problem was that they couldn't accept that a young boy who was supposed to become a free citizen could be dominated and used as an object for someone's pleasure. A woman, a slave, could be passive: such was their nature, their status. All this reflection, philosophizing about the love of boys—with always the same conclusion: please, don't treat a boy as a woman—is proof that they could not integrate this real practice in the framework of their social selves.

You can see through a reading of Plutarch how they couldn't even imagine reciprocity of pleasure between a boy and a man. If Plutarch finds problems in loving boys, it is not at all in the sense that loving boys was antinatural or

232

something like that. He says "It's not possible that there could be any reciprocity in the physical relations between a boy and a man."

Q: There seems to be an aspect of Greek culture, that we are told about in Aristotle, that you don't talk about, but that seems very important—friendship. In classical literature, friendship is the locus of mutual recognition. It's not traditionally seen as the highest virtue, but both in Aristotle and in Cicero, you could read it as really being the highest virtue because it's selfless and enduring, it's not easily bought, it doesn't deny the utility and pleasure of the world, but yet it seeks something more.

A: But don't forget *L'Usage des plaisirs* is a book about sexual ethics, it's not a book about love, or about friendship, or about reciprocity. And it's very significant that when Plato tries to integrate love for boys and friendship, he is obliged to put aside sexual relations. Friendship is reciprocal, and sexual relations are not reciprocal: in sexual relations, you can penetrate or you are penetrated. I agree completely with what you say about friendship, but I think it confirms what I say about Greek sexual ethics: if you have friendship, it is difficult to have sexual relations. If you look at Plato, reciprocity is very important in a friendship, but you can't find it on the physical level; one of the reasons why they needed a philosophical elaboration in order to justify this kind of love was that they could not accept a physical reciprocity. You find in Xenophon, in the *Banquet,* Socrates saying that between a man and a boy it is obvious that the boy is only the spectator of the man's pleasure. What they say about this beautiful love of boys implies that the pleasure of the boy was not to be taken into account, moreover, that it was dishonorable for the boy to feel any kind of physical pleasure in a relation with a man.

What I want to ask is, Are we able to have an ethics of acts and their pleasures which would be able to take into account the pleasure of the other? Is the pleasure of the other something which can be integrated in our pleasure, without reference either to law, to marriage, to I don't know what?

Q: It looks like nonreciprocity was a problem for the Greeks all right, but it seems to be the kind of problem that one could straighten out. Why does sex have to be virile? Why couldn't women's pleasure and boy's pleasure be taken account of without any big change to the general framework? Or is it that it's not just a little problem, because if you try to bring in the pleasure of the other the whole hierarchical, ethical system would break down?

A: That's right. The Greek ethics of pleasure is linked to a virile society, to dissymmetry, exclusion of the other, an obsession with penetration, and a kind of threat of being dispossessed of your own energy, and so on. All that is quite disgusting!

Q: OK, granted that sexual relations were both nonreciprocal and a cause of worry for the Greeks, at least pleasure itself seems unproblematic for them.

A: Well, in *L'Usage des plaisirs* I try to show, for instance, that there is a growing tension between pleasure and health. When you take the physicians and all the concern with diet, you see first that the main themes are very similar during several centuries. But the idea that sex has its dangers is much stronger in the second century A.D. than in the fourth century B.C. I think that you can show that for Hippocrates the sexual act was already dangerous, so you had to be very careful with it and not have sex all the time, only in certain seasons and so on. But in the first and second centuries it seems that, for a physician, the sexual act is much closer to *pathos*. And I think the main shift is this one: that in the fourth century B.C., the sexual act was an activity, and for the Christians it is a passivity. You have a very interesting analysis by Augustine which is, I think, quite typical concerning the problem of erection. The erection was for the Greek of the fourth century the sign of activity, the main activity. But since for Augustine and the Christians the erection is not something which is voluntary, it is a sign of a passivity—it is a punishment for the first sin.

Q: So, the Greeks were more concerned with health than with pleasure?

A: Yes, about what the Greeks had to eat in order to be in good health we have thousands of pages. And there are comparatively few things about what to do when you have sex with someone. Concerning food, it was the relation between the climate, the seasons, the humidity or dryness of the air and the dryness of the food, and so on. There are very few things about the way they had to cook it, much more about these qualities. It's not a cooking art; it's a matter of choosing.

Q: So, despite the German Hellenists, classical Greece was not a Golden Age. Yet, surely we can learn something from it?

A: I think there is no exemplary value in a period which is not our period . . . it is not anything to get back to. But we do have an example of an ethical experience which implied a very strong connection between pleasure and desire. If we compare that to our experience now, where everybody—the philosopher or the psychoanalyst—explains that what is important is desire, and pleasure is nothing at all, we can wonder whether this disconnection wasn't an historical event, one which was not at all necessary, not linked to human nature, or to any anthropological necessity.

Q: But you already illustrated that in *The History of Sexuality* by contrasting our science of sexuality with the oriental *ars erotica*.

A: One of the numerous points where I was wrong in that book was what I said about this *ars erotica*. I should have opposed our science of sex to a contrasting practice in our own culture. The Greeks and Romans did not have any *ars erotica* to be compared with the Chinese *ars erotica* (or at least it was not something very important in their culture). They had a *techne tou biou* in which the economy of pleasure played a very large role. In this "art of life" the notion of exercising a perfect mastery over oneself soon became the main issue. And the Christian hermeneutics of the self constituted a new elaboration of this *techne*.

Q: But, after all you have told us about nonreciprocity and obsession with health, what can we learn from this third possibility?

A: What I want to show is that the general Greek problem was not the *techne* of the self, it was the *techne* of life, the *techne tou biou*, how to live. It's quite clear from Socrates to Seneca or Pliny, for instance, that they didn't worry about the afterlife, what happened after death, or whether God exists or not. That was not really a great problem for them; the problem was which *techne* do I have to use in order to live as well as I ought to live. And I think that one of the main evolutions in ancient culture has been that this *techne tou biou* became more and more a *techne* of the self. A Greek citizen of the fifth or fourth century would have felt that his *techne* for life was to take care of the city, of his companions. But for Seneca, for instance, the problem is to take care of himself.

With Plato's *Alcibiades*, it's very clear: you have to take care of yourself because you have to rule the city. But taking care of yourself for its own sake starts with the Epicureans—it becomes something very general with Seneca, Pliny, and so on: everybody has to take care of himself. Greek ethics is centered on a problem of personal choice, of aesthetics of existence.

The idea of the *bios* as a material for an aesthetic piece of art is something which fascinates me. The idea also that ethics can be a very strong structure of existence, without any relation with the juridical per se, with an authoritarian system, with a disciplinary structure. All that is very interesting.

Q: How then did the Greeks deal with deviance?

A: The great difference in sexual ethics for the Greeks was not between people who prefer women or boys or have sex in this way or another, but was a question of quantity and of activity and passivity. Are you a slave of your own desires or their master?

Q: What about someone who had sex so much he damaged his health?

A: That's hubris, that's excess. The problem is not one of deviancy but of excess or moderation.

Q: What did they do with these people?

A: They were considered ugly, they had a bad reputation.

Q: They didn't try to cure or reform such people?

A: There were exercises in order to make one master of oneself. For Epictetus you had to be able to look at a beautiful girl or a beautiful boy without having any desire for her or him. You have to become completely master of yourself.

Sexual austerity in Greek society was a trend or movement, a philo-sophical movement coming from very cultivated people in order to give to their life much more intensity, much more beauty. In a way it's the same in the twentieth century when people, in order to get a more beautiful life, tried to get rid of all the sexual repression of their society, of their childhood. Gide in Greece would have been an austere philosopher.

Q: In the name of a beautiful life they were austere, and now in the name of psychological science we seek self-fulfillment.

A: Exactly. My idea is that it's not at all necessary to relate ethical problems to scientific knowledge. Among the cultural inventions of mankind there is a treasury of devices, techniques, ideas, procedures, and so on, that cannot exactly be reactivated, but at least constitute, or help to constitute, a certain point of view which can be very useful as a tool for analyzing what's going on now—and to change it.

We don't have to choose between our world and the Greek world. But since we can see very well that some of the main principles of our ethics have been related at a certain moment to an aesthetics of existence, I think that this kind of historical analysis can be useful. For centuries we have been convinced that between our ethics, our personal ethics, our everyday life and the great political and social and economic structures there were analytical relations, and that we couldn't change anything, for instance, in our sex life or our family life, without ruining our economy, our democracy, and so on. I think we have to get rid of this idea of an analytical or necessary link between ethics and other social or economic or political structures.

Q: So, what kind of ethics can we build now, when we know that between ethics and other structures there are only historical coagulations and not a necessary relation?

A: What strikes me is the fact that in our society, art has become something which is related only to objects and not to individuals, or to life. That art is something which is specialized or which is done by experts who are artists. But couldn't everyone's life become a work of art? Why should the lamp or the house be an art object, but not our life?

Q: Of course, that kind of project is very common in places like Berkeley where people think that everything from the way they eat breakfast, to the way they have sex, to the way they spend their day, should itself be perfected.

A: But I am afraid in most of those cases, most of the people think if they do what they do, if they live as they live, the reason is that they know the truth about desire, life, nature, body, and so on.

Q: But if one is to create oneself without recourse to knowledge or universal rules, how does your view differ from Sartrian existentialism?

A: I think that from the theoretical point of view, Sartre avoids the idea of the self as something which is given to us, but through the moral notion of authenticity, he turns back to the idea that we have to be ourselves—to be truly our true self. I think that the only acceptable practical consequence of what Sartre has said is to link his theoretical insight to the practice of creativity—and not of authenticity. From the idea that the self is not given to us, I think that there is only one practical consequence: we have to create ourselves as a work of art. In his analyses of Baudelaire, Flaubert, etc., it is interesting to see that Sartre refers the work of creation to a certain relation to oneself—the author to himself—which has the form of authenticity or of inauthenticity. I would like to say exactly the contrary: we should not have to refer the creative activity of somebody to the kind of relation he has to himself, but should relate the kind of relation one has to oneself to a creative activity.

Q: That sounds like Nietzsche's observation in *The Gay Science* [no. 290] that one should create one's life by giving style to it through long practice and daily work.

A: Yes. My view is much closer to Nietzsche's than to Sartre's.

The Structure of Genealogical Interpretation

Q: How do the next two books after *The History of Sexuality* volume 1, *L'Usage des plaisirs* and *Les Aveux de la chair,* fit into the structure of your genealogy project?

A: Three domains of genealogy are possible. First, an historical ontology of ourselves in relation to truth through which we constitute ourselves as subjects of knowledge; second, an historical ontology of ourselves in relation to a field of power through which we constitute ourselves as subjects acting on others; thirds, an historical ontology in relation to ethics through which we constitute ourselves as moral agents.

So, three axes are possible for genealogy. All three were present, albeit in a somewhat confused fashion, in *Madness and Civilization*. The truth axis was studied in *The Birth of the Clinic* and *The Order of Things*. The power axis was studied in *Discipline and Punish*, and the ethical axis in *The History of Sexuality*.

The general framework of the book about sex is a history of morals. I think, in general, we have to distinguish, where the history of morals is concerned, acts and moral code. The acts *(conduites)* are the real behavior of people in relation to the moral code *(prescriptions)* which are imposed on them. I think we have to distinguish between the code which determines which acts are permitted or forbidden and the code which determines the positive or negative value of the different possible behaviors—you're not allowed to have sex with anyone but your wife, that's an element of the code. And there is another side to the moral prescriptions, which most of the time is not isolated as such but is, I think, very important: the kind of relationship you ought to have with yourself, *rapport à soi*, which I call ethics, and which determines how the individual is supposed to constitute himself as a moral subject of his own actions.

This relationship to oneself has four major aspects: The first aspect answers the question, Which is the aspect or the part of myself or my behavior which is concerned with moral conduct? For instance, you can say, in general, that in our society the main field of morality, the part of ourselves which is most relevant for morality, is our feelings. (You can have a girl in the street or anywhere, if you have very good feelings toward your wife.) Well, it's quite clear that from the Kantian point of view, intention is much more important than feelings. And from the Christian point of view it is desire—well, we could discuss that, because in the Middle Ages it was not the same as the seventeenth century . . .

Q: But, roughly, for the Christians it was desire, for Kant it was intentions, and for us now it's feelings?

A: Well, you can say something like that. It's not always the same part of ourselves, or of our behavior, which is relevant for ethical judgment. That's the aspect I call the ethical substance *(substance éthique).*

Q: The ethical substance is like the material that's going to be worked over by ethics?

A: Yes, that's it. And, for instance, when I describe the *aphrodisia* in *L'Usage des plaisirs,* it is to show that the part of sexual behavior which is relevant in Greek ethics is something different from concupiscence, from flesh. For the Greeks, the ethical substance was acts linked to pleasure and desire in their unity. And it is very different from flesh, Christian flesh. Sexuality is a third kind of ethical substance.

Q: What is the difference ethically between flesh and sexuality?

A: I cannot answer because all that can only be analyzed through a precise inquiry. Before I studied Greek or Greco-Roman ethics, I couldn't answer the question, What exactly is the ethical substance of Greco-Roman ethics? Now I think that I know, through the analysis of what they mean by *aphrodisia,* what the Greek ethical substance was.

For the Greeks, when a philosopher was in love with a boy, but did not touch him, his behavior was valued. The problem was, does he touch the boy or not. That's the ethical substance: the act linked with pleasure and desire. For Augustine it's very clear that when he remembers his relationship to his young friend when he was eighteen years old, what bothers him is what exactly was the kind of desire he had for him. So, you see that the ethical substance has changed.

238

The second aspect is what I call the mode of subjection *(mode d'assujettissement),* that is, the way in which people are invited or incited to recognize their moral obligations. Is it, for instance, divine law, which has been revealed in a text? Is it natural law, a cosmological order, in each case the same for every living being? Is it a rational rule? Is it the attempt to give your existence the most beautiful form possible?

Q: When you say "rational," do you mean scientific?

A: No, Kantian, universal. You can see, for instance, in the Stoics how they move slowly from an idea of an aesthetics of existence to the idea that we have to do such and such things because we are rational beings—as members of the human community we have to do them. For example, you find in Isocrates a very interesting discourse, which is supposed to be held with Nicocles, who was the ruler of Cyprus. There he explains why he has always been faithful to his wife: "Because I am the king, and because as somebody who commands others, who rules others, I have to show that I am able to rule myself." And you can see that this rule of faithfulness has nothing to do with the universal and Stoic formulation: I have to be faithful to my wife because I am a human and rational being. In the former case it is because I am the king! And you can see that the way the same rule is accepted by Nicocles and by a Stoic is quite different. And that's what I call the *mode d'assujettissement,* the second aspect of ethics.

Q: When the king says, "because I am the king," is that a form of the beautiful life?

A: Both aesthetic and political, which were directly linked. Because if I want people to accept me as a king, I must have a kind of glory which will survive me, and this glory cannot be dissociated from aesthetic value. So political power, glory, immortality and beauty are all linked at a certain moment. That's the *mode d'assujettissement,* the second aspect of ethics.

The third one is, What are the means by which we can change ourselves in order to become ethical subjects?

Q: How we work on this ethical substance?

A: Yes. What are we to do, either to moderate our acts, or to decipher what we are, or to eradicate our desires, or to use our sexual desire in order to obtain certain aims like having children, and so on—all this elaboration of ourselves in order to behave ethically. In order to be faithful to your wife you can do different things to the self. That's the third aspect, which I call the self-forming activity *(pratique de soi)* or *l'ascétisme*—asceticism in a very broad sense.

The fourth aspect is, Which is the kind of being to which we aspire when we behave in a moral way. For instance, shall we become pure, or immortal, or free, or masters of ourselves, and so on. So that's what I call the telos *(teleologie).* In what we call morals there is the effective behavior of people, there are the codes and there is this kind of relationship to oneself with the above four aspects.

Q: Which are all independent?

A: There are both relationships between them and a certain kind of independence. For instance, you can very well understand why, if the goal is an absolute purity of being, then the type of techniques of self-forming activity, the techniques of asceticism you are to use, is not exactly the same as when you try to be master of your own behavior. In the first place you are inclined to a kind of deciphering technique, or purification technique.

Now, if we apply this general framework to pagan or early Christian ethics, what would we say? First, if we take the code—what is forbidden and what is not—you see that, at least in the philosophic code of behavior, you find three main prohibitions or prescriptions: One about the body—that is, you have to be very careful with your sexual behavior since it is very costly, so do it as infrequently as possible. The second is, when you are married, please don't have sex with anybody else but your wife. And with boys—please don't touch boys. And you find this in Plato, in Isocrates, in Hippocrates, in late Stoics, and so on—and you find it also in Christianity, and even in our own society. So I think you can say that the codes in themselves didn't change a great deal. Some of those interdictions changes; some of the prohibitions are much stricter and much more rigorous in Christianity than in the Greek period. But the themes are the same. So I think that the great changes which occurred between Greek society, Greek ethics, Greek morality and how the Christians viewed themselves are not in the code, but are in what I call the ''ethics,'' which is the relation to oneself. In *L' Usage des plaisirs* I analyze those four aspects of the relation to oneself, through the three austerity themes of the code: health, wives or women, and boys.

Q: Would it be fair to say that you're not doing the genealogy of morals, because you think the moral codes are relatively stable, but what you're doing is a genealogy of ethics?

A: Yes, I'm writing a genealogy of ethics. The genealogy of the subject as a subject of ethical actions, or the genealogy of desire as an ethical problem. So, if we take ethics in classical Greek philosophy or medicine, what is the ethical substance? It is the *aphrodisia*, which are at the same time acts, desire, and pleasure. What is the *mode d'assujettissement?* It is that we have to build our existence as a beautiful existence; it is an aesthetic mode. You see, what I tried to show is that nobody is obliged in classical ethics to behave in such a way as to be truthful to their wives, to not touch boys, and so on. But, if they want to have a beautiful existence, if they want to have a good reputation, if they want to be able to rule others, they have to do that. So, they accept those obligations in a conscious way for the beauty or glory of existence. The choice, the aesthetic

240

choice or the political choice, for which they decide to accept this kind of existence—that's the *mode d'assujettissement*. It's a choice, it's a personal choice.

In late Stoicism, when they start saying "Well, you are obliged to do that because you are a human being" something changes. It's not a problem of choice; you have to do it because you are a rational being. The *mode d'assujettissement* is changing.

In Christianity what is very interesting is that the sexual rules for behavior were, of course, justified through religion. The institutions by which they were imposed were religious institutions. But the form of the obligation was a legal form. There was a kind of the internal juridification of religious law inside Christianity. For instance, all the casuistic practice was typically a juridical practice.

Q: After the Enlightenment, though, when the religious drops out, is the juridical what's left?

A: Yes, after the eighteenth century, the religious framework of those rules disappears in part, and then between a medical or scientific approach and a juridical framework there was competition, with no resolution.

Q: Could you sum this all up?

A: Well, the *substance éthique* for the Greeks was the *aphrodisia;* the *mode d'assujettissement* was a politicoaesthetical choice; the *form d'ascèse* was the *techne* which were used—and there we find, for example, the *techne* about the body, or economics as the rules by which you define your role as husband, or the erotic as a kind of asceticism toward oneself in loving boys, and so on—and the *teleologie* was the mastery of oneself. So, that's the situation I describe in the two first parts of *L'Usage des plaisirs*.

Then there is a shift within this ethics. The reason for the shift is the change of the role of men within society, both in their homes toward their wives and also in the political field, since the city disappears. So, for those reasons, the way they can recognize themselves as subjects of political, economic behavior changes. We can say roughly that along with these sociological changes something is changing also in classical ethics—that is, in the elaboration of the relationship to oneself. But, I think that the change doesn't affect the ethical substance: it is still *aphrodisia*. There are some changes in the *mode d'assujettissement,* for instance, when the Stoics recognize themselves as universal beings. And there are also very important changes in the *asceticism,* the kind of techniques you use in order to recognize, to constitute yourself as a subject of ethics. And also a change in the goal. I think that the difference is that in the classical perspective, to be master of oneself meant, first, taking into account only oneself and not the other, because to be master of oneself meant that you were able to rule others. So, the mastery of oneself was directly related to a dissymmetrical relation to others. You should be master of yourself in a sense of activity, dissymmetry, and nonreciprocity.

Later on, due to the changes in marriage, society, and so on, mastery of oneself is something which is not primarily related to power over others: you have to be master of yourself not only in order to rule others, as it was in the case of Alcibiades or Nicocles, but you have to be master of yourself because you are a rational being. And in this mastery of yourself, you are related to other people, who are also masters of themselves. And this new kind of relation to the other is much less nonreciprocal than before.

So, those are the changes, and I try to show those changes in the three last chapters, the fourth part of *L'Usage des plaisirs*. I take the same theme—the body, wives or women, and boys and I show that these same three austerity themes are linked to a partially new ethics. I say "partially" because some of the parts of this ethics do not change: for instance, the *aphrodisia*. On the other hand, others do, for instance the techniques. According to Xenophon, the way to become a good husband is to know exactly what your role is inside your home or outside, what kind of authority you have to exercise on your wife, what are your expectations of your wife's behavior, and so on. All this calculation gives you the rules for behavior, and defines the way you have to be toward yourself. But for Epictetus, or for Seneca, for instance, in order to be really master of yourself you don't have to know what your role in society or in your home is, but you do have to do some exercises like depriving yourself of eating for two or three days, in order to be sure that you can control yourself. If one day you are in prison, you won't suffer from being deprived of food, and so on. And you have to do that for all the pleasures—that's a kind of asceticism you can't find in Plato or Socrates or Aristotle.

There is no complete and identical relation between the techniques and the *tele*. You can find the same techniques in different *tele*, but there are privileged relations, some privileged techniques related to each telos.

In the Christian book—I mean the book about Christianity!—I try to show that all this ethics has changed. Because the telos has changed: the telos is immortality, purity, and so on. The asceticism has changed, because now self-examination takes the form of self-deciphering. The *mode d'assujettissement* is now divine law. And I think that even the ethical substance has changed, because it is not *aphrodisia*, but desire, concupiscence, flesh, and so on.

Q: It seems, then, that we have a grid of intelligibility for desire as an ethical problem?

A: Yes, we now have this scheme. If by sexual behavior, we understand the three poles—acts, pleasure, and desire—we have the Greek "formula," which is the same at the first and at the second stage. In this Greek formula what is underscored is "acts," with pleasure and desire as subsidiary: <u>acte</u>—*plaisir*—

242

(désir). I have put desire in brackets because I think that in the Stoic ethics you start a kind of elision of desire, desire begins to be condemned.

The Chinese "formula" would be *plaisir—désir—(acte)*. Acts are put aside because you have to restrain acts in order to get the maximum duration and intensity of pleasure.

The Christian "formula" puts an accent on desire and tries to eradicate it. Acts have to become something neutral; you have to act only to produce children, or to fulfill your conjugal duty. And pleasure is both practically and theoretically excluded: *(désir)—acte—(plaisir)*. Desire is practically excluded —you have to eradicate your desire—but theoretically very important.

And I could say that the modern "formula" is desire, which is theoretically underlined and practically accepted, since you have to liberate your own desire. Acts are not very important, and pleasure—nobody know what it is!

From the Classical Self to the Modern Subject

Q: What is the care of the self which you have decided to treat separately in *Le Souci de soi?*

A: What interests me in the Hellenistic culture, in the Greco-Roman culture, starting from about the third century B.C. and continuing until the second or third century after Christ, is a precept for which the Greeks had a specific word *epimeleia heautou*, which means taking care of one's self. It does not mean simply being interested in oneself, nor does it mean having a certain tendency to self-attachment or self-fascination. *Epimeleia heautou* is a very powerful word in Greek which means working on or being concerned with something. For example, Xenophon used the word *epimeleia heautou* to describe agricultural management. The responsibility of a monarch for his fellow citizens was also *epimeleia heautou*. That which a doctor does in the course of caring for a patient is *epimeleia heautou*. It is, therefore, a very powerful word; it describes a sort of work, an activity; it implies attention, knowledge, technique.

Q: But isn't the application of knowledge and technology to the self a modern invention?

A: Knowledge played a different role in the classical care of the self. There are very interesting things to analyze about relations between scientific knowledge and the *epimeleia heautou*. The one who cared for himself had to choose among all the things that you can know through scientific knowledge only those kinds of things which were relative to him and important to life.

Q: So, theoretical understanding, scientific understanding, was secondary to and guided by ethical and aesthetic concerns?

A: Their problem and their discussion concerned what limited sorts of the

243

knowledge were useful for *epimeleia*. For instance, for the Epicureans, the general knowledge of what is the world, of what is the necessity of the world, the relation between world, necessity and the gods—all that was very important for the care of the self. Because it was first a matter of meditation: if you were able exactly to understand the necessity of the world, then you could master passions in a much better way, and so on. So, for the Epicureans there was a kind of adequation between all possible knowledge and the care of the self. The reason that one had to become familiar with physics or cosmology was that one had to take care of the self. For the Stoics, the true self is defined only by what I can be master of.

Q: So knowledge is subordinated to the practical end of mastery?

A: Epictetus is very clear on that. He gives as an exercise to walk every morning in the streets looking, watching. And if you meet a consular figure you say, "Is the consul something I can master?" No, so I have nothing to do. If I meet a beautiful girl or beautiful boy, is their beauty, their desirability, something which depends on me, and so on? For the Christians things are quite different; for Christians the possibility that Satan can get inside your soul and give you thoughts you cannot recognize as Satanic but that you might interpret as coming from God leads to uncertainty about what is going on inside your soul. You are unable to know what the real root of your desire is, at least without hermeneutic work.

Q: So, to what extent did the Christians develop new techniques of self-mastery?

A: What interests me about the classical concept of care of the self is that we see here the birth and development of a certain number of ascetic themes ordinarily attributed to Christianity. Christianity is usually given credit for replacing the generally tolerant Greco-Roman life-style with an austere life-style marked by a series of renunciations, interdictions, or prohibitions. Now, we can see that in this activity of the self on itself, the ancients developed a whole series of austerity practices that the Christians later directly borrowed from them. So, we see that this activity became linked to a certain sexual austerity which was subsumed directly into the Christian ethic. We are not talking about a moral rupture between tolerant antiquity and austere Christianity.

Q: In the name of what does one choose to impose this life-style upon oneself?

A: In antiquity, this work on the self with its attendant austerity is not imposed on the individual by means of civil law or religious obligation, but is a choice about existence made by the individual. People decide for themselves whether or not to care for themselves.

I don't think it is to attain eternal life after death, because they were not

244

particularly concerned with that. Rather they acted so as to give to their life certain values (reproduce certain examples, leave behind them an exalted reputation, give the maximum possible brilliance to their lives). It was a question of making one's life into an object for a sort of knowledge, for a *techne* —for an art.

We have hardly any rem ant of the idea in our society, that the principle work of art which one has to take care of, the main area to which one must apply aesthetic values is oneself, one's life, one's existence. We find this in the Renaissance, but in a slightly academic form, and yet again in nineteenth-century dandyism, but those were only episodes.

Q:　But isn't the Greek concern with the self just an early version of our self-absorption which many consider a central problem in our society?

A:　You have a certain number of themes—and I don't say that you have to reutilize them in this way—which indicate to you that in a culture to which we owe a certain number of our most important constant moral elements, there was a practice of the self, a conception of the self, very different from our present culture of the self. In the California cult of the self, one is supposed to discover one's true self, to separate it from that which might obscure or alienate it, to decipher its truth thanks to psychological or psychoanalytic science, which is supposed to be able to tell you what your true self is. Therefore, not only do I not identify this ancient culture of the self with what you might call the Californian cult of the self, I think they are diametrically opposed.

What happened in between is precisely an overtuning of the classical culture of the self. This took place when Christianity substituted the idea of a self which one had to renounce because clinging to the self was opposed to God's will for the idea of a self which had to be created as a work of art.

Q:　We know that one of the studies for *Le Souci de soi* concerns the role of writing in the formation of the self. How is the question of the relation of writing and the self posed by Plato?

A:　First, to bring out a certain number of historical facts which are often glossed over when posing this problem of writing, we must look into the famous question of the *hypomnemata*. Current interpretors see in the critique of the *hypomnemata* in the *Phaedrus* a critique of writing as a material support for memory. Now, in fact, *hypomnemata* has a very precise meaning. It is a copybook, a notebook. Precisely this type of notebook was coming into vogue at Plato's time for personal and administrative use. This new technology was as disrupting as the introduction of the computer into private life today. It seems to me the question of writing and the self must be posed in terms of the technical and material framework in which it arose.

Secondly, there are problems of interpretation concerning the famous critique of writing as opposed to the culture of memory in the *Phaedrus*. If you read the *Phaedrus*, you will see that this passage is secondary with respect to another one which is fundamental and which is in line with the theme which runs throughout the end of the text. It does not matter whether a text is written or oral—the problem is whether or not the discourse in question gives access to truth. Thus the written/oral question is altogether secondary with respect to the question of truth.

Thirdly, what seems remarkable to me is that these new instruments were immediately used for the constitution of a permanent relationship to oneself— one must manage oneself as a governor manages the governed, as a head of an enterprise manages his enterprise, a head of household manages his household. This new idea that virtue consists essentially in perfectly governing oneself, that is, in exercising upon oneself as exact a mastery as that of a sovereign against whom there would no longer be revolts, is something very important which we will find, for centuries—practically until Christianity. So, if you will, the point at which the question of the *hypomnemata* and the culture of the self comes together in a remarkable fashion is the point at which the culture of the self takes as its goal the perfect government of the self—a sort of permanent political relationship between self and self. The ancients carried on this politics of themselves with these notebooks just as governments and those who manage enterprises administered by keeping registers. This is how writing seems to me to be linked to the problem of the culture of the self.

Q: Can you tell us more about the *hypomnemata?*

A: In the technical sense, the *hypomnemata* could be account books, public registers, individual notebooks serving as memoranda. Their use as books of life, guides for conduct, seems to have become a current thing amongst a whole cultivated public. Into them one entered quotations, fragments of works, examples, and actions to which one had been witness or of which one had read the account, reflections or reasonings which one had heard or which had come to mind. They constituted a material memory of things read, heard, or thought, thus offering these as an accumulated treasure for rereading and later meditation. They also formed a raw material for the writing of more systematic treatises in which were given arguments and means by which to struggle against some defect (such as anger, envy, gossip, flattery) or to overcome some difficult circumstance (a mourning, an exile, downfall, disgrace).

Q: But how does writing connect up with ethics and the self?

A: No technique, no professional skill can be acquired without exercise; neither can one learn the art of living, the *techne tou biou,* without an *askesis* which must be taken as a training of oneself by oneself: this was one of the traditional principles to which the Pythagoreans, the Socratics, the Cynics had for a long time attributed great importance. Amongst all the forms this training took (and which included abstinences, memorizations, examinations of conscience, meditations, silence and listening to others), it seems that writing—the fact of writing for oneself and for others—came quite late to play a sizeable role.

Q: What specific role did the notebooks play when they finally became influential in late antiquity?

A: As personal as they were, the *hypomnemata* must nevertheless not be taken for intimate diaries or for those accounts of spiritual experience (temptations, struggles, falls, and victories) which can be found in later Christian literature. They do not constitute an ''account of oneself''; their objective is not to bring the *arcana conscientiae* to light, the confession of which—be it oral or written— has a purifying value. The movement that they seek to effect is the inverse of this last one. The point is not to pursue the indescribable, not to reveal the hidden, not to say the nonsaid, but on the contrary, to collect the already-said, to reassemble that which one could hear or read, and this to an end which is nothing less than the constitution of oneself.

The *hypomnemata* are to be resituated in the context of a very sensitive tension of that period. Within a culture very affected by traditionality, by the recognized value of the already-said, by the recurrence of discourse, by the ''citational'' practice under the seal of age and authority, an ethic was developing which was very explicitly oriented to the care of oneself, toward definite objectives such as retiring into oneself, reaching oneself, living with oneself, being sufficient to oneself, profiting by and enjoying oneself. Such is the objective of the *hypomnemata:* to make of the recollection of the fragmentary *logos* transmitted by teaching, listening, or reading a means to establish as adequate and as perfect a relationship of oneself to oneself as possible.

Q: Before we turn to the role of these notebooks in early Christianity, could you tell us something about how Greco-Roman austerity differs from Christian austerity?

A: One thing that has been very important is that in Stoic ethics the question of purity was nearly inexistent or rather marginal. It was important in Pythagorean circles and also in the neo-Platonic schools and became more and more important through their influence and also through religious influences. At a certain moment, the problem of an aesthetics of existence is covered over by the problem of purity, which is something else and which requires another kind of technique. In Christian asceticism the question of purity becomes more and more important; the reason why you have to take control of yourself is to keep yourself pure. The problem of virginity, this model of feminine integrity, becomes much more important in Christianity. The theme of virginity has nearly nothing to do with sexual ethics in Greco-Roman asceticism. There the problem is a problem of self-domination. It was a virile model of self-domination and a woman who was temperate was as virile to herself as a man. The paradigm of sexual self-restraint becomes a feminine paradigm through the

247

theme of purity and virginity, based on the model of physical integrity. Physical integrity rather than self-regulation became important. So the problem of ethics as an aesthetics of existence is covered over by the problem of purification.

This new Christian self had to be constantly examined because in this self were lodged concupiscence and desires of the flesh. From that moment on, the self was no longer something to be made but something to be renounced and deciphered. Consequently, between paganism and Christianity, the opposition is not between tolerance and austerity, but between a form of austerity which is linked to an aesthetic of existence and other forms of austerity which are linked to the necessity of renouncing the self and deciphering its truth.

Q: So Nietzsche, then, must be wrong, in *The Geneaolgy of Morals,* when he credits Christian asceticism for making us the kind of creatures that can make promises?

A: Yes, I think he has given mistaken credit to Christianity, given what we know about the evolution of pagan ethics from the fourth century B.C. to the fourth century after.

Q: How was the role of the notebooks transformed when the technique of using them to relate oneself to oneself was taken over by the Christians?

A: One important change is that the writing down of inner movements appears, according to Athanase's text on the life of Saint Anthony, as an arm in spiritual combat: while the demon is a force which deceives and which makes one be deceived about oneself (one great half of the *Vita Antonii* is devoted to these ploys), writing constitutes a test and something like a touchstone: in bringing to light the movements of thought, it dissipates the inner shadow where the enemy's plots are woven.

Q: How could such a radical transformation take place?

A: There is, indeed, a dramatic change between the *hypomnemata* evoked by Xenophon, where it was only a question of remembering the elements of a diet, and the description of the nocturnal temptations of Saint Anthony. An interesting place to look for a transitional set of techniques seems to be the description of dreams. Almost from the beginning one had to have a notebook beside one's bed upon which to write one's dreams in order either to interpret them oneself the next morning or to show them to someone who would interpret them. By means of this nightly description, an important step is taken toward the description of the self.

Q: But surely the idea that the contemplation of the self allows the self to dissipate shadows and arrive at truth is already present in Plato?

A: Yes, but this is an ontological and not a psychological form of contemplation. This ontological knowledge of the self takes shape, at least in certain

248

texts and in particular in the *Alcibiades,* in the form of the contemplation of the soul by itself in terms of the famous metaphor of the eye. Plato asks, ''How can the eye see itself?'' The answer is apparently very simple, but in fact it is very complicated. For Plato, one cannot simply look at oneself in a mirror. One has to look into another eye, that is, one *in* oneself, however in oneself in the shape of the eye of the other. And there, in the other's pupil, one will see oneself: the pupil serves as a mirror. And, in the same manner, the soul contemplating itself in another soul (or in the divine element of the other soul) which is like its pupil, will recognize its divine element.

You see that this idea that one must know oneself, i.e. gain ontological knowledge of the soul's mode of being, is independent of what one could call an exercise of the self upon the self. When grasping the mode of being of your soul, there is no need to ask yourself what you have done, what you are thinking, what the movements of your ideas or your representations are, to what you are attached. That's why you can perform this technique of contemplation using as your object the soul of an other. Plato, never speaks of the examination of conscience—never!

Q: It is a commonplace in literary studies that Montaigne was the first great autobiographer, yet you seem to trace writing about the self to much earlier sources.

A: It seems to me that in the religious crisis of the sixteenth century—the great rejection of the Catholic confessional practices—new modes of relationship to the self were being developed. We can see the reactivation of a certain number of ancient Stoic practices. The notion, for example, of proofs of oneself, seems to me thematically close to what we find among the Stoics where the experience of the self is not a discovering of a truth hidden inside the self, but an attempt to determine what one can and cannot do with one's available freedom. Among both the Catholics and Protestants, the reactivation of these ancient techniques in the form of Christian spiritual practices is quite marked.

Let me take as an example the walking exercise recommended by Epictetus. Each morning, while taking a walk in the city, one should try to determine with respect to each thing (a public official or an attractive woman), one's motives, whether one is impressed by or drawn to it, or, whether one has sufficient self-mastery so as to be indifferent.

In Christianity one has the same sort of exercises, but they serve to test one's dependence on God. I remember having found in a seventeenth-century text an exercise reminiscent of Epictetus, where a young seminarist, when he is walking, does certain exercises which show in what way each thing shows his dependence vis-à-vis God—which permit him to decipher the presence of divine providence. These two walks correspond to the extent that you have a case with Epictetus of a walk during which the individual assures himself of his own sovereignty over himself and shows that he is dependent on nothing. While in the Christian case, the seminarist walks and before each thing he sees, says, "Oh, how God's goodness is great! He who made this, holds all things in his power, and me, in particular," thus reminding himself that he is nothing.

Q.   So discourse plays an important role but always serves other practices even in the constitution of the self.

A: It seems to me, that all the so-called literature of the self—private diaries, narratives of the self, etc.—cannot be understood unless it is put into the general and very rich framework of these practices of the self. People have been writing about themselves for two thousand years, but not in the same way. I have the impression—I may be wrong—that there is a certain tendency to present the relationship between writing and the narrative of the self as a phenomenon particular to European modernity. Now, I would not deny it is modern but it was also one of the first uses of writing.

So, it is not enough to say that the subject is constituted in a symbolic system. It is not just in the play of symbols that the subject is constituted. It is constituted in real practices—historically analysable practices. There is a technology of the constitution of the self which cuts across symbolic systems while using them.

Q: If self-analysis is a cultural invention, why does it seem so natural and pleasurable to us?

A: It may have been an extremely painful exercise at first and required many cultural valorizations before ending up transformed into a positive activity. Techniques of the self, I believe, can be found in all cultures in different forms. Just as it is necessary to study and compare the different techniques of the production of objects and the direction of men by men through government, one must also question techniques of the self. What makes the analysis of the techniques of the self difficult is two things. First, the techniques of the self do not require the same material apparatus as the production of objects, therefore they are often invisible techniques. Second, they are frequently linked to the techniques for the direction of others. For example, if we take educational institutions, we realize that one is managing others and teaching them to manage themselves.

Q: Let's move on to the history of the modern subject. To begin with, was the classical culture of the self completely lost, or was it, rather, incorporated and transformed by Christian techniques?

A: I do not think that the culture of the self disappeared or was covered up. You find many elements which have simply been integrated, displaced, re-utilized in Christianity. From the moment that the culture of the self was taken up by Christianity, it was, in a way, put to work for the exercise of a pastoral power to the extent that the *epimeleia heautou* became essentially *epimeleia tonallon*—the care of others—which was the pastor's job. But in so far as individual salvation is channeled—to a certain extent at least—through a pastoral institution which has the care of souls as its object, the classical care of the self disappeared, that is, was integrated and lost a large part of its autonomy.

What is interesting is that during the Renaissance you see a whole series of religious groups (whose existence is, moreover, already attested to in the Middle Ages) which resist this pastoral power and which claim the right to make their own statutes for themselves. According to these groups, the individual should take care of his own salvation independently of the ecclesiastical institution and of the ecclesiastical pastorate. We can see, therefore, a reappearance, up to a certain point, not of the culture of the self which had never disappeared, but a reaffirmation of its autonomy.

In the Renaissance you also see—and here I refer to Burkhardt's text on the famous aesthetics of existence—the hero as his own work of art. The idea that from one's own life one can make a work of art is an idea which was undoubtedly foreign to the Middle Ages and which reappears at the moment of the Renaissance.

Q: So far you have been treating various degrees of appropriation of ancient techniques of self-mastery. In your own writing, you always show a big break between the Renaissance and the classical age. Was there an equally significant change in the way self-mastery was related to other social practices?

A: That is very interesting, but I won't answer you immediately. Let us start by saying that the relationship between Montaigne, Pascal, and Descartes could be rethought in terms of this question. First, Pascal was still in a tradition in which practices of the self, the practice of asceticism, were tied up to the knowledge of the world. Second, we must not forget that Descartes wrote "meditations"—and meditations are a practice of the self. But the extraordinary thing in Descartes's texts is that he succeeded in substituting a subject as founder of practices of knowledge, for a subject constituted through practices of the self.

This is very important. Even if it is true that Greek philosophy founded rationality, it always held that a subject could not have access to the truth if he did not first operate upon himself a certain work which would make him susceptible to knowing the truth—a work of purification, conversion of the soul by contemplation of the soul itself. You also have the theme of the Stoic exercise by which a subject first insures his autonomy and independence—and he insures it in a rather complex relationship to the knowledge of the world, since it is this knowledge which allows him to insure his independence and it is only once he has insured it that he is able to recognize the order of the world as it stands. In European culture up to the sixteenth century the problem remains "What is the work which I must effect upon myself so as to be capable and worthy of acceding to the truth?" To put it another way: Truth always has a price; no access to truth without ascesis. In Western culture up to the sixteenth century, asceticism and access to truth are always more or less obscurely linked.

Descartes, I think, broke with this when he said "To accede to truth, it suffices that I be *any* subject which can see what is evident." Evidence is substituted for ascesis at the point where the relationship to the self intersects the relationship to others and the world. The relationship to the self no longer needs to be ascetic to get into relation to the truth. It suffices that the relationship to the self reveals to me the obvious truth of what I see for me to apprehend that truth definitively. Thus, I can be immoral and know the truth. I believe that this is an idea which, more or less explicitly, was rejected by all previous culture. Before Descartes, one could not be impure, immoral, and know the truth. With Descartes, direct evidence is enough. After Descartes we have a nonascetic subject of knowledge. This change makes possible the institutionalization of modern science.

I am obviously schematizing a very long history, which is, however, fundamental. After Descartes, we have a subject of knowledge which poses for Kant the problem of knowing the relationship between the subject of ethics and that of knowledge. There was much debate in the Enlightenment as to whether these two subjects were completely different or not. Kant's solution was to find a universal subject, which, to the extent that it was universal could be the subject of knowledge, but which demanded, nonetheless, an ethical attitude—precisely the relationship to the self which Kant proposes in *The Critique of Practical Reason*.

Q: You mean that once Descartes had cut scientific rationality loose from ethics, Kant reintroduced ethics as an applied form of procedural rationality?

A: Right. Kant says, "I must recognize myself as universal subject, that is, I must constitute myself in each of my actions as a universal subject by conforming to universal rules." The old questions were reinterpreted: "How can I constitute myself as a subject of ethics? Recognize myself as such? Are ascetic exercises needed? or simply this Kantian relationship to the universal which makes me ethical by conformity to practical reason?" Thus Kant introduces one more way in our tradition whereby the self is not merely given but is constituted in relationship to itself as subject.

Foucault's Interpretive Analytic of Ethics

Methodological Refinements

INTERPRETIVE DIAGNOSIS

In *The History of Sexuality*, vol. 1, Michel Foucault presents a description of our current practices as the product of a confluence of Christian techniques of self-decipherment and Enlightenment technologies for the rational policing of populations, all of which he calls bio-power. Foucault does not explain why he selects these techniques for study, but as we argued in the first edition of this book, Foucault's method, which we called interpretive analytics, must begin, at least implicitly, with a diagnosis of what we called our common distress. Foucault now has given a name to this situation in which the genealogist finds himself and which provokes both his analytical and practical response. He speaks, still somewhat elusively, of combating the current danger. It is as if he has moved from an autobiographical account of his choice of practices to be undermined to an almost impersonal assessment of an objective threat.

We continue to think that what motivates archaeological and genealogical work is neither as subjective nor as objective as Foucault suggests. We maintain that he is performing an interpretive act which focuses and articulates, from among the many distresses and dangers which abound in our society, those which can be seen as paradigmatic. The resulting interpretation is neither a subjective invention nor an objective description, but it is an act of imagination, analysis, and commitment.

Since the publication of our book three years ago, Foucault has become more and more interested in the fact that our society increasingly emphasizes the formation of individuals as deep selves. The resulting historical and methodological complexity has caused Foucault to recast his project for a history of sexuality. Volumes 2 and 3 of *The History of Sexuality*, *L'Usage des plaisirs* and

253

Les Aveux de la chair, lay the foundation for a complex genealogy of the modern subject. A third book, *Le Souci de soi*, complementary to *The History of Sexuality*, analyzes the great attention the ancient world paid to the care of the self—by showing the several stages through which techniques of self-mastery developed.

It is important to note that, at least temporarily, this has skewed Foucault's project in the direction of an undermining of the Christian/Freudian hermeneutic subject. This is a comprehensible strategy given current politics and thought. Foucault seems to be saying that until we free ourselves from our obsession with deciphering the truth of our desires, we will continue to be entangled in our selves and in the power/knowledge complex which claims to help us uncover this truth. Since Christianity hardly seems a dangerous force in the modern world, and since Reichian-Marcusian sexual liberation has spent itself, and since Lacan is dead, Foucault takes this be an opportune moment for renewed thought about an ethical life. He does not seek to deconstruct the subject but to historicize thoroughly the deep self in order to open the possibility of the emergence of a new ethical subject.

This is not to say that debilitating concern with the self is a unique, or the most important, or the enduring form of danger for the world today—but it is one that Foucault thinks is ripe for change. However, as we shall argue later, Foucault's focus on technologies of the self may have deflected concern from what his work has singled out as the even greater and longer range dangers of Weberian rationalization, Heideggerian technology, and the normalization and destruction inherent in bio-power. At this point, however, Foucault is devoting his attention to an area that, according to his diagnosis, is more open to change, while bearing in mind that he will eventually have to return to a full-scale analytics of bio-power.

GENEAOLOGY

Volume 2 of *The History of Sexuality* was to have begun with an analysis of the early Christian confessional practices which constituted a hermeneutics of desire. This was to include an introductory chapter on the relation of sexuality and self-mastery in ancient culture. The chapter soon became problematic for two reasons. First, perhaps not surprisingly given Foucault's analysis of sexuality as a historical construct, the Greeks and the Romans had nothing to say about sexuality per se, and little to say about specific kinds of sexual acts, although they do talk at length about the relation of sexual activity to health and ethics. Second, Foucault was surprised to find that Greek thinkers paid elaborate attention to techniques of self-care, and that these concerns endured for six centuries, during which the practices evolved through several stages. Foucault thus had to modify his original hypothesis that elaboration of techniques of self-analysis and control was a Christian invention.

He now claims in *Le Souci de soi* that the Christians took over for their own hermeneutic purposes an elaborate technology of self-examination which was already in place by the time of the Stoics. The Christian innovation was to break the pagan "economy of bodies and pleasures" in which desire and pleasure were linked in an unproblematic way. They radically separated pleasure and desire and appropriated the classical techniques of self-care in the service of a constant concern with the hidden truth and dangers of desire. Classical techniques of austerity which were a means to self-mastery were transformed into techniques whose purpose was the purification of desire and the elimination of pleasure, so that austerity became an end in itself. Thus the Christians took an old set of practices as a form to which they gave a new content and a new goal.

If Nietzschean genealogy is "the appropriation of a system of rules, . . . in order to bend it to a new will, to force its participation in a different game,"[1] then Foucault has here serendipitiously come upon a text book example. However, according to Foucault, Nietzsche notwithstanding, austerity does not begin with the Christians. It is a well-developed element in the techniques of self-mastery, which the Christians, as Nietzsche himself saw, privileged as an end in itself.

Moreover, in the course of this genealogical investigation, Foucault reveals that despite his radical questioning of our tradition, Nietzsche had accepted the Christian appropriation of the Greeks as their predecessors. Foucault offers a counterinterpretation to Nietzsche's claim that Socrates' injunction "know thyself" was an early form of the Christian attempt to unearth the self's deepest truths. According to Foucault, the attempt to put the truth of the self into words is a uniquely Christian perversion of Greek forms of self-examination. "Know thyself" carved on the temple of Apollo simply meant "be sure of your questions before consulting the oracle." Socrates presumably was recommending an examination of one's concepts and their relation to one's acts, not a suspicious examination of one's fantasies, impulses, and intentions.

ARCHAEOLOGY

Most important of all, Foucault has excavated an ethical system which, like the pagan buildings over which Christians built their churches, was partly covered up, partly dispersed, and partly appropriated in the new Christian structures. Foucault devotes volume 2 of *The History of Sexuality,* to a systematic presentation of Greek sexual ethics. He reconstructs the rest of the edifice—the techniques of self-mastery—in *Le Souci de soi*. His reconstruction is guided by an overall schema in which he distinguishes the *telos*, or goal of the ethical life (in the Greek case, a beautiful life); the ethical substance which is to be formed into such a life (in the Greek case, acts, pleasure/desire); and the

---

1. Michel Foucault, "Nietzsche, Genealogy, History," in *Language, Counter-Memory, Practice,* ed. by Donald F. Bouchard (Ithaca: Cornell University Press, 1977), pp. 151–52.

interpretations and techniques (such as self-mastery) which operates on the ethical substance to actualize the telos (See interview, pages 238–43).

When archaeology serves genealogy, it takes on a different function than it had in Foucault's earlier works. This new function only becomes clear in the books on the ancient world. The genealogist is led back to find the system whose partial appropriation is contemporaneous with the beginnings of the cultural conditions he is seeking to understand. And it is this prior system in its integrity which the archaeologist unearths and seeks to make intelligible.

All archaeology reconstructs systems of practices which have an internal intelligibility from which the archaeologist distances himself. Once he has established the internal rationality of a particular set of discourses and practices, he has the option of making them seem more or less familiar. We have seen examples of both strategies in Foucault's previous work. On one hand, *Madness and Civilization* and *Discipline and Punish* begin with descriptions of what seem to be totally alien practices—the mad who cruised Europe's rivers on the ships of fools and the gruesome torture of Damiens—which Foucault shows to be both internally coherent and plausible responses to recognizable problems. On the other hand, attempts to treat madness as a disease and humanitarian prison reforms are shown to have an internal coherence but also a disturbing distance from what we think of as their rational and humane intent.

Foucault combines both these archaeological strategies in *L'Usage des plaisirs*. Nothing would seem to be more familiar to us and continuous with our ideals than the Greek ethical system. Yet when he steps back from it and examines its systematic coherence, Foucault as archaeologist shows that care of the self was not focused on desires and their truth but on social acts. For example, sex was not understood in terms of desire. Rather, sexual acts, desire, and pleasure were connected by the Greeks in a manner which, once made internally intelligible, can be seen to be alien to our current understanding of sexuality. Yet, at the same time, Foucault lets us see that the Greeks had a plausible way of relating acts, desire, and pleasure, and thus that there is in our tradition a basis for an ethical life and for an economy of bodies and pleasures different from the one we have come to take for granted.

Foucault calls the Greek ethical system an aesthetic of existence. It enabled the Greek aristocrats at least to inhabit a shared, social world in which bodily pleasure, perfection of character, and service to the polis could be cultivated without being grounded in norms underwritten by religion, law, or science. This seemingly attractive alternative within our own tradition is worth piecing together in detail, because only then can we see it as a working system which confronted a problem similar to the one we confront. And at the same time, such a detailed reconstruction shows precisely that the classical period was not a Golden Age. Foucault's analysis of *chresis*—the Greek understanding of when, where, and with whom sexual acts *(aphrodisia)* were appropriate—reveals a world of generalized and institutionalized inequality, in which masters exploited slaves, men dominated women, and older men subjugated boys, a world obsessed with active and passive roles, where relations of reciprocity between selves were possible only in those areas cut off from *aphrodisia*.

Thus Foucault's interpretive analytics starts with our current danger—that by trying to ground our norms in religion, law, and science, we have been led to seek the truth of our desires and have thereby become entangled in our selves and governed by a normalizing web of law and medicine. He then defines our current problem as how to construct a different ethics. Next he traces the lineage of the Christian self-understanding which produced our danger, in order to break its grip on us, and at the same time unearths the system that immediately precedes our self-understanding. This earlier system, the Greeks', had an ethics unrelated to religion, law, or science and so was free of our dangers, but it had its own dangers and is therefore no solution for us. Foucault is emphatic that this elaborate analysis does not offer any solutions or alternatives. It shows, however, that an ethical problem similar in form to our own has been confronted before in our history, and his analysis thus gives us a new perspective on our problem.

Norms, Reasons, and Bio-Power

Even if Foucault is right that the current understanding of the self is changing, and even if the problem of how to live a beautiful life which Foucault finds in the ancient world were once again to become our problem, this would hardly be the end of the story. A shift in ethical substance from desire to pleasure, and in telos from autonomy to an aesthetics of existence, could offer only a qualified hope. The deep self our Christian history has made us into is a likely target for practices of purification and repentance to begin with, later for knowledge of the true character which underlies our acts, and most recently for therapeutic normalization. A self that, as its ethical activity, constituted itself as an ongoing public creation by giving a unified style to its acts would, in contrast, be much less vulnerable to currently available techniques of power/ knowledge. But even as a changed understanding of the self wards off old dangers, it carries with it new ones.

It seems obvious that a revived culture of the self concretized in new reciprocal relationships is, although a change from entanglement in the deep self, as an isolated achievement, thoroughly vulnerable. Any such culture could be appropriated by expertise, the same expertise we continually resort to in order to make the individual and community healthy, normal, and productive. We see such an appropriation happening already in the area of sex counseling. No longer does this counseling help us to decipher our desires (and this is indeed a significant step away from the deep self). Now it attempts to improve the pleasure of the body. After Masters and Johnson, sex therapists do not merely tell us that it is normal and beneficial to masturbate, but offer us films and demonstrations of techniques, applicable from infancy to old age, for optimizing efficiency and pleasure. This does not free us from bio-power; rather this appropriation enmeshes us even more.

So even if genealogy undermines the notion of a true self which has a truth which must be put into words, by showing the subject to be a historical construction whose way of working requires that it hide the fact that it is a historical construction—even then our normalizing practices would not lose their efficacy. And even if the created self, as Foucault understands it, is not isolated and self-absorbed, but publicly active and, like a work of art, always working out of a shared understanding of style, it is eminently vulnerable to all current dangers. This indicates that, in order to overcome our present danger, one needs an interpretive analytics not only of the modern subject but also of bio-power.

In *The Order of Things*, Foucault identified Kant as the exemplary figure for the understanding of human beings as subject/object doubles. But there, Foucault was only analyzing the systematicity of the discursive practices of the human sciences, and he found the notion of man convoluted and unstable but not dangerous. When in *Discipline and Punish*, Foucault turns to the power relations which govern *nondiscursive* practices, he sees the human sciences and the colonizing norms they promote as ominous.

In *Discipline and Punish* and in the part of *The History of Sexuality* devoted to bio-power, Foucault begins his diagnosis by pointing to the peculiar way modern norms work, which he calls normalization. Among all the rich assortment of techniques, practices, knowledges, and discourses Foucault has discussed, normalization is at the core. Of course, all societies have norms and socialize their members into them. Foucault, however, shows us that our kinds of norms and our methods of socialization are unique, and uniquely dangerous. Foucault has called attention to the peculiar and to him disquieting fact that our norms can be read as having a special kind of strategical directedness—what he calls a strategy without a strategist. Our norms are always on the move if their goal was to bring every aspect of our practices together into a coherent whole. To this end various experiences are identified and annexed as appropriate domains for theoretical study and intervention. Within all these domains, the norms do not rest but, at least in principle, are endlessly ramified down to the finest details of the micropractices, so no action that counts as important and real falls outside the grid of normality. In addition, as in normal science, the normalizing practices of bio-power define the normal in advance and then proceed to isolate and deal with anomalies given that definition.

Our norms have this special type of normativity. They tend toward ever greater totalization and specification. We try to ground our norms in reason, but it is as if reason, which for the Greeks corresponded to static natural kinds, has become unmoored and no longer corresponds to anything beyond itself. As Kant argued in *The Critique of Pure Reason*, scientific rationality, once cut off from things in themselves, must seek ever more general principles under which to subsume more and more phenomena, and ever more refined categories into

258

which to subdivide the phenomena. Thus reason becomes procedural, the demand for greater and greater systematization for its own sake.

Once the interpretive analyst has established the danger of normalization, he needs a genealogy of how our norms got connected with procedural rationality. The genealogist looks for the moment in our history when human reality in its three dimensions (truth, power, and ethics) was first restructured in a way that set up a space in which the kind of rationality that could lead to our current norms could work itself out. One might expect to find a set of relatively benign practices from an older articulation of reality being given a new content. And indeed, Foucault finds in a topical piece Kant wrote for a German newspaper in response to the question. What is Enlightenment? terms reminiscent of Stoicism being used to articulate a new problem and a new solution, a solution which has become our predicament.

On the basis of this essay, Foucault sees Kant as the first philosopher to assume the task of posing the problem of the meaning of his present situation. Kant takes the challenge of the Enlightenment to be, Can humanity reach its maturity by using its reason to overcome its subservience to anything but its own rational capacities? Kant argues that the culture will gain maturity when the state, in this case Frederick the Great, takes over the task of assuring the onward march of reason in every sector of society. And since reason no longer corresponds to objective reality but is now seen as man's capacity for the critical examination and systematic ordering of everything, this amounts to a new understanding of the state as the administrator and embodiment of procedural rationality. Kant concludes, ''But only one who is himself enlightened, is not afraid of shadows, and has a well-discipline army to ensure public peace can . . . treat men . . . in accordance with their dignity.''[2]

Kant's problem is still with us; we must still use our reason to achieve autonomy and maturity. But genealogy shows the disastrous implications of Kant's solution. It thus prevents us from succumbing to proposed ''solutions'' which seek to select the supposedly liberating aspects of the enlightenment, namely, critical reason, and which ignore procedural and instrumental reason and Frederick's well-disciplined armies.

Like Heidegger, Foucault sees critical reason as revealing the absence of traditional, religious, and rational grounding for our understanding of ourselves and the world, and he sees Kant as proposing to fill this empty space with the regulative ideal of a pure reason, which organizes reality so that it has a field in which to pursue greater and greater coherence and specificity. Thus procedural reason fills the empty space opened by critical reason by constituting a realm ideally adapted to its endless progressive activity. Now that the project of using instrumental reason to fill the space opened by critical reason has been

---

2. Immanuel Kant, *What is Enlightenment,* trans. Lewis White Beck (New York: Liberal Arts Press), pp. 91–92.

all too successful, some modern theorists are attempting to return to the enlightenment concern with maturity and critical reason, making the activity of driving away darkness an end in itself. When this in turn reveals its procedural emptiness, they are driven to substitute for the true order of the cosmos the true needs of the self and society. The work of critical reason then becomes the endless task of clearing away distortions which impede the endless task of bringing forth this truth.

But Foucault has already shown that the imperative to use reason to discover a deep truth about ourselves and our culture is a historical construction which has to hide its history in order to function as goal for us. Moreover, the belief that there is a deep truth in the self leads directly to the application of scientific rationality to the self and thus to the very normalization one seeks to avoid. So the genealogist sees the Enlightenment solution as either frankly and totally empty or contributing to the very problem it seeks to solve.

Having located the danger and the point in the past where the understanding of reality that produced it was introduced, the genealogist is in a position to turn archaeologist and seek out the system which the Enlightenment preempted. Kant's emphasis on reason as the means for achieving maturity and autonomy is obviously Stoic, but only when Foucault goes back and reconstructs in detail the Stoic understanding of the relation between ethics and politics does it become clear that the Stoics faced a problem similar to Kant's, although they arrived at an entirely different solution.

The Stoics faced the problem of living their lives according to norms in a time when tradition, religion, and the polis no longer carried authority. Their solution was to live in conformity with universal reason. Since all rational beings had to live in accordance with this order, autonomy did not mean withdrawal from society; rather, the mature person sought to fill his role according to what reason demanded of someone in his position. Since reason corresponded to the static order of the cosmos, the norms to which the mature person adhered were not empty, expanding, procedural norms.

Thus archaeology reveals an understanding of reason free from the dangers of procedural rationality which genealogy has traced back to the beginning of the Enlightenment. This understanding enabled the Stoics to face problems similar in form to our own, but its organization depended upon a notion of cosmic order no longer plausible to us. Nonetheless, this different notion of rational maturity in our past gives us evidence that reason need not compensate for its emptiness by subsuming all dimensions of life under more and more totalizing principles.

Substantive rather than procedural reason allowed the Stoics to establish the relative importance of a plurality of goals. Goods which were valuable but not unconditionally required were referred to as "preferred goods." Thus, for example, the Stoics recognized the importance of the health of individuals and communities, but they did not think of health and welfare as absolutes. Rather, they held that once they had done their rational duty, of course, health was to be preferred over illness.

For us, with our procedural and welfare-oriented understanding of reality, the relative importance of individual choice and public health is no longer questionable. But, up to the time of D'Alembert, the question of whether vaccination for public health overrode individual rights was still disputed. Stoic "preferential reason" endured far into the Enlightenment, and of course, outside the domain of theory—trivialized and taken for granted—it endures to this day.

Beyond Foucault

In *The History of Sexuality,* volume 1, when Foucault wanted to make us see that our concern with the truth of sexual desire was highly unusual, he could only contrast it with the oriental *ars erotica.* This does give the reader the sense that things might have been otherwise but not that *we* might have been otherwise. Ancient yogic techniques for intensifying and maintaining pleasure do relativize our own obsession with sexual meaning, but they do not seem a viable alternative for modern Western human beings who are the product of two thousands years of practices which, as Nietzsche would say, have given us even the bodies we have. We would have to do violence to our souls and bodies to become anything other.

But this does not show that we are stuck with our attempt to know our sexuality and put it into words. In Foucault's three books on ancient ethics, we find a developing sense of those practices and techniques which were once important but have been eclipsed by our post-Christian practices so that they no longer link up in an essential way with who we are. What the reconstruction of these pagan practices now allows us to consider is not the kind of violence which would require us to jump out of our cultural skins and become members of another civilization, but rather the sort of violence which would require us to repudiate many of the practices central to our Christianized self-understanding and to take up others which have been marginalized and trivialized, but which have, nonetheless, helped shape our bodies and are still within our reach.

Foucault realizes that the discovery of the Greek ethical system radically different from our own yet in our tradition is an important advance, but his method does not allow him to say why. To understand why he cannot say why, it is important to remember that Foucault has chosen as the title of his chair at the Collège de France, Professor of the History of Systems of Thought. We maintain that the very strengths of Foucault's method also define its limits. He is so good at the history of *systems* of thought (practices), that he cannot deal with thoughts and practices when they are not systematically interrelated.

To see the intrinsic limitations of Foucault's method we must distinguished three different but interrelated realities: the understanding of what counts as real in the everyday practices, linguistic and otherwise; the understanding of what counts as physical reality according to natural science; and the understanding of what counts as social reality in the disciplines which claim knowledge in this area. Foucault is very clear that it is only this third type of reality in which he is interested. In his discursive period Foucault elaborated a method for dealing only with systems of thoughts, materialized in discursive practices. The categories for analyzing discursive formations are laid out in *The Archaeology of Knowledge*. In the works more concerned with power, Foucault turns to systems of actions which govern other actions. He sketches the categories for analyzing these systems of power relations in the two essays in the first edition of this book. In the interview included in this Afterword, he gives us the system of categories for analyzing practices for forming ethical selves. Relations of truth, power, and ethics constitute human reality at a given time.

As has often been noted, Foucault, unlike Nietzsche, does not try to explain how a system of thought emerges. For Nietzsche the early Church did not invent its concerns out of whole cloth but focused, systematized, and proclaimed what was already present in the culture.[3] Foucault, in contrast, when he deals with Christianity narrows genealogy to the appropriation of one already organized set of practices (techniques of self-examination) as the form for another already functioning set of concerns (self-decipherment for the sake of salvation). He does not tell us how either system emerged, although he has a lot to tell us about the systematic working and the systematic transformations of each.

It is less often noted that Foucault's emphasis on systems leads him to lose sight of those practices which once had a central importance in what it meant to be an ethical human being but which were disconnected from what was taken to be important and were thus trivialized but not eliminated in the shift from one system, such as the pagan, to another, such as the Christian. Among such marginalized practices, one might expect to find friendship, temperance, amateur sports, and the pleasures of the body. Thus friendship from Homer to Cicero is always among the highest virtues because it is in relation to friendship that human beings can achieve reciprocity and thereby actualize most fully what it means to be human. With the appearance of Christianity, however, this primacy of friendship is no longer possible because any intense human involvement is seen as deflecting a love that should be directed toward God. So, for example, Augustine interprets his suffering over his friend's death as evidence of the hazards of directing one's love towards a finite being. Because it has no central place in the Christian understanding of human reality, friendship

---

3. "Founders of religion [take up] a way of life [which] was usually there before, but alongside other ways of life and without any sense of its special value. [They] bestow on this life style an *interpretation* that makes it appear to be illuminated by the highest values" (Fredrich Nietzsche, *The Gay Science,* Aphorism no. 353).

disappears as a philosophical theme. It also disappears if one is studying the history of systems of thought. Yet it obviously continues in a variety of forms as a marginal Western cultural practice.

We can now see the importance of Foucault's archaeological reconstruction of a non-Christian form of ethical substance from our own past. If one sees how new systems of practices are formed by focusing practices that are already present but do not count as real, we can go beyond Foucault and see how an ethical system can come into existence and thus how a new ethical system might emerge for us. Whatever the new economy of bodies and pleasures, which Foucault seems to be hinting is about to appear, its ethical substance may well be acts and pleasure/desire, and its telos may be an aesthetics of existence. But its content, its practices, cannot be the nonreciprocal practices of the Greeks, let alone the self-decipherment and concern with purity essential to the Christian understanding of human reality. The new economy of bodies and pleasures presumably will focus among its elements those species of marginalized practices which have accompanied Christianity as trivial and unreal and for that very reason have survived its passing. Thus only if one is prepared to study not only systems of thought and the human reality they constitute, but also those practices which persevere even though they seem to be trivial and even subversive can one understand how a new ethical system emerges and focuses human reality in a new way. The move to replace central practices by those which are now marginal might thus provide the basis of a more satisfactory account of a nonreactive kind of resistence than Foucault has thus far been able to offer.

Of course, should such a new ethical system emerge and overcome our most pressing dangers, there is no reason to think that it would give us a golden future. Foucault has interpreted the nonreciprocity of the Greek system as its distressing danger regardless of its other virtues, and although Foucault does not read it this way, one could see Christian universal brotherhood as a successful response to this danger. But as Foucault has been showing in greater and greater detail, this new ''solution'' carries its own dangers. Likewise, any new ethical system will presumably bring new dangers which it will be the job of interpretive analytics to discover and resist. Although Foucault has no argument to buttress this interpretation of social reality as perpetually changing because it is perpetually dangerous, it does seem to be the ''unthought'' of his historical ontology.

Although this may sound Hegelian, it is radically opposed to all dialectical thought. Foucault has absolutely no sense that the truth is the whole and that these archaeological and genealogical transformations are stages in a process converging on an ideal community. Moreover, although Foucault is immensely indebted to Nietzsche for his genealogical method, if the Nietzschian genealogist as free thinker is dedicated to showing, just for its own sake, that all we take for natural is simply layers of interpretation, then Foucault's interpretive analytics is quite far from this active nihilism. Deconstruction as an end in itself has never interested Foucault. He only seeks to undermine those practices which he takes to be important elements in our current danger. And although Foucault's presentation of bio-power as our current danger is reminiscent of Heidegger's portrayal of technology as the total ordering of all beings, Heidegger is both bleaker and more hopeful. Whereas Heidegger thinks that the steady decline of the West has reached its culmination and that we now face "the greatest danger," Foucault is not interested in telling a story of decline.

What is important for Foucault is not that some particular danger is the culmination of our history; rather, he seeks to diagnose and confront whatever the danger is at the time. Furthermore, Foucault shows no trace of the Christian hope for salvation. Heidegger's phrase "only a God can save us now;" while no Christian invocation of the supernatural, does express the hope that some new and safer cultural paradigm could focus our practices in such a way as to avoid the danger which has increasingly flattened our understanding of Being since before pre-Socratic Greece. On Foucault's interpretation, such a new paradigm would not be safer but would bring its own dangers. Thus, in contrast to Heidegger's receptive waiting, Foucault proposes "hyperactive pessimism." This is his way of understanding the kind of maturity that Kant saw as the opportunity offered by the Enlightenment.

It might seem that if Foucault wants to give up one set of dangers for another, he owes us a criterion of what makes one kind of danger more dangerous than another. Foucault is clear that he cannot justify his preference for some dangers over others by an appeal to human nature, our tradition, or universal reason. His silence on this matter, while consistent, is nonetheless a source of confusion. His practice suggests, however, that he realizes that his diagnosis of the current dangers of a Christian striving for purity and salvation and of an Enlightenment faith in universal reason, as well as his preference for an ethics which is an aesthetics of existence with *its* dangers, is ultimately an interpretation to be judged in terms of its reasonance with other thinkers and actors and its results.

Index

Index to Afterword (1983)